BLACK RADICAL

Also by Nelson Peery from The New Press

Black Fire:
The Making of an American Revolutionary

BLACK RADICAL

The Education of an American Revolutionary

NELSON PEERY

THE NEW PRESS

NEW YORK
LONDON

Requests for permission to reproduce selections from this book should be mailed to:
Permissions Department, The New Press, 38 Greene Street, New York, NY 10013.

Published in the United States by The New Press, New York, 2007
Distributed by W. W. Norton & Company, Inc., New York

LIBRARY OF CONGRESS CATALOGING-IN-PUBLICATION DATA

Peery, Nelson, 1925–
Black radical : the education of an American revolutionary / Nelson Peery.
p.   cm.
Includes index.
ISBN 978-1-59558-145-7 (hc.)
1. Peery, Nelson, 1925–   2. African Americans—Biography.
3. Revolutionaries—United States—Biography.   4. African American political
activists—Biography.   5. African American radicals—Biography.
6. Racism—United States—History—20th century.   7. African Americans—
Civil rights—History—20th century.   8. United States—Race relations—
History—20th century.   I. Title.
E185.97.P44A3 2007
973'.04960730092—dc22
[B]
2007009181

The New Press was established in 1990 as a not-for-profit alternative to the large,
commercial publishing houses currently dominating the book publishing industry.
The New Press operates in the public interest rather than for private gain, and is
committed to publishing, in innovative ways, works of educational, cultural, and
community value that are often deemed insufficiently profitable.

www.thenewpress.com

Composition by dix!
This book was set in Minion

Printed in the United States of America

2   4   6   8   10   9   7   5   3   1

Dedicated to the memory of my wife, Sue Ying,
and our decades of struggle for the better world

Contents

Preface

Black Fire: The Making of an American Revolutionary, published by The New Press in 1994, is my memoir of growing up in the rural North and moving, as millions of African Americans did, from the farms and small towns to the urban ghettos. The first half of that book is the story of the development of my social consciousness during the Great Depression. The second half of the memoir deals with the Black soldiers in World War II and the deepening of my racial consciousness as a soldier in the all-Black Ninety-third Infantry Division. *Black Fire* ends abruptly with the ending of the war. Many friends and some people I do not know who read the book encouraged me to write a sequel. It has been a long time birthing. This sequel to *Black Fire* is the recollection of my integration back into civilian life and the development of my revolutionary consciousness as I fought to move from first-class soldier to first-class civilian. It is a participant's view of the struggle of the radical left to bring to life the ideals we fought for in World War II.

Radicals and revolutionaries in America have legitimacy not found in any other country. The world we fight for is enshrined in the documents of our Revolution, the Civil War, and Emancipation. American revolutionaries strive to extend to the economy the democracy we struggle for in the political arena. Thus, an American revolutionary can truthfully sing, "O beautiful for spacious skies" with the same emotion that he or she sings, "Arise, ye wretched of the earth."

This is also the story of my family, the freedom movement, and the experience of African Americans as a whole during the crucial postwar period from 1946 through 1966.

In the way of acknowledgments, the memoir probably wouldn't have been written without the encouragement and professional advice of Michael McColly, professor of creative writing, author, world traveler, AIDS activist, and dear friend.

Special thanks are given to Sandra Reid, dear family friend and comrade for over thirty years. Her patiently prodding me to finish the work made it possible. Her quite efficient handling of the endless indispensable organizational details that go into publishing a book made it happen.

Nelson Peery
Chicago, Illinois
January 2007

BLACK RADICAL

A GRATEFUL NATION WELCOMES YOU HOME. No soldier returning from the Pacific war will forget the sight of the huge white rocks spelling out that greeting on the hills of San Francisco Bay. I hoped and at least partly believed that the sign included us. I tried to set aside the misgivings developed while serving in a segregated Black infantry division. We fought the good fight. We contributed more than our share to defend a democracy that thus far excluded us. A grateful nation! This could be a new beginning. The greatest catastrophe in human history was at an end. Caught up in the euphoria of victory and peace, there was reason to believe a new world was in birth and America, too, would change.

PART I

Minneapolis, 1946

1

I glanced over my blue and silver combat infantry badge and the rows of campaign ribbons with their battle stars pinned to my new olive drab jacket. Who said you can't go home again? Yes! Yes, you can! I opened the door, taking the final step out of the army.

On January 23, 1946, after three and a half years of war, I was home again. Home! After slogging across that great wasteland, I had come to the place of cool waters. Giddy with happiness, I gulped it in. The laughing, rough-and-tumble greetings from my six brothers did not hide their happiness. Mom's prolonged embrace left a touch of tears on my shirt. She seemed so thin and tiny. I looked onto that toil-worn, loving face and tried to imagine the gnawing fears and prayers that had been her life while we were overseas.

A younger brother had returned from the navy a few days before. We were all home. After the welcoming hugs and kisses, after we exhausted the questions and superficial talk, I left for the corner tavern to reunite with my childhood friends. After the beer with the few friends who remained in the city, after inquiring about those who left, I went home. Everyone had gone to bed. I sat alone in the dark living room, thinking how decisively the past twenty-three years had been severed and how murky the road that lay ahead.

A homeboy coming home has social obligations to fulfill. The next day I set out to visit family friends and relatives. Buck Curry, a fellow postal worker and longtime friend of my father, had lost his wife and one of his sons while I was away. I went first to his house to offer my condolences. Surprised to see me, he set a beer in front of me, saying, "I guess you're a man now." We talked of war—him speaking of the First World War, me speaking of the Second. It all seemed to have been so futile. When the beer bottle was empty I stood up and told him how sorry I was to learn of the death of his wife and son. He looked at me for a moment, then embraced me with a bear hug. "God bless you, son."

I turned to leave, tears welling up in my eyes.

After seeing the minister and relatives, I sat down to contact the white schoolmates I'd stayed in touch with. Rather than possibly embarrassing the several women who'd kept up a correspondence, I called them, telling them how much their letters had meant to a soldier in the Pacific.

Steve Tanner had been a friend since ninth grade. We maintained a correspondence throughout the war. His parents had never failed to send cookies and cards for the holidays. I would have to go and thank them. In spite of rational thinking, I was a bit apprehensive. For three and a half years I had seldom spoken to a white person without standing at attention and answering, "Yes, sir" and "No, sir." Steve had been home for several weeks, and we spent a pleasant hour reminiscing about a world we knew was gone forever.

Dale Gaffin's parents always had mailed crumbling holiday cakes to Choisel, Kolombangara, Emiru, and the other unheard-of islands where I had fought the war. His father, a fireman, had always let me know that I was welcome in their home. A whooping yelp answered my phone call. Dale informed me he was getting married the next morning and invited me to the wedding.

Still a bit apprehensive, I begged off, saying I had an appointment I couldn't break. After a moment's pause he said, "OK, the reception is in the afternoon. You come or I'll send my squad after you."

That afternoon I ironed my uniform and walked the few blocks to his house. After the backslapping and small talk, we got into the cars for the drive to the reception. After the years of living in a battalion of eight hundred Black men and eight white officers, I felt out of place, being the only Black person going to the reception.

Someone had miscounted. There was not enough room. One of the bridesmaids, whom I didn't know, motioned for me to take her seat, then, holding up her long skirt, sat on my lap. After eighteen womanless months in the Pacific, the half-hour ride to Lake Minnetonka with that lady on my lap was almost unbearable. When we finally got there and the other passengers had left the car, she slid off my lap. As I helped her from the car she leaned close to me. "How long were you in the Pacific?"

"Two years."

"It must have been terrible."

"Yeah, it was."

She leaned against me, her lips brushing my jugular vein. "Just because they made it hard for you, don't hold it against me." She broke out into peals of laughter, took my hand, and pulled me, embarrassed and speechless, toward the reception.

I sat down with my wineglass and plate of food, thinking about America. *How do we separate the decent, hardworking people from the Theodore Bilbos, John Rankins, and Klansmen that are lynching my people? How do we identify and separate these two Americas?* By the time I got back home, I knew that although I sometimes had thought in such terms, I could never be caught up with the idea of race war. I would have to find another way.

2

With the rest of the recently discharged veterans, I clumsily tried to integrate myself into civilian life. The January, thirty-degrees-below-zero Minneapolis weather was the same, but the old house no longer felt like home. I didn't know how to connect with my brothers. I was eighteen when I left home and twenty-three when I returned. During those years we lived in different worlds.

Talking to the guys in the tavern, I realized how much they hadn't changed, and how much I had. I'd thought I could pick up where I'd left off. I couldn't. There was no point of connection. Even when we agreed, we disagreed. Those who were political at all were anxious to fight for the equal rights promised them during the war. The myth of Minnesota liberalism made the reality of rigid segregation in the city all the more unbearable, but since they knew very little of the fight for freedom raging through China, India, the East Indies, Indochina, and the Philippines, they could only imagine a fight within the system. I had been there and knew our fight was part of the unfolding struggle in the colored, colonial world—a fight against the system.

Over the next few weeks, as we kept up the pretense of "welcome home," I slowly withdrew from them. They seemed to know little about how much we, the million Black veterans returning home, were determined to gain for ourselves the democracy we had given so much to secure for others. If army segregation—the enforced isolation of the Black troops—had no other effect, it turned us inward, touching and nurturing deep roots of love and a sense of responsibility for our people. It was a consciousness that could not have developed had I stayed in Minneapolis. It wasn't so much that we veterans came home and said, "I'm not going to accept the Jim Crow and the discrimination." We had been first-class soldiers. Even in a segregated army we had rights protected by the Articles of War. We had the same pay as the white soldiers and were issued the same uniforms and rations. We never rebelled against segregation. We were rather proud of our all-Black outfits. We did not accept the brutal discrimination and galling inequality in the army and could not accept it at home.

Every returning Black veteran knew we could not get rid of the inequality without destroying segregation. We were prepared to make that fight. It was not difficult to make a first-class soldier out of a second-class citizen. It would prove next to impossible to make a second-class citizen out of a first-class soldier.

As I was coming home from the war, in January 1946, one hundred Black veterans waving their discharge papers marched through Birmingham, Alabama, demanding the right to vote. By the end of the month, the police had murdered five of them. The scene haunted me. It was as if a company of soldiers, surrounded by the enemy, was bravely fighting, confident that their comrades would come to their rescue. I could not drink a beer without thinking of them. I didn't know what to do. It was my fight, too, and I knew I could not avoid it.

Our neighborhood had changed. Most of my friends who had not served in the army had left the stultifying atmosphere of our little eight-block ghetto, never to return. I could not join what was left of the old gang, hanging out on the corner, drinking beer, and swapping stories. Instead, I drifted into an informal little group of veterans who, like me, had entered the army as teenagers.

Having left one world and not knowing how to enter the other, without the mission or sense of self-worth that made us soldiers, we were lost and lonesome. We spent the weekends together, talking about the good parts of the war, drinking more and more whiskey, covering our depression with loud laughter and crude jokes. I knew when the partying was over, alone in their rooms, disconsolate, like me, they pondered the worth of a life without purpose. In World War I they called this depression "shell-shock." In World War II they called it "combat fatigue." It was something deeper. This depression did not smother every veteran or every combat veteran. Those who matured in the years of combat and camaraderie were the ones who suffered. We became men conditioned by the order and discipline that existed within the confusion and destruction of war. Every day of our lives was with a purpose. The hours of battle were bearable because we knew the soldiers at our side protected our flanks and were driving toward the same goal—all confident of each and each of all. We were part of a machine, a machine that nurtured and protected us as it oppressed and destroyed us. Without it, we were adrift.

The year 1946 was the end of an era. The war and the government's calls for freedom and democracy stopped in concert. In every segregated section of every city and town, African Americans knew that their minuscule wartime social and economic gains were in jeopardy. Even if they did not know the facts, they understood what had happened in history and that it was about to repeat itself.

During the war, in order to mobilize the people, the rulers extended a promise of democracy and freedom. We African Americans gained a few concessions. As the war ended and the people demanded fulfillment of wartime promises, the goals of whites and Blacks were separated. The Blacks were isolated and driven back. The weakened movement collapsed and the wartime vision died a-birthing.

At the end of the Civil War there also had been a moment when a democratic path could have been followed, but the intertwined demands of Blacks and whites were separated and defeated. Then again, at the end of World War I, there was a brief moment when America could have become a multiracial democracy. The blood-drenched Red Summer of 1919 was testimony to the desperate fight for—and the merciless crushing of—that vision.

In 1946, the sharp rise in Black joblessness, lynchings, police brutality, and mob violence showed that postwar reaction was again on the offensive. Although the goal was to drive the African Americans back, the vision of Roosevelt's Four Freedoms, the possibility of peace and progress, and the future of organized labor were in the line of fire.

At eighteen, when I went to war, I knew all about America's racism, from the petty insults and humiliations to the mob violence. I hated it and fought against it. In Indonesia and the Philippines, I began to understand it. It was more than the brutal economic exploitation of the African American. It was the way the rulers kept all whites united, despite their class differences. That unity was the foundation of their wealth and the stability of the system.

Before the war, we too often shrugged helplessly when confronted with the reality of race. Returning home, and beginning to understand the why of that racism, made it unbearable. We had become conscious defending other people's freedom. That consciousness made us half free. As with most of the million Black veterans, I began to realize that the war we just completed was a prelude to the one we now had to fight.

3

Not a week went by without a lynching or some other form of mob violence in America. Between June 1945 and September 1946, fifty-six African American veterans were lynched. The actual death toll was far greater. The Klan, as part of and in league with the police, had developed a terrible new weapon. Outspoken Blacks simply disappeared. The African

American press carried long columns seeking help in locating a disappeared loved one. An appeal to the sheriff for help was asking the goat about the cabbage.

White America, caught up in the giddy economic expansion, had little time for anything save their immediate problems. Official America decided "they" were asking for too much and turned a deaf ear to the cry for justice, turned a blind eye to the torture and murders, turned its back to the stench of burning flesh. I couldn't.

Sunday afternoon was quiet time in our house. My brothers were reading books or the Sunday paper or thoughtfully staring at the chessboard. I read a story about the lynching of one of those Black veterans from the stack of eight *Chicago Defenders* that I had saved over the past two months. Too tired from the rat race of reentering civilian life and too drunk from partying with my fellow vets to read what was happening to and with our people, I'd simply saved the papers. I hadn't been able to throw them away because reading our press was an obligation for any socially conscious African American.

I read the paper slowly, memorizing the scene. This was the fork in the road that I had tried to avoid. To not know and do nothing was one thing; to know and do nothing was something else. I knew I could not desert my fellow Black veterans any more than I could desert my platoon in combat. And they were in the most mortal of struggles. I read on.

John Jones, of Cotton Valley, Louisiana—Corporal John Jones of the United States Army a few months earlier—was arrested along with a teenager named Albert Harris on suspicion of attempting to rob a garage. The owner, Mrs. Sam Mettrick Jr., could not identify them. The two young Black men were released from the jail into the hands of a lynch mob that included her husband. The mob, determined to "drive the niggers back into their place" now that the war was over, attacked the men with axe handles and rifle butts. Screaming their innocence, the two men fell under the blows. The sheriff closed the door of the jail so he could testify that he did not see what happened. Beaten with clubs, stomped and kicked in the face and groin, the two half-conscious youths were thrown onto a truck and driven into the woods.

Dragged from the truck, Harris staggered to his feet and attempted to run. One of the white men raised his pistol and fired. The bullet hit Harris in the shoulder. He fell and lay still. The white man calmly walked over to the blood-soaked body and kicked. Harris remained still. The lyncher walked back to the mob and joined in torturing the young veteran. One of the white men had brought along an ugly, thick, four-foot whip used to drive cattle. Laughing at the moans and pleading, one after the other they lashed the half-conscious bloody body. Tiring of their sport, one of the white men went to the truck and returned with a double-bit axe. Jones was jerked to a kneeling position. One of the lynchers kicked him in the face, knocking him over onto his back. The lyncher raised the axe and with one blow severed Jones' arm between the wrist and the elbow. Screaming in pain, Jones attempted to rise and was knocked back to the ground. The axe, swung again, severed the other hand from the wrist. Cursing and laughing at his death agony, one of the white men lit a blowtorch and directed the flame at the stumps of Jones' arms, stopping the gushing blood. Then the flame was turned to the testicles and up to the stomach and the chest. His face engulfed with searing agony, Jones, screaming in pain, sucked in the flame, burning his lungs and mercifully ending his life.

After tossing Jones's burned, broken, dead body onto the flatbed, a few of the men turned to pick up Harris's body. It was gone. Harris's father had followed the lynchers. While they tortured Jones, he dragged his wounded son to a waiting car and sped off toward Texarkana. Infuriated, the lynchers headed for Jones's home, intending to kill his wife and newborn baby. Spirited through the back woods, however, his family was already on their way to the relative safety of Michigan.

The NAACP questioned Harris and other eyewitnesses to the sadistic murder. The *Chicago Defender* published the lynchers' names: Sidney Dean, deputy sheriff of Cotton Valley; Charley Edwards, deputy sheriff of Spring Hill; Oscar Haynes, deputy sheriff of Webster Ferry; and ten others. I wrote down each name so I would never forget them. The names were given to the FBI, but they were too busy hounding "Communists." President Truman was appealed to. He was too busy fighting for democracy in Bulgaria and did nothing for his Black citizens. A reality sank deeper into my consciousness: *They don't care. Nobody cares. The war is over, we are no longer needed, and they no longer care.*

I turned the page. Shocked by the rising tide of racist violence, Robert Hutchins, president of the University of Chicago, sadly stated, "America is conquered by the ideologies of Hitler." A few days later, a mob of two thousand of Chicago's whites attacked the home of a Black couple moving into "their" neighborhood. I read on. February 25, 1946, Columbia, Tennessee: After a dispute over the repair of a radio, two white men attacked nineteen-year-old navy veteran James C. Stevenson Jr. and his mother. Stevenson defended himself, knocking one attacker through a plate glass window. Three other white men ran across the street, beating and stomping both Stevenson and his mother. The police arrived and joined in the beatings. They took both mother and son to jail. The Black community raised the bail money. An infuriated mob of whites formed to lynch the mother and son.

The Black community, led by 150 veterans, formed an armed defense team. A lynching had occurred not quite a year before, and they were taking no chances this time.

The lynch mob, led by the city police, attacked the barricaded Black veterans with rifles, submachine guns, pistols, and shotguns. The veterans returned fire, wounding four cops. The mob withdrew for a few hours while the Tennessee National Guard, backed by the mob, moved in with armored cars and machine guns. Overwhelmed, the Black veterans surrendered. The entire Black community was looted and burned. The cops and National Guardsmen savagely beat the 101 captives. In the security of the jail, they murdered the two leaders, Gorton and Johnson, recently discharged veterans.

The African American people were fighting back. The scattered resistance, led by the veterans, was slowly coalescing into a fighting movement for equality. Senator Theodore Bilbo of Mississippi, ranting from the security of the Senate well, called for whites to use any means necessary to stop African Americans from voting.

It was a terrible time of indecision. I couldn't ignore the brutality and violence just because it hadn't hit me personally. The segregated army had given me too much of a collective spirit. It was either go back to a mission and sanity or stay with my drinking buddies and sink deeper into the depression and the frantic search for the "good times."

I folded the papers, put them aside, pulled on my army overcoat, and walked to the Dreamland Café, where the guys would be drinking beer and talking nonsense. It was a ritual of good-bye. I knew I could not stay with them.

As I left the bar, a neighbor kid passed by, nonchalantly singing the Jim Crow lyrics of a popular tune: "They hang you high, up in the sky, deep in the heart of Texas."

4

Subconsciously I began looking for some organized, militant movement. Movements and revolutions, however, do not come in neat packages. They start as street brawls and riots. In Minneapolis, the movement I was looking for began in that way. I'd been out of the army three months, but the war and its aims were still the number one topic on the corner and in the Dreamland Café. A group of us were having a discussion late on a Saturday evening. One of the men, Wilbur Wright, hadn't been in the army and mostly listened. A lean, dark-complexioned, five-foot-ten man, he was a fighter and would have made a good soldier. However, he'd spent most of the war in the Minnesota state prison at Sandstone.

Perhaps because of his prison experience, he was a loner and didn't tell anyone of his plans. That night, instead of going down to Seven Corners—the integrated, rowdy slum area—he stopped at a bar on Seventeenth and Cedar. The area was all white and dangerous for Black people. Wilbur tried to be served. In the fight that ensued the bartender was shot dead. The patrons closed in on Wilbur, beating and kicking him.

When the police arrived, Wilbur was more dead than alive. Three months later, with a plate in his skull, he appeared in court to face the charge of murder. A sympathetic judge gave him three years.

While one man's action isn't a movement, Wilbur Wright's attempt to integrate that bar was the beginning of something new in Minneapolis. Not everyone agreed with the way he went about it, but something had to be done. People were proud of him because, right or wrong, he took a stand.

brother, loaned him the funds to set up a forge in Oswego, Kansas. As a free man, he worked as the town's only blacksmith. Mom was born there on October 24, 1894.

By the time I was fifteen, this story, part of our often-told family history, posed questions I had to answer to myself. How could a father sell his daughter into a New Orleans whorehouse? How could a father sell his son into the short and ugly life of a slave on a sugar plantation? How does one enslave his brother? What kind of people were these? Consciously or subconsciously, every African American confronts this question. People who answer it by saying that something is inherently wrong with white people organize their lives around some form of Black nationalism. People for whom the answer is that the capitalist *system* strips mankind of its humanity become political progressives or revolutionaries. Early on, I rejected the first answer and by doing so unconsciously began my development as a revolutionary.

Kansas hated slavery, but it also hated the slave and later the freedmen and strictly enforced its segregation laws. One of those laws declared that a county could not build a school for colored children if there were fewer than twenty in attendance. The few African American children in the county depended upon their slave-born parents for education. Mom's mother, able to read and write, prepared her as best she could.

When Mom was fourteen, the extended family raised the money to send her to relatives in Kansas City, where she could go to school. After graduation she was introduced to Madam C.J. Walker, an African American who was America's first self-made female millionaire. A chemist and shrewd businesswoman, she created a line of cosmetics for the dark skins, tightly curled hair, and full lips of America's Black women. Walker lived modestly and used a great amount of her fortune to "uplift her people." One of her initiatives was to underwrite the education of bright African American women if they would agree to spend five years in the Deep South as teachers. Mom gave her word (that's all Madam Walker required) and graduated from Drake University Teachers College when she was twenty-four. After a year of "acclimation" in Atlanta, she accepted a teaching position in Greenwood, Mississippi. A year after that she moved to Mound Bayou.

The things she saw and participated in during those years in Mississippi shaped her social outlook. She believed deeply in W.E.B. Du Bois's notion that the educated tenth of the African American people bore the responsibility of "uplifting the race." She passed that sense of responsibility on to her sons.

Though quiet and unassuming, she was an activist. She took part in the demonstrations demanding the ballot for women and voted in the first election after that right was secured in 1920. She was a charter member of the Women's International League for Peace and Freedom. One hundred and seven years old at the time of her death in 2000, she was its oldest continuously active member.

The joy of her sons returning home from the war was dampened by the fact that her marriage was breaking up. Mom and Dad had been on the road to divorce since before the war, but our leftward drift gave our father an excuse to distance himself from the family. Pop was completing his final year with the Railway Mail Service as the McCarthy-led anti-Communist hysteria got under way in 1947. He had good reason to fear that he would be fired without his pension for associating with Communists—who were his sons. It never occurred to him that it was McCarthy and the fascist movement, not his sons, who threatened him, his job, and his pension. Worse, by our open support of the Communist Party we seemed to publicly challenge his position as head of the family. The quarrel transcended politics and became the bitterest of struggles between father and sons. We, his sons, felt that Pop was using anti-Communism as a way to socially justify distancing himself from the heavy responsibilities of a large family and to prepare a new life for himself and the woman with whom he was having an affair.

We didn't reject him. He was still our father. We were hurt, but we were open to him. However, like most African American families, we were centered around our mother.

With his flair for the dramatic, Pop assumed the aura of a loving father betrayed by his sons, who were caught up and brainwashed by Communism. At the meetings of his segregated American Legion post and in the corner tavern, he let it be known that he was forced to choose between patriotism and his sons. Publicly and tearfully he chose patriotism, to the applause of the professional anti-Communists, who then opened doors otherwise closed to him. As in the rise of German fascism, the first fatality was the family.

Ben, my older brother, held a job as a draftsman and was the sole support of the family for several months. I was still in the "52-20 club"—the government gave returning vets twenty bucks per week for a year as unemployment compensation. We couldn't pass that up—especially the guys who had been in the infantry, where we were on duty twenty-four hours a day, seven days a week. When the new semester began in September 1946, Ben went back to the University of Minnesota. I went to work as a construction laborer on the "Big Inch" gas pipeline for the unheard-of wage of ninety-nine cents an hour. (I had never earned more than thirty-two cents an hour before the war.) The other brothers, except the two youngest, found various jobs. We felt like a rich corporation. At the end of the week we would pile our money on the table. Mom would take out what was needed to run the house and feed the family, and divided the rest equally amongst us.

Through the Depression and the war years the family had grown close. As my brothers and I began dating and drifting away from the house, the women passed a joke around our little community: "Don't ever take up with a Peery boy. First time you have a fight he'll go home to his brothers."

Of the seven boys, I was always the one to stick his neck out first and furthest. I never knew why until the battle for Biak, an Indonesian island. While on patrol, we were fired on. Unable to see the enemy, my first instinct was to get away, to run. The patrol, frightened and unsure, hugged the ground. I knew if I didn't move forward, I would run back. I moved forward. It was the proper thing to do. The patrol moved with me. Later, one of the men asked me, "Why did you do that? You could have gotten shot."

"I had to," I replied.

I did not know how to tell him that I did it because I was terrified—terrified of getting shot, and more terrified of being a coward. For the first time, I realized that I seldom considered the middle ground.

When my mind was clear as to what I wanted to do with my life, I sat down with Mom and told her of my plans. When she asked why I was joining the Communists, I told her, "Because I have to." I knew she understood. I didn't know how to tell her that I had awoken and could never, ever go back to sleep.

I often thought about Harriet Tubman's saying: "If they would have understood their slavery, I could have saved thousands more." A slave who has not awakened bears his slavery as the natural order of things. But that slavery is unbearable to those who are awake. I tried to tell Mom that I was joining because I couldn't let them do this to me and to us. Now that I knew the why of the lynchings, the humiliations, and the exploitation, I had to fight them or become their dog. I reminded her of my great-grandfather who, after years of struggle and defeats, finally said, "We're mud on the white man's boots. The only place we're going is where he carries us." I had awakened and could no longer be that mud.

Mom didn't oppose my joining the Party. Terribly worried about my safety, she said, "If a revolution ever happens in this country, it will be because millions of white people are drawn into it. During slavery we had to wait until the white people began fighting one another, then we could talk about freedom. Let it happen again. They got us into this mess, let them get us out."

I quietly reminded her that both her grandfathers had fought in the Civil War. As usual, she accepted what was fact and began thinking in terms of how to protect me as I prepared to go forth into the struggle.

I again spoke to my brother Ben about joining the Party. He thought for a moment and said, "I believe in what the Party is doing. That doesn't mean I have to join it. I want to make my contribution as a scientist—as a teacher. I don't think I can do that as a member. You join, you are burning a lot of bridges and restricting what you can do. You had better think it over."

6

The mechanization of southern agriculture reduced the need for the unpaid farm labor that segregation and second-class citizenship provided. The question shifted from the level of economic necessity to the level of morality. America could not avoid asking itself whether it was American, Christian, or ethical to deny citizens their civil and equal rights simply because of color or former condition of slavery. I at least partially understood that a fight against what was considered "economic necessity" could not be won. I knew that a fight on the moral battlefield could be won, but it would be a fight that demanded everyone's participation.

It was no longer possible to quantify African American liberation. There was only one struggle left. That was the fight for complete equality and all that it implied. The Communists fought for it. The liberals could not visualize it.

In the face of this great danger and opportunity, the African American movement was undergoing a new level of splits. On one hand, such giants as W.E.B. Du Bois and Paul Robeson, energized by the human rights declarations of the United Nations and the developing national liberation movements, called for a militant, united fight against not only the lynchers but also the system that spawned and protected them. On the other hand, the so-called moderate Black leaders, notably Walter White and Roy Wilkins of the NAACP, lined up against them. The split was historic and irreconcilable. Both sides deeply believed their tactic would bring about real equality while anything else would result in destruction of their people.

This division of tactics began with the defeat of post–Civil War Reconstruction and the withdrawal of the Union army from the South. Delivered into the hands of their vengeful former masters, the freedmen had to find a path of survival. Those who chose to stand and fight were met with unspeakable mob violence, mass lynchings, and entire communities burned to the ground. As during the days of slavery, the defeated movement turned to those able to speak to and find accommodation with their oppressors. Under slavery they'd turned to the house servants. After Reconstruction, they turned to their progeny, who now worked in government and social service. In both eras they were betrayed.

Something akin to a bureaucratic Black bourgeoisie based in the social services and the segregated educational system developed and gained control of the African American movement. Their economic and social privileges depended on the tactic of accommodation. On the other hand, small-business owners, farmers, and a growing corps of cultural and industrial workers began to coalesce. Their existence depended upon creating space to grow. That depended upon struggle.

The educated, articulate sector of the African American people was so narrow they all knew each other and at times had worked together. Consequently, the split was not simply political. It was deeply personal and left its mark on the movement. The average African American did not speak of supporting "accommodation" or "militancy"; rather, he or she spoke of support for either Wilkins of the NAACP or Paul Robeson. The spreading, deepening, veteran-led spontaneous fight for freedom was shaking up both sides.

The prestige of the world Communist movement was at its height. Wherever there was a progressive struggle the Communists were leading it. The Communist Party was accepted in the Black neighborhoods because it was the only integrated organization. The church—the so-called moral leader—was the most segregated. Black workers didn't listen closely to the anti-Communist propaganda. They knew that if the government was serious about democracy and human rights, it would do something about the murders, the mob violence, and the lack of civil rights here in America.

My literary idol, Theodore Dreiser, America's greatest living writer, joined the Party. Former Marine colonel Evans Carlson (leader of the famous "Carlson's Raiders") joined with Paul Robeson to chair the "Win the Peace" conference. Robeson, near exhaustion, was fighting on all fronts, lending his name and voice in the struggle against some of the more fascistic anti-Black violence.

When Robeson came to Minneapolis on his cross-country tour in 1947, we timidly sent him a note asking if he had time to meet with our youth group for a few moments. We proceeded with our regularly scheduled meeting, not daring to hope that he would come by. In the middle of the meeting Robeson walked in, holding out his hands and smiling the smile that endeared him to millions around the world. After the handshakes and a short talk about the importance of the work we were doing, he gave a five-minute portrayal from *Othello* followed by a stanza of his signature song, "Old Man River." I sat enraptured, thinking how this man was giving his everything to the struggle—international prestige, fame, and an open road to a great fortune. Unlike Robeson, I had nothing to lose and no right to hold back.

Du Bois, who after a 1923 visit to the Soviet Union declared himself "Communist forever," began speaking at meetings sponsored by the Party and Party-influenced groups. Some eleven international unions, led by Communists or pro-Communists, were clearing the way for the politicization of the mass of workers. The left, riding high, inspired and excited me with the possibility of bringing real democracy not only to the African American people but also to the nation. I knew that to win in a decisive battle, every person had to carry out his or her responsibilities. I became more active.

I was asked to say a few words at a meeting of the Farmer-Labor Association, the left wing of the former Farmer-Labor Party. After the merger of the Farmer-Labor Party with the Democratic Party, the association independently carried on its populist-socialist program. I spoke of how the oppression of Black people led to the domination of Congress by reactionaries who were passing the anti-labor laws that affected Minnesota. The people liked what I said, and afterward I was introduced to a number of trade union and political leaders, among them the former governor, Elmer Benson. Governor Benson was the last of the left-wing populists who did so much to reconfigure Minnesota's political landscape. The governor, with a smile and a firm handshake, said, "I'm happy to meet you. We are going to need all the young people we can get."

I knew he meant it. Proud to meet the governor and to be part of a movement that included such leaders, I assured him that I intended to fight to the finish.

People I respected, older people who stayed out of trouble but contributed to the fight in a quiet way, warned me about joining the Party. They warned that I was bound to get in trouble with the law. I should be afraid of a police force that was almost an adjunct of the Ku Klux Klan? I thought that it was a pretty poor soldier who is afraid of those he has to fight. Right-wing Black fighters warned that the Party, being white, would use African Americans to gain their ends and then drop us. Paul Robeson's answer was that he hoped more people would use us in that manner. I remembered the day that I decided to join the army. I hated the U.S. Army. I hated its southern white generals, its segregation, its hatred of me. Yet I had to fight Hitler. The army was fighting Hitler, and so I joined it. With much the same outlook, I made up my mind that I would join the Party and, if possible, learn to be a Communist organizer.

I didn't know how to go about joining. I only knew of Communists who were underground, and even to ask about them made it appear as if you were in league with the police. It never occurred to me that Communists in America—in Minnesota—were completely open and secure. It never occurred to me that they would have an office. When I finally got the courage to ask one of the people I believed to be in the Party how to join, he suggested I go down to their office. I tried to cover my naiveté with a "Thanks, I should have thought of that."

The next morning I grabbed the streetcar and got off at Fifth Street and Hennipen. Glancing at the address, I walked up the stairs and knocked on a door that had the small letters CPUSA. A grandmotherly-looking woman with glasses and graying hair twisted into a bun atop her head opened the door and invited me into the large, airy office. I glanced quickly at the two empty desks. Behind the third sat a balding, ruddy-faced person in his late thirties or early forties. I smiled at the woman and told her my name and that I wanted to join the Party. She smiled and, introducing herself as Rose, nodded toward the seated comrade and said, "Good! You want to talk to Bob."

I walked over and shook his hand. He reached into the top drawer of his desk and pulled out a card. Folding it carefully down the center, he wrote in my name, so that it read, "Nelson Peery is a member in good standing of the CPUSA." The card was not unlike a regular union dues book except for the CPUSA logo and the slogan "Workers of the world—unite!"

After saying good-bye and shaking hands I started down the stairs thinking of the significance of what I had done. The period of being just another angry militant was over. I had volunteered again. I knew that, again, it was for the duration. Lost in such thoughts, I opened the door and noticed a car across the street as the driver calmly photographed me. I knew it was the FBI and gave him an infantryman's salute by extending my doubled-up fist and hitting the inside of my elbow. He glared at me. I glared back, crossed the street, and boarded the waiting streetcar.

7

Retail stores in Minneapolis followed a policy of not hiring Blacks. One of the record shops, the Melody, on Hennepin Avenue, catered to what white people called "race music" and had a near monopoly on Black trade. As a concession, or perhaps to secure that monopoly, they decided to hire a Black clerk to stock records. My younger brother Norm was seventeen at the time, clean-cut and handsome. He needed a job and applied at the Melody. The owners felt that he would be an asset to the place and hired him.

He was Black and they were white, so they assumed that if they put him in the section with the race records, he would steal some of them. They put him in the section that contained the classical music, sure that he had no use for any of those albums. If they thought he was a thief, he would be one. Every other week Norm walked out of the Melody with a classical record under his sweater.

The first record he brought home was Tchaikovsky's *Romeo and Juliet*. We all knew the story from high school, and part of our evening fun was acting out or shouting the part when there was a shift from one movement to the next. We eagerly awaited each new record, and it was a collective after-dinner treat when Norm came home with one.

We had just begun a second playing of "Sabre Dance" when Ira, our next-door neighbor, walked in. We were listening intently and no one bothered to say hello. Ira sat and listened for a few moments, then mumbled, "Man, that's some deep music. Who wrote it?"

"Khachaturian."

"Where's he from?"

"Georgia."

Ira listened for a few more moments, "That figures. The cat's got soul."

No one commented. Comrades in Soviet Georgia had soul just like brothers in the Ku Klux Klan's Georgia.

Between meetings and demonstrations I tried to maintain my ties with the guys and young women in the neighborhood. We seldom talked politics, but sometimes I would hear a snide remark to the effect that "Nelson is riding the gray train," which meant they felt I would rather spend my time with white people than with them. I was drifting away from them—I no longer got a thrill from the frantic parties and the heavy drinking that took the place of a social life we were barred from. Yet I wanted to stay close to them. As African Americans and as working people, they were who and what I was fighting for. I'd grown up with them, and I valued our relationship. Like so many Black Communists, I lived in two worlds and tried to keep them balanced.

8

The Party was ill-prepared to meet the anti-Communist offensive. A Communist Party with a membership base that has nothing to lose but their chains can withstand almost any pressures reaction turns against it. We had no such base. During the war, the Party became more of an anti-fascist movement than a party of the working class. When the war ended and the economy began to expand, it could not recover its working-class base. Instead, it tried to consolidate the thousands of outstanding intellectuals who came close to or joined the Party on the basis of anti-fascism. After I joined, I soon learned how fragile this base was.

The Red-baiting attacks were cranked up against any prominent person who spoke out against lynching or the muzzling of progressive intellectuals. Led by Walter Reuther, the trade union right wing, assisted by the FBI, the courts, and the monopoly press, gained victory over the left wing. Dizzy with success, the Red-baiters turned on the intelligentsia. I don't believe anywhere on earth an intelligentsia collapsed before reaction with such abject rapidity as in America. Here, joining the intelligentsia was hardly a calling. It was the path to wealth and prestige. By contrast, in Italy and Germany the intelligentsia often put their social responsibility ahead of their economic well-being and paid the price. The CPUSA's academics, under attack on all sides, fought back as best they could, but the reactionaries crushed the thin line of progressive intellectuals who attempted to make a stand. Democratic journalists were wiped out; lawyers who defended the legal rights of those on the left were disbarred. Progressive authors could not find a publisher. Teachers were fired for advocating equal rights or speaking out for peace. Schools moved to outlaw teachers' unions as well as a whole slew of books such as John Steinbeck's *Grapes of Wrath* and Lillian Smith's *Strange Fruit.* New York State's Feinberg Law not only compelled a loyalty oath from teachers but required that they spy and squeal on one another. In 1937, Nazi Germany passed a law allowing for the firing of tenured employees on the grounds of disloyalty. In 1947, America passed the same law.

The mass of the intelligentsia not only surrendered but provided an intellectual base for the reaction. Serious revolutionaries should never forget that the wholesale desertion of the intellectuals from the side of progress was the most severe and unexpected blow we suffered during that period. Our vision of a brave new world faded as the specter of fascism, armed with the seemingly irresistible weapons of racism and anti-Communism, arose.

Working-class comrades became a minority in the Party. Far more vulnerable than the academics, attacked by union and boss, they had little choice but to leave a Party that could not defend them. The Party began taking on more and more of a middle-class and especially academic face.

William Z. Foster, chairman of the Party and a worker himself, moved to strengthen what he saw as a serious weakening of the Party. He proposed that wherever possible working-class comrades should be merged into clubs that were top-heavy with cultural workers and academics. In line with this proposal, the section organizer informed me that I was being transferred to the club at the university.

I learned a lot at my first meeting. A political summary was the first point on the agenda. The depth and breadth of the comrades' grasp of world affairs astonished me. Later, they showed me the great number of magazines and journals they'd used in preparing the report. I had never seen or heard of any of them and was amazed that anyone had time to read them all. I began partly to understand why academics knew so much.

When the meeting was over, only a few said they had to leave. The rest stayed on for the coffee, sweets, and casual discussion. It took only one smiling invitation for me to stay. It was fascinating to seeing the fragile, human side of professors respected by the entire academic world. The small talk and corny jokes made me feel that if these common, ordinary human beings could master their intellectual crafts, any normal person could. I began to lose my fear of books and reports. The talk turned to classical music. I had no idea what the points and counterpoints they spoke of were. Conscious of the necessity of including me in their discussions, Mary Shaw, the head of the philosophy department, turned to me and asked, "Have you had a chance to study classical music?"

Instead of simply saying no, I made my ignorance more profound. "I like listening to some things, but I'm not much into the long-hair stuff." I could sense the shock in the room.

Mary was the first to recover. She smiled knowingly. "Comrade Nelson," she said, "it's classical because it has endured through the centuries. Anyone can enjoy music, but to get the most out of it, like anything else, it has to be studied."

I knew I'd better worm my way out of this, and thought of some of the records Norm had liberated and brought home. As softly as possible I said, "At home we listen to things like *El Amor Brujo* and *Prince Igor*. I know we don't understand everything, but we like them."

Mary smiled warmly. I liked the way she talked to me. I was a "comrade worker," not a "Negro comrade," and she was a respected intellectual. She was just as quick and sincere with her criticism as with her smiles.

"If you'd like," Mary said, "I'll arrange for you to audit a class in music appreciation. I think you'll like it."

I surely didn't need another night taken away from my time on the corner, but there was no way to say, "No, thank you."

"Thanks, Mary," I said, trying to sound sincere, "I'd really like to."

I liked my new club, since all they'd talked about in my former Party club was the situation in the unions. I intended to enter the university and did not want to be assigned to union work.

The following week I took a seat in the back of the music room and for six weeks I listened to the professor play, dissect, and explain the German classic *Till Eulenspiegel.*

I laughed to myself—a Black laborer studying a Gothic classic. It was a tough six weeks, but the tales of Till, as he outsmarted the nobility and defended the peasants, taught me the universality of culture in the struggle for democracy. Regardless of national forms, the content of democratic culture is the same the world over.

9

My time at the University of Minnesota was the happiest and most important period of my life. I would never again learn so much in such a short time, nor be so free to shape my own space and activity. The fifty bucks a month I received under the GI Bill was enough for personal needs, and all university expenses were paid.

In the latter years of World War II, the Party had struggled to broaden its base. Liquidating the Young Communist League in 1943 in favor of a broader organization, the American Youth for Democracy (AYD), was part of that struggle. Young, well-known radicals such as Frank Sinatra joined and lent their names to this new organization. I went to my first meeting of the University of Minnesota branch. As usual, I was late. As quietly as possible, I slipped into the room and sat beside a young white fellow. Just to be sure, I leaned over and asked him.

"This is the AYD?"

"Must be. It looks like an Association of Yids and Darkies."

I wasn't sure if I should laugh or belt him one. With a second glance, I was sure he was Jewish. It did seem that the meeting consisted of a few African Americans with the rest being Jews.

The meeting was educational. A "chalk-talk" artist rapidly drew rough sketches to illustrate the points in his lecture. He said, "Here's a man running down the street in his underwear. Must be crazy, no?"

Then he continued his sketching, showing the man running from a house with flames billowing from the doors and windows. Then he said, "No, he's not crazy. He's smart. But you would never know it if you didn't know the conditions. So the first step in any evaluation is to know the conditions."

I sat nodding to myself. I never forgot that lesson, and it would sustain me through the years.

When the meeting ended, most of us sauntered up to the Gopher Café for a beer and to continue the introductions. I knew I was going to like working with the AYD. Before the evening was over I felt the warmth that held the comrades together.

10

By 1948 it was clear to the FBI and revolutionaries alike that the groundswell of struggle created by the African American people throughout the nation was of historic importance. The heroic determination of the Black masses, the Cold War rhetoric about freedom and democracy, and the decline of southern agriculture created a situation where the ruling class could not control Blacks in the same old way. Conversely, the African American masses refused to be controlled in the same old way. Led by the veterans and determined to get some of the Four Freedoms they had fought and died for, they were no longer afraid of the Klan and the sheriffs. This was the specific form in which the worldwide wave of national liberation washed ashore in America. The winds of change generated by the war against fascism were finally blowing across Mississippi and Alabama.

The FBI claimed the upsurge was due to subversion by the Communists. A huge section of white America believed them, and anti-Black and anti-Communism ideology became even more tightly linked. The Civil

Rights Congress, with the full support of the Party, stood almost alone in exposing and fighting the increasing oppression.*

The more determined the struggle of the African American people for freedom, the more vicious became the assault against them. In Martinsville, Virginia, seven young African Americans were arrested on the standard charge of rape and sentenced to death. The case of Willie McGee of Mississippi, another so-called rape case, became a center of our activity. A court in Trenton, New Jersey, sentenced six African American youths to death for a murder they could not possibly have committed. An African American veteran and his wife were murdered on the steps of the Atlanta courthouse when they attempted to register to vote. A Georgia landlord assaulted Rosa Ingram, one of his sharecroppers, and her two young sons came to her assistance; the three of them were jailed for life. Amy Mallard had the courage to publicly identify the white man who murdered her husband. The white man was never arrested and Amy Mallard was sent to prison.

11

Our little Communist club at the university could not see the historic parameters of the struggle, but like the rest of politicized America, we were swept into it.

We never put the point on the agenda of our meetings, but the weakest link in our Party unit was the lack of African American women members. Of the small number of African American women at the university, three or four of the more politically advanced were close to the Party. A few nominally joined the AYD. A combination of history and society kept them at arm's length from us. History taught them that with an education and a

---

* The Civil Rights Congress was formed in 1946 by a merger of the International Labor Defense (which led the struggle for Sacco and Vanzetti, Tom Mooney, and the Scottsboro Boys), the National Negro Congress, and the National Federation for Constitutional Liberties.

clean record, they could slowly move ahead economically and socially. If they rocked the boat and angered the ruling class, they would remain day workers, shackled to the mops and kitchens of people with less sense and often less education. Society taught them that joining the revolutionary movement very often placed them, as relatively politically unsophisticated Black women, in unequal competition with white women for the attention of their men. It was easier to simply stay away even as they supported the struggles of the Communists.

Marion was an exception. I'd known her slightly before the war. She grew up on the far North Side of Minneapolis, away from our tight little ghetto. With few close friends, most of them neighborhood white girls she grew up with, she was one of the few Black women I knew at the time who felt at ease with whites. She was majoring in sociology, and as she was surrounded by Jewish liberals from her college, it was only a matter of time before she came to a meeting of the AYD.

I saw her before she noticed me. She stood quite at ease talking to Sheila, her arms crossed, holding a book to her breast. One foot rested on the first of the marble stairs of the student union. The spring breeze ruffled her skirt, outlining the straight athletic legs.

As I approached, she turned, smiling. "I saw the announcement that you were giving a talk. Thought I'd come by and see if you remember me."

"Sure, I remember you. I heard you were here at school. I'm glad to see you." I was happy she'd come to the meeting. She made it more legitimate. More than that, the more time I spent with the comrades, the less I spent with the guys on the corner or with the few Black students at school. I didn't like being known as a Black guy who would rather hang around with whites than with his own color, but I couldn't back off from my commitments to the movement. The only way out of the contradiction was to recruit Black students into the AYD.

I took her arm and we went up the steps to the meeting.

After it was over the students stood around for a few moments discussing the political points raised during the meeting and then drifted away. After the room emptied, the Party members grouped together for the walk to the café and a sum-up of the meeting. I invited Marion to come with us. With a warm smile she stepped beside me. I had the uncomfortable feeling the comrades assumed, because we were African Americans, that she was my date rather than a contact we all had responsibility for.

From the beginning, I felt drawn to her. It was more than the easy laughter, the slender healthy body, or the way she incorporated every new word from her Psych I class into her conversation ("the teaching assistant has a fixation on me"). I understood her. Marion was lonesome the way I was lonesome. The way she thought, her white friends, and the social goals she held tended to isolate her from Minneapolis's tiny Black community, except for the Sunday services. Unable because of color to fully fit into the social stratum that reflected her education and culture, she, like me, lived in the lonely periphery of both societies, belonging to neither. I had a large, warm, boisterous family. I had the Party and my twenty-four-hours-a-day, seven-days-a-week schedule to keep me from thinking about the contradictions. She had none of this, and aside from a minimal social life, she spent her hours maintaining a straight-A average at the university.

We connected at an opportune time. Longing for a stable relationship, I was terrified by the possibility. Stability meant responsibility, and that meant dividing my life. I never admitted it to myself, but I knew without the intensity and discipline of nearly full-time Party life, I would slide back into the postwar emotional depression, the whiskey, and whatever lay beyond. I reached for what she offered, knowing it would kill me should I take it.

12

Our club meetings sometimes went on for hours as we strained to determine what we could do to influence the developing struggle. At one such meeting I raised the point that the University of Minnesota was one of the nation's great schools, yet it did not have a single Black professor. I thought that might be a campaign that would gather real support for the Party on campus. There was prolonged discussion as to how to get started. Some thought it would be most effective if comrades on the faculty raised the issue. Some thought it would not become a student issue if raised by the faculty. I agreed with the majority that we should raise it through the AYD, which would openly carry out and lead the struggle. Then comrades on the faculty would support it. We agreed to make an appeal to the students' morality, to their sense of fair play, and thereby get them into motion. We finally decided that we would open the campaign by distributing a leaflet and calling a demonstration. At the demonstration, I would speak with a bullhorn from the steps of the student union. I was assigned to get a permit from student affairs.

The next day I went to student affairs to ask for the permit to speak. Viola handled most of the permits. She wasn't a comrade, but if there was any such thing as a fellow traveler, it was Viola.

"What is going to be the subject of the demonstration?" she asked.

I didn't want to appear too radical on this most radical question facing the country.

"We feel that it is time for the university to hire a Negro professor. Other schools are integrating their faculty and we thought it would be good for the U to do that, too."

Viola looked at me for a few moments, nodding slightly as if the idea of a Black professor had never occurred to her but she thought it was a good one. She said, "I'll have to take this to the dean. Can you come back tomorrow?" I assured her I could and left.

The next morning, the student paper, the *Gopher*, came out. I quickly turned to the letters page. Sure enough, the letter I had written in the name of the Party club was prominently printed. The letter was signed, "For the combined Communist clubs, Nelson Peery." Ben had cautioned me that signing such a statement was too much of a challenge for the university to accept and it wasn't necessary. I did it because I felt we had to assert our right to speak as a legitimate part of the campus. I knew the letter would cause a stir; I didn't know how much.

The following day I went back to student affairs. Viola, unsmiling, came to the counter. I knew something was wrong.

"Did they deny the permit?" I asked.

"No, at least not yet. The dean wants to speak with you."

"Now?" I asked.

"Yes."

I knew the dean did not have time to speak to students about trivial things.

"Is it something real bad?"

"Probably about the letter in the *Gopher*," she said.

She opened the gate and motioned down the hall toward the ornate office of Dean Edmund Williamson. I started down the hallway thinking, *The university is the last citadel of free speech in the country, and unless that free speech is used, it is useless.* By the time I reached his door, I was determined to be defiant and hold my ground. I knocked lightly and pushed the door open. The dean rose, motioning to a big leather chair in front of his desk.

"Come in, Mr. Peery, have a seat."

Thanking him, I sat down, glancing at the open *Gopher* on his desk. The dean pressed the tips of his thumbs and fingers together and looked at me as if thinking, *How do I get this across to a person who under these conditions openly identifies himself as a Communist?*

"Mr. Peery"—he leaned slightly toward me—"do you know how this university is run?"

"Sir, I think the university administration is doing a fine job."

"No, no. I mean do you know what it takes to run this university?"

I hesitated, so he continued. "It takes money. Millions of dollars. Money for buildings, for salaries, for research. Millions of dollars. Do you know where it comes from?"

Again I hesitated.

"That money is appropriated by the state legislature. The legislature is dominated by downstate, conservative, rural representatives."

I sat quietly, waiting for the inevitable.

"They are informed about this university." He nodded toward the *Gopher*. "They read this paper. I don't know what they will say, but I don't think they will be much inclined to meet our budget requests this year."

"Sir, I had no intention of harming the university. We felt we had to speak about the attacks on academic freedom under the guise of anti-Communism. We only wanted to let people know that we are students, not some foreign conspiracy."

"I'll defend your right to speak. This is a university. I'm just asking you to think about timing. And please stop calling me 'sir.' "

"All right, Dean, if you stop calling me 'Mr.' "

The atmosphere relaxed, and the dean glanced from the paper to me.

"So you want to bring a Negro professor to the campus."

"We thought it would make the university appear more democratic and it would help the white students learn to respect Negroes. And it would help if the few Negro students saw what was possible."

"It might help you to know that we have been privately discussing this for some time. You will get your permit, and I'll probably lose the new dormitory and perhaps the agricultural building and maybe my job."

I smiled at the dean and said, "Then we'll really hold some rallies."

Smiling too, he rose, signaling that the interview was over. I thanked him and left the room. After years of watching leading academics kowtow to the thought-control police, I realized what a democratic, committed man Dean Williamson was.

The following Friday morning we passed out leaflets stating the purpose of the afternoon rally. We didn't talk about it, but we all knew that beneath the democratic surface of the university, the majority of the white students did not believe that any African American was qualified to teach. Sadly, the majority of the Black students shared that opinion. Excelling in this or that subject, yes. But teaching? A man born in slavery lived down the street from us! Even to speak of getting an education would have gotten him a severe beating not that long ago. After three hundred years of successful whites telling unsuccessful Blacks that they were not capable, some of it was bound to sink in, and it did. In order to fight for our rights, we had to first fight ourselves. We had to conquer ourselves, make ourselves stand up and repeat that "everyone on earth is just as good as we are" until we understood and believed it.

To our surprise, the students seemed interested. By two o'clock small groups began assembling at the foot of the steps of the student union. We knew we were going to have a successful rally.

The comrades arrived with their assigned papers and pamphlets. Bob and Jay showed up with the bullhorn and the rally began. I spoke for half an hour and then handed the bullhorn to other comrades who passionately demanded the university stop Jim Crowing education. After several hours we were worn out and our audience began to dissipate. We called a halt to the rally, knowing we had taken a solid step toward a victory. The glum looks on the faces of the FBI agents covering the rally told us we were winning.

A month later, a brilliant young African American academic, Forrest Wiggins, was appointed to the Philosophy Department.

13

The Party was an education machine. There was so much to learn! It seemed that culture, not Marx, lay at the heart of the movement. With the rest of the comrades, I set about learning the songs and culture of the peoples of the earth. To do otherwise, we were convinced, would be crass chauvinism. My brother Al had a good voice and soon was singing with the Party chorus. He was sharp-faced and thin-lipped, with a hawk-like nose, and he sang the Yiddish songs so well that two old Jewish revolutionaries asked him if he was from the lost tribe. In perfect Yiddish he assured them that he was.

I learned the stirring words of our anthem, "The International." Written in 1871 by Eugène Pottier, a working-class fighter of the Paris Commune, before he faced the firing squad, it is the most beloved of all revolutionary music. Full of pride and conviction, my voice was always the loudest:

Arise, ye prisoners of starvation,
Arise, ye wretched of the earth,
Justice thunders condemnation!
A better world's in birth.

Being a student meant access to books and time to read them. I literally dove into Marxism. Nothing is so exhilarating as learning, and for a time I was on a high with new ideas. No matter the misunderstandings, the misconceptions, or the lack of a base in philosophy or economics, no matter the number of times I had to go to the dictionary, I was learning to think! At the club educationals, I began to understand the engines of history and the role of individuals in making that history. Idea by idea and page by page, I became a communist.

There was more to education than books. If one aspect was intellectually stimulating, the other aspect was fun. As the repression increased and the fellow travelers who connected us to the world deserted us, more and more we turned inward and our social life became an appendage of our political life.

Guitars, songs, and Red Mountain wine mixed with Marx and Engels at our impromptu little socials. My youngest brother, Dick, never formally joined with us in the Party or the youth movement, but he often came to the events and outings. At one such outing after the political discussion, someone pulled out a guitar. We sang "I've Been Working on the Railroad," and after the line "Someone's in the kitchen with Dinah," one of the young white comrades said we shouldn't sing that song since it was chauvinistic. Dick, fifteen at the time, quietly asked her, "Why do you think Dinah is colored?" I felt sorry for the embarrassed comrade. I, too, had always assumed she was.

Every two weeks the AYD held a dance class. Along with learning songs, we learned folk dances of various nations. I was almost always the only African American present. We weren't successfully contacting the social sector we wanted to recruit from. Finally one of the organizers suggested that we hold the classes at the Phyllis Wheatley Settlement House. This institution, located in the poorest area on the North Side of Minneapolis, was the only settlement house serving the Black community.

I had grave doubts about a group of young white men and women going there, but I didn't say anything. We were for integration, and that meant white kids had the right to go to that settlement house, just as we were fighting for my right to go to the settlement houses in the white areas.

The two leaders of the AYD, who were white, went to the settlement house and presented their plan for teaching the dances of various European nationalities. It would have been unthinkable for the administration to say no despite their misgivings. The date was agreed upon and the orga-nization went to work guaranteeing success.

A professional square dance caller (probably a Party member) was en-gaged. Records of the polka and other European dances were gathered. To the consternation of the young Black nationalists who were struggling to gain control of the settlement house, we passed out leaflets in the area inviting all the neighborhood youth to come.

The dance was a great success. Some twenty Black youth showed up and had a wonderful time learning the square dance and polka. It again showed me that people are naturally curious about other cultures and peo-ples. National hostilities had to be taught.

14

A few of us were hanging out at the AYD office. My younger brother Car-roll, who as a baby we nicknamed "Ki," was mumbling about the need to connect to the masses. He was such a hot-rod radical that within the secu-rity of the house we called him "LBL"—Little Black Lenin. Mom once called him a monomaniac. Chuck Rollins, the state chairman, looked up from his paper and said, "What do you know! Leadbelly is going to be at the university this afternoon."

"Good. Do you want to go see him?" Ki asked, taking the paper. When he finished the article, his eyes shifted to the adjoining page. "Hey, the Dean of Canterbury is in town. He's a leader of the Episcopalian Church. That's the church I grew up in."

"I guess you want to see him, too," I said.

We all laughed. Folks like us didn't go see a leader of the Church of En-gland. An hour later we were sitting in the university auditorium laughing and applauding Leadbelly's booming voice singing the gutsy folk songs from the cotton patch and chain gangs.

Alan Lomax had met Huddie Ledbetter (no Black Mississippi chain gang prisoner was going to pronounce that name, hence the nickname

Leadbelly) while touring southern prisons, recording Negro folk music for the Library of Congress. Under Lomax's guidance, Leadbelly became an internationally known source of African American country blues.

Ki, always the wheeler and dealer in the family, headed backstage. We followed him. Mobbed by adoring college students, Leadbelly, sweating and grinning, was looking for a way out. When he saw Ki, the only black face in the crowd, he walked over and introduced himself as if no one knew who he was. They started talking. Ki, the master jive artist, met Leadbelly's every down-home cliché with one of his own. They were hitting it off. After a few moments of banter, two sharp-looking white men approached Ki and introduced themselves as Leadbelly's managers.

"Do you think you can get this guy out of sight for the next twenty-four hours?" they asked.

Ki, stunned, blinked his eyes for a moment. "What do you mean?"

"Well, could you take him to your house or something like that? I'll give you ten dollars to cover with."

Ki grinned, "You've got a deal."

We took Leadbelly home. We talked a bit and then Ki looked up and said, "Hey, guys—I just remembered reading somewhere that the Dean of Canterbury once said that he was a champion of southern Negro music. Do you think we could get these guys together and let them have a conversation?"

We all looked at one another, thinking, *The frocked, staid Dean of Canterbury and ruckus-raising Leadbelly having a discussion?* We all broke out laughing at the thought of it. Then Ki said, "Why not?" None of us could answer that.

We went to the church where the dean, Hewlett Johnson, was speaking that night. Ki always believed in solving problems by tackling them head-on. He walked up to the dean's traveling secretary, whose name was Carr, and said, "We have Leadbelly, the great Negro folksinger, at our house. I understand the dean is interested in that kind of music. Why don't you bring him over to say hello?"

It turned out that the dean's secretary was also a lover of folk music. Dr. Carr broke into a slow smile and said, "Where do you live?"

Ki gave him the address. Carr thought for a moment and said, "That's a small colored neighborhood over there."

"That's right," Ki said

"We'll be there tonight."

We left, and when we got home Leadbelly was gone. We panicked. The Dean of Canterbury was coming over and, typically, our man had gone in search of some action.

Three of us jumped into the car and raced down to Leadbelly's hotel. After pounding on the door for a few moments, we cornered one of the bellhops we knew and asked him to see if Leadbelly's guitar was in his room. That would give us some indication where he wasn't—and maybe where he might be. When it was safe, the bellhop looked in and told us both guitars were there.

"I know what's going on," Ki said. "We've got to get up to Olson Highway right away."

We started where Olson Highway entered the Black area and bar by bar searched the neighborhood. We were ready to give up when we entered the Keystone, the roughest bar in town. With such a small Black population, everybody knew all the Black bartenders, and we knew this one.*

"Hey, man, how you doin?" That was Ki's standard opening when he wanted something.

"All right. What you want?"

"Man, I'm supposed to be taking care of Leadbelly. Did he come in here?"

"Yeah, he's here. He's downstairs."

"Can I go down and get him?"

The bartender gave a slow, lascivious grin. "You don't want to go down there."

---

* In 1946 there were five thousand African Americans living in Minneapolis. The majority lived on the North Side, with a smaller enclave on the South Side of the city. Minneapolis was rigidly segregated, especially in employment. The unions and employers cooperated in barring African Americans from most industrial jobs. The African American community provided the waiters, janitors, bellhops, and other service workers to the city. A major employer was the railroad.

"Well, can I send a message down there?"

"Yeah, I'll take it down." The barkeep wrote down Ki's name and disappeared through the door to the basement. He returned in a few moments, grinning. "Go down and knock on the door with the slot in it."

We went down and knocked on the described door. A big ornery-looking guy with a long razor scar on his face slowly opened the door.

"You the guy lookin' for Leadbelly?"

"Yeah."

"What you want with him?"

"Just tell him I'm here and got to speak to him."

When he turned, we looked into the big room with its gaudy furniture and dim blue and red lights. It was early in the evening, and three or four women lounged on the sofa or the overstuffed chairs. Leadbelly was sitting in an easy chair with a woman on his lap. Scarface shambled over and whispered to him. Leadbelly, with a sheepish grin, motioned to Ki, and my brother went in. He quietly explained the situation to him and said we would have to get back home right away.

Leadbelly gave a sigh of resignation and said, "That sounds right to me." Turning to the woman sitting on his lap, he told her, "I'm sorry, babe, but the date's off this time. Next time, we really gonna have a date."

"Honey, you ain't gonna dump me now—not for some preacher?"

"I'm sorry, but I got to do what I got to do." He pulled a five-spot out of his pocket, gave it to her, and stood up, almost dumping her on the floor. He flashed his big grin to the ladies and walked out the door.

Getting back to the house before the dean arrived, we served Leadbelly the promised collard greens and smoked pig knuckles. Then we set about picking up the place and arranging the chairs.

Things were just about ready when we saw the two limousines pull up in front of the house. Our neighbor, Ira, saw them too. Having watched *I Led Three Lives,* he was convinced that this was a FBI raid on his Communist neighbors. Grabbing his stash of marijuana, he fled out his back door.

We all wished we had cleaned the walks as the dean and his entourage made it through the snow and ice and up the eight concrete steps to the top of the terrace. The dean, in a gray tunic and sporting his famous gaiters, smiled broadly as he approached the house. Everyone stood and cheered as he entered. Hewlett Johnson, the Dean of Canterbury! The Red Dean! The author of *The Secret of Soviet Power*, which so upset the world's Christian community, the friend of the Soviet people, was in our house! The pictures I had seen of him did not do him justice. The Anglo-Saxon nose and the sharp Dickensian face exuded a Christian goodwill and communist blessings over everyone present.

When the dean entered the room, Leadbelly, being very polite, rose grinning. He thought, given the dean's position in the church, it would be proper to bow. Leadbelly gave an awkward curtsy. Ki introduced them. Grinning, Leadbelly said, "I sure am pleased to meet you, Mr. Dean."

The dean replied, "And I am certainly most pleased to meet you, Mr. Belly."

After the dean was seated, Carr leaned over and asked him if he would like a glass of beer. The dean graciously answered that he would like one at room temperature. We all smiled; we had never heard anyone order warm beer.

Slowly the party got under way. Leadbelly tuned his big twelve-string guitar and began to sing some of his better-known songs. His great, countrified, prison-molded voice boomed through the house and out into the street.

The Episcopalians and leftists from the suburbs got wind of the party and began arriving in their Cadillacs and Lincoln Continentals. The students from the university got the word and began arriving. Comrades with a radar sense of the gathering mingled with the highbrow from the suburbs in the classless swaying to the beat of the twelve-string guitar. Someone tipped off the press, and they came elbowing their way into the living room. The neighbors leaned out of the windows trying to see what in the world was going on.

Soon there were more than two hundred people crowded into our house. With the doors open to the cold November night, they packed the porch. They overran the living and dining room. They jammed the entryway, the area leading to the stairs, and even the stairway leading up to the bathroom. Given the swaying and milling of two hundred people, I thanked the Lord that I had just the week before set up steel stanchions to underpin our already sagging floor.

The dean sat listening with the quiet attention of the English. Lead-belly noticed he wasn't swaying or tapping his foot. He couldn't allow that. He turned to the dean. "Mr. Dean, here's how the people in the Episcopal Church sing this song." He slowly strummed the guitar and sang in a slow, dignified manner:

Shine on me, shine on me.
Let the light of the lighthouse shine on me.

"And here's how the Baptists sing it." The rhythm and tempo increased, and some of the people were caught up as he sang to the new beat:

Oh, shine on me, shine on me.
Let the light from the lighthouse shine on me.

"And," Leadbelly shouted above the laughter, "here's the way the Holy Rollers sing it." His big sausage-like fingers flew up and down the neck of the guitar, slapping and pounding out an almost boogie-woogie beat:

Yes Lord, Let it shine on me. Shine on me.
Let that light from the light house shine on me.

I looked over at the dean. He was smiling and tapping his foot to the rhythm. I got the feeling that he was the only Englishman I ever met that we might have transformed into a sure-enough African American.

The dean and Leadbelly found themselves separated by this restless sea of people. There was a pensive look on the dean's face. He rose, saying, "This man is a marvelous genius," and elbowed his way to Leadbelly's chair. Bending down to sit on the floor, the dean said, "It is my honor to sit at your feet, sir."

I'll never know where the beer and the wine came from, but they were plentiful, and soon people began working their way through the crowd and up the stairs to the only bathroom. With seven guys, Mom, and Grandma living in the house, there was always something wrong with the toilet. Either it wouldn't flush or the water kept running, threatening to overflow.

Finally it happened and the word was passed down the stairs that the toilet was overflowing. It was not possible to elbow one's way up the stairs. My brother Ross went outside and got the ladder we used to put on the storm windows, which was still leaning against the house. He climbed through the window and fixed the toilet. Another guest stood patiently waiting for him to leave the bathroom. Mr. Supac, the millionaire manufacturer of snowsuits, smiled and told Ross he would take care of things. Ross climbed back out the window and Supac graciously adjusted the toilet after every use.

Leadbelly wore the night away, bubbling with his famous, charming little speeches and anecdotes. Once he stopped playing, looked at the dean, and said, "Mr. Dean, why do you wear that frock?"

The dean's answer was lost in the embarrassed laughter, and I was glad to hear the music start again. By eleven, Leadbelly kept looking with increasing concern at the dean. After a moment he asked, "You all right, dean?"

The dean, a frail-looking, intense man, answered, "Oh, yes. I'm quite all right and am enjoying myself immensely."

Finally, Carr said, "It's been a marvelous night, and we could stay here until nine in the morning, but I think we'd better get Dean Johnson in for a bit of rest."

We all joined in singing "Goodnight Irene" as the crowd filed out the door. That ended the night, and Fourth Avenue would never be the same.

15

Henry Wallace, former vice president and leader of the People's Progressive Party (PPP), made huge inroads into the Democratic Party's turf. A public opinion poll of June 1948 indicated that Wallace would get ten million votes in that fall's presidential election. Defying the death threats and demonstrations by the Klan, Wallace toured the South, speaking only to integrated audiences. His Progressive Party became the target of every

African-American-hating Red-baiter in the country. The Detroit police commissioner, John Ballenger, proclaimed that Progressive Party members "ought to be either shot, thrown out of the country, or put in jail."

After carefully analyzing the election of 1940, in which Roosevelt had been elected to a third term, Clark Clifford, advisor to President Harry S. Truman, told Truman that he would lose the election if he didn't get the Black vote. That vote was increasingly swinging to Wallace and his promise of democracy. The political establishment panicked, and the isolation of the PPP became the center of election politics. The Americans for Democratic Action (ADA) was formed to destroy the PPP. It immediately moved to identify Wallace's party with the Communists. Lester Granger, head of the Urban League, leading the pack, declared that the Communist Party had formed the Progressive Party. Buoyed up by the congratulations of those in Congress who filibustered every half step toward equality, Granger secured his place alongside the scores of "house Negroes" who betrayed every rebellion of the field hands.

W.E.B. Du Bois, the respected leader and intellectual soul of the NAACP, was fired as editor of its magazine, *The Crisis*, when he endorsed Wallace and the PPP. After an attempt to murder him in Jefferson City, Iowa, Paul Robeson, a prime mover in the formation of the PPP, abandoned his successful concert stage career to devote himself to that party. President Truman, dropping his racist positions, issued the executive order desegregating the armed forces and asked congress to create a permanent Fair Employment Practices Commission. The Dixiecrats walked out of the Democratic Party rather than accept any form of racial equality. The base of Black support for the PPP began to crack, and we were suddenly on the defensive.

16

At home things went from bad to worse. As the Red-baiting and repression increased, Pop stayed away from the house. I could imagine what happened when FBI agents interrogated him about his loyalty considering his seven pro-Communist sons. Pop was a professional at this sort of game. He quickly became the chief Red-baiter in his Jim Crow American Legion post and was the cardinal anti-Communist in the state's American Legion. He became a mentor to George Putnam, who went on to become the ultra-right, Red-baiting newscaster in Los Angeles. Years later, Putnam read the eulogy at Pop's funeral.

Pop was away from home for longer and longer periods. When he did come home, there was such tension and bitter arguments that we seldom missed him. Not so with Mom; for her, the impending divorce was the beginning of the breakup of the family she had borne so much to hold together.

I was twenty-four and knew what went on in the world. I abstractly understood what happens when people who have been married for twenty-six years decide to divorce. But these were my parents, and some-how, no matter how difficult things had become, I believed the family would stay together.

I was not prepared when I came home and heard the muffled sobbing upstairs. Not knowing what to expect, I ran up the stairs two at a time. Mom was lying across the bed sobbing as if her heart would break. Beside her was an opened gift box. Flung out, partly on the bed and partly on the floor, was an expensive, quilted maroon man's bathrobe. A little flowered card was signed, "Love, Dolly."

Even if I couldn't admit it, from the time I came home from the war I'd known that Pop had another woman. Everything that Mom had sus-pected was now a fact. I sat at the edge of the bed and held her for a few mo-ments. The trusting little girl in her was lost and betrayed and hurt. She seemed so tiny and fragile, so much in need of protection. I had never seen her cry before, and for the first time, I saw her not just as Mom but as a woman. Sorrow welled up for all the times I'd never considered her needs. She put those needs aside to care for us. She wanted the family to stay to-gether. We would give her that. We were still a family—he was no longer part of it.

17

At the university we held a special Party club meeting to elect delegates to the state convention. I knew that as the most public African American comrade, I would be elected as a delegate from our club.

The convention, held in the summer of 1948, was to discuss the Party's draft political resolution and elect delegates to the national convention, to be held in New York. The resolution explained the fundamental political line the party was to follow for the next two years. It was a moment when all officials resigned and everyone at the convention was organizationally equal. In this moment of equality, criticism would be evaluated on its merit, not by who said it. I was naive enough to believe that.

I intended to bring up several questions concerning Party policy. One of these questions was around Josip Broz Tito, the general secretary of the Yugoslav League of Communists. At that time, Tito was the darling of the communist movement. I considered the apolitical adulation to be contrary to the spirit of communist collectivity. More importantly, I thought that his recent articles on the relationship of the Party, state, and government were fundamental deviations from Marxist doctrine and intended to say so.

The convention opened on a Friday evening in an uneasy atmosphere. After the preliminaries, such as the reading of the political resolution, the floor was turned over to the delegates for debate. I sat and listened for a long time, trying to muster the courage to attack the writings of a world leader of the movement. I felt I had to do it because we were political equals and I believed Tito to be wrong. The convention followed the usual pattern. First a discussion of the resolution was held, then a discussion of international affairs and local politics, and finally a discussion on the Party itself.

After the almost mandatory self-praise of the Party—much of it earned in the increasingly difficult struggle—the discussion turned to some criticism of past mistakes. At this point, I thought I should present my case against Tito. I was confident that the carefully written paper, with references to the classical writings of Marx and Lenin, would be a contribution to our convention. I raised my hand and asked for the floor. With polite applause from the sixty-odd delegates, I was called upon.

"Comrades, I would like to present a criticism of the article by Comrade Tito that was printed in last month's *Political Affairs.*"

A deathly silence fell over the room. I knew at once that I was in trouble. I also knew that to simply follow leaders that I felt were wrong was a betrayal of the revolutionary spirit. I continued reading to the end of the report. "Hence"—that was the way Stalin ended his reports—"it seems clear that the theory of placing the state, the government, and the Party on the same level does away with the leading role of the Party."

The usual polite applause that accompanied each speaker was missing. A tense silence smothered the room. I knew that a criticism of Tito was, in the minds of most comrades, an implied criticism of Stalin and the Soviet Communist Party. I thought, though, that the comrades in Minnesota were much more freethinking that those of New York. I was wrong.

Carl Ross, the secretary of the district, took the floor. A Finn in a Party struggling against the "Jewish communist" stereotype, Carl was catapulted into the leadership of the Young Communist League and later into the leadership of the Minnesota district. Taking a long drag on his pipe for effect, he opened with the New York jargon we'd learned was the prelude to expulsion.

"Why does the comrade come to this district convention and carry out a slanderous attack against Comrade Tito? Is it not true that Comrade Tito led the International Brigades in Spain? Is it not true that Comrade Tito led the partisan resistance against the fascist invaders? Is it not true that Comrade Tito, unifying the Yugoslav peoples for the first time, is Stalin's closest comrade?"

By the time he finished, I knew that my expulsion was inevitable. I was angry that they should invite criticism and evaluation and then attack anyone who attempted it. I took the floor.

"Comrades, I have not attacked Comrade Tito. I criticized an article I believe to be incorrect." I could feel the convention splitting. Some instinctively came to the defense of a Black comrade. Some wanted more democracy in the Party. Others believed that, under attack, the Party had to close ranks. Through it all, I felt the hand of the FBI. Never exposing themselves by taking firm positions, always in lukewarm support of the organizational leaders, they knew how to take advantage of every opportunity to undermine the internal legality and solidarity of the Party. Two delegates later exposed as agents supported Carl Ross in his attack against me. Then the discussion turned to how to handle this hot potato. Sam Davis, editor of the *CIO News*, took the floor. Holding the back of a chair to ease the pain of a hip shattered in an automobile accident, he said, "Comrades, Comrade Nelson has presented a paper for consideration. An ideological attack on a theoretical paper is not Marxism. I propose that a committee study the paper and bring back a report tomorrow."

Martin Mackie, the district chair, was well aware that my expulsion would result in the loss to the party of my four brothers who had joined. The expulsion of the Peery family would be a major blow to the stability of the Party in the African American community. He gratefully welcomed the proposal, accepted its seconding, and, noting the late hour, called for adjournment. I hurriedly left the building, not wanting to explain anything to anyone. If they threw me out for thinking, I was in the wrong party. At the same time, I could not visualize life without the Party and the sense of purpose that held us all in close and warm comradeship. The Party connected us to the struggle in the neighborhood and internationally. It was our vehicle for achieving the vision of a peaceful and orderly world. Expulsion from the Party was almost unthinkable.

I got little sleep that night and rose early to prepare for the 9:00 A.M. meeting. After washing up, I stepped outside to get the morning paper. One glance at the headlines sent my heart pounding in my throat: "Stalin Expels Yugoslavia's Tito." I hurriedly read through the excerpts from the statement by the Communist Information Bureau. Some of the criticisms of Tito were close to what I had written. Delighted, I left for the convention knowing I had the winning weapon, if anybody still wanted to fight.

Warm congratulations replaced yesterday's cold shoulder. At the end of the convention Mackie, Bob Kelly, labor secretary of the Minnesota district, and I formed the elected Minnesota delegation to the fourteenth national convention of the Party to be held in August 1948. I felt it was a real honor and intended to do everything a delegate should do.

I left the state convention happy that I had made a contribution and was going to the national convention, but there was a sense of uneasiness. Comrades I respected swung 180 degrees on the basis of the statements of leaders rather than thinking things through. Marxism had taught me the only revolutionary weapon is the human mind. Being criticized when I used my mind and applauded by people who wouldn't use theirs left me uneasy. Worse, I saw how the sense of loyalty and the desperate need for unity was easily transposed into weapons that intellectually deadened and threatened to destroy the Party.

Meridel LeSueur was a close and long-time friend of Alexander Trachtenberg, the founder of International Publishers, which printed most of the Party's books and pamphlets. Vague rumors had it that he had been part of the personal financial network of the czar while a secret member of the Bolshevik Party. He saw to it that the czar "donated" the money to found the publishing house. Before I left for the convention in New York, Meridel wrote to him asking that I be allowed to take a tour of the publishing house. Trachtenberg, steeped in the courtesy of the Russian nobility, would treat the friend of his friend to more than a tour of a workshop.

I arrived in New York a day before the convention. As planned, I met Trachtenberg (who immediately insisted that I call him Alex) at the office of the publishing house. After the introductions, we caught a cab to the Russian Tea Room, beside Carnegie Hall in Manhattan. While in the cab, I tried to steal a few glances at Alex. I imagine he must have cut quite a dashing figure in pre-revolutionary Russia. The finely chiseled face, the neat little mustache, and the patrician bearing made me wonder how such a person became caught up in the revolution and forsook a life of luxury to serve the international working class.

As we left the cab and approached the restaurant, the doorman fixed a cold stare at me. Then, realizing I was with Alex, he opened the door, speaking Russian with a deference that must have been the norm between servants and noblemen in czarist times. It reminded me of the excessive courtesy shown by Black doormen at upper-class white clubs. I didn't like it.

Next, Alex stopped at a small booth just inside the door and gave the man two twenty-dollar bills. That was a lot of money. I almost instinctively understood that these noblemen so hated everything bourgeois that they paid up front so they wouldn't have to undergo the humiliation of paying the check in front of others.

As my eyes grew accustomed to the soft lights, candles, and blazing salamanders, I could see that the clientele was indeed the Russian émigré nobility. They all knew Alex and greeted him warmly as we threaded our way to the table that perhaps was always his.

I must have said something about how cordial they were to him, a leading communist. Alex went on to explain that these people hated the capitalists more than any other class. Communists were near the end of the list of political groups they hated, since communists, too, hated the capitalists.

The waiter came to our table with a bottle of iced vodka and a platter of cheeses, salami, and other tidbits. When the food was gone along with half the vodka, the waiter rolled up a salamander and cooked a most scrumptious Russian feast at the table.

Alex told stories of the Lenin he knew until I felt that I, too, knew and understood the man and would never betray him or his cause. Then there were stories of the Russian workers and the structure of the Soviet system. There were stories of Stalin as the Soviets prepared for and fought single-handedly the greatest war in human history. Alex talked. I listened, ate, and drank. Each of us thoroughly enjoyed the other.

Finally Alex politely glanced at his watch. My God, we had been there six hours! I mumbled apologies for taking up so much of his time, but he laughingly told me what a pleasure it was for him to talk to a working-class communist. As we left the Russian Tea Room, I realized we'd drunk a quart of vodka. With all that food, however, we were stone sober.

Alex instructed the cabby to take me to the hall, where a welcoming party for the delegates was held, and went back to his office.

I was early for the social and the hall was empty. Each table held a bottle of cheap whiskey and a plate of salami and cheese. Taking a table toward the rear and out of the way, I leaned back, closed my eyes, and waited for my delegation to show up. Half dozing, I slowly woke up to the sound of muffled voices. A heavyset, tall Black man was earnestly talking to a white woman. I had no intention of eavesdropping, but they had not noticed me and it never occurred to me to politely cough or scrape my chair so they would be aware of me. I recognized the man as Comrade Ben Davis, central committee member and New York City councilman. The woman was Comrade Peggy Dennis, wife of Gene Dennis, the general secretary of the Party. As they talked, they would touch each other's hand or arm for emphasis. I was deeply impressed by these two leading figures in the party talking together in a warm, respectful, and comradely relationship. Here, it seemed to me, was a microscopic expression of all I fought for and dreamed of. This is the way all people would relate to one another after the defeat of capitalism. Nothing important was happening, but this was the high point of my emotional linking of the Party to a vision of equality and comradeship.

The CPUSA's fourteenth convention would be remembered as a turning point in the struggle to stabilize the Party. The convention agreed that the fight for peace would continue to be the center of our work. William Z. Foster, the respected chair of the Party, stated that if we could raise the membership from 150,000 to 200,000, a qualitative change would take place in the fight for peace and African American rights. We believed him, never understanding the forces poised to crush us.

Rising wages, the destruction of the left-led unions by the Taft-Hartley Act, the combination of CIA agents and right-wing labor leaders, the establishment of the state of Israel, and the growing terror of the McCarthy inquisition all worked against us. Most of all, the deepening penetration of FBI agents at all levels spelled the destruction rather than an expansion of the Party. I could not have imagined that John Lautner, the head of Party security and in charge of the defense team in the trial of the twelve central committee members for violating the Smith Act by conspiring to advocate the overthrow of the government, was an FBI agent. I never again believed that numerical growth meant quantitative development or was the road to qualitative changes.

I came home from New York totally committed to the revolution. I was soon to learn that no amount of ideological steadfastness or willingness to sacrifice could overcome objective conditions.

By 1949 the frightful shadow of fascism lay over the land. J. Edgar Hoover now had 105 million sets of fingerprints. Across the country thousands of teachers who stood up for academic freedom were fired from their jobs. A high school principal in Oregon was fired for refusing to remove *Grapes of Wrath* from the school library. The political vermin crept out of the woodwork. Proven liars became rich as informers and "experts" on communism, while university professors who refused to lie or inform became laborers. A few months before, J. Edgar Hoover had proudly announced that the leading communists were "in the can or on the lam." Now he was saying that the FBI had achieved a majority on the Central Committee. I'll never know if this was the truth or simply a statement to panic the comrades, but the desertion rate from the Party ranks increased.

18

Hegel wrote that history repeats itself. Marx added, "First as tragedy and secondly as farce." It was tragic that the German Socialist Party refused to work with the Communists when together they could have defeated Hitler. It was farcical to see Norman Thomas, the leader of the American Socialist Party, call upon Congress to round up all known or suspected Communists and place them in concentration camps.

At this moment, Albert Einstein, already marginalized in the scientific community, published his little book, *Why Socialism?* I took heart at this, but at the same time I watched with disgust as the weak-kneed fled the Party. Like an infantryman marching to the front, I sensed some men were going to die, but it wouldn't be me.

The struggle against fascist Germany was only a few years in the past, and we remembered the lessons. The FBI tapped our phones so they could record any conversation in the area. We responded by building little padded boxes to hold the phone and a small radio that could override any discussion in the room. Agents followed us everywhere we went. We learned to lead them on wild-goose chases or to slummy taverns. One cold, rainy evening, Meridel LeSueur asked the agents tailing her for a ride since they were all going to the same meeting. We learned never to discuss serious business in the house. We walked; we met in libraries and restaurants. We forced them to commit more resources than we were worth.

Sensationalism was the lifeblood of the witch-hunts, and the House Un-American Activities Committee could be counted on to provide a new circus whenever another grew stale. One of their biggest circuses began unfolding around a gentle, balding little German refugee, Gerhardt Eisler. Representative J. Parnell Thomas, head of the House Un-American Activities Committee, dramatically announced Eisler was the leader of the Comintern (Communist International) spy network inside the United States.

In 1936, Gerhardt Eisler escaped from a German concentration camp and made his way to Spain. There, he became a leader of the German brigade that fought on the side of the elected Spanish government against Franco's fascist rebellion. When the legal government fell, he escaped to France. Just before the German invasion, he escaped to the United States. After the war, Eisler wanted to return to his home in what had become East Germany. The anti-Communist hysteria had set in, and the U.S. government, citing his membership in the prewar German Communist Party, would not allow him to leave. In 1947, Louis Budenz, the former editor of the *Daily Worker*, finally came out as a highly paid informer. He suddenly "discovered" Eisler and named him as the master spy in the United States.

Representative Thomas subpoenaed Eisler to appear before his committee. Thomas paid and produced Eisler's sister, who denounced him as the perfect terrorist type. Just as in Nazi Germany, relatives were spying and informing on one another. Outstanding progressives such as Thomas Mann, Linus Pauling, and Cary McWilliams understood the danger of the proceedings and spoke out strongly in defense of Eisler. At the committee hearings, Eisler refused to name names and was cited for contempt of Congress. Out on bail, in 1950 he went on a speaking tour to raise money for his defense. His last stop was Minneapolis.

Bob, Hubert, my brother Ben, and I arrived at the tavern about the same time. Bob, chairman of our Party club, called us individually asking if we felt like a beer. We knew he wasn't talking about beer, and knew better than to ask questions. After the greetings and the slaps on the back, Hubert asked, "What's up, Bob?"

Bob nodded toward the door and we walked out. We knew something important was up. We stood in a little circle and Bob said, "I had a talk with Carl this afternoon. Gerhardt Eisler is in town. They're getting ready to frame him and throw away the key. I guess he's trying to get out of the country before they issue any indictments. The FBI is tailing him so they can arrest him the moment the indictment is out. The Party is asking us to get him on a plane to New York, but first we have to be sure we've lost the FBI."

"Wow!" Hubert said. "That's an assignment!"

"It sounds bigger than it actually is. There is nothing illegal. Eisler is going to New York and we're going to put him on the plane."

After a few moments of discussion we came up with a simple plan. Eisler was staying with a newly rich comrade in the suburbs. We knew the FBI was staked out in front of the house. We couldn't shake them there. Our plan was to get into the city and into a tavern, and perhaps with enough people milling about, we could get him out unnoticed.

We drove out to the suburbs and walked past the two agents parked in front of the house. Both looked to be in their thirties, with crew cuts and sharp, expressionless faces with thin, tight-lipped slits for mouths—replicas of Hitler's SS. I had no idea how we would lose them. They seemed absolutely determined to get Eisler.

Irene Paull, head of the Local Civil Rights Congress and in charge of raising money for Eisler's defense, met us at the door.

"I'm so glad you're here. You should leave right away. It will take time to shake them."

We stepped inside. Irene went from room to room calling Gerhardt. He seemed to have disappeared. As I went into the bathroom I saw him sitting cross-legged on the floor of the kids' room engaging them in a game of jacks.

I closed the door of the bathroom thinking, *That little balding man playing jacks with the kids doesn't look very dangerous to me.*

We pulled away from the curb; the FBI tailed us closely all the way into town. We finally pulled over in front of a tavern between Sixth and Seventh on Hennepin. Once inside we all lined up at the bar and ordered beer. The plan evolved quite spontaneously. Every time one of us went to the restroom, one of the FBI agents would follow to make sure it wasn't Gerhardt trying to escape. We began going to the restroom in twos. Then two of us went to one end of the bar, two to the other, and two to the restroom. It was clear that the pair of agents could not keep an eye on three teams at once.

Bob kept looking at his watch. The time for the plane to depart was near, and whatever we were going to do had to be done quickly.

Bob slipped out the front door, brought the car through the alley to the back door, and reentered through the front. Hubert and Gerhardt went to the restroom and exchanged hats and overcoats. The Feds kept their eye on Hubert's turned back. As if by signal, Hubert, Ben, and I bolted out the front door. The FBI, convinced we were making a run for it, followed in hot pursuit. Bob and Gerhardt slipped out the back and drove away. He barely made the plane. The FBI completely lost him and did not discover his whereabouts until he was at sea aboard a Polish ship heading home, where he became the German Democratic Republic's minister of culture. We were happy that we had contributed a little comma to history. It was party time. The Grain Belt beer and Red Mountain wine flowed that night.

As Eisler slipped through their dragnet, the FBI detained Gerhardt's wife to make sure she didn't escape before they deported her to East Germany. Parnell Thomas was sent to the Federal penitentiary for illegally hiring relatives. With poetic justice, the warden assigned him the appetizing task of cleaning up chicken shit in the prison's coops.

19

At the university, our Party unit was the hub of much of the campus political activity. I tried to apply everything I learned in the army about organization, plus everything I gleaned from Lenin's *Party Work in the Masses*. We veterans had a deeper sense of organization than the average student. My three years as battalion operations sergeant in the army served me well. The Party unit was the core of the continuous activity of the AYD, and members of AYD were influential in other organizations. My close friend Jerry Stoll formed the American Veterans Committee on the campus. It soon had four thousand members out of the twelve thousand veterans who attended the thirty-thousand-student university.

These veterans, along with others we indirectly influenced, carried bits and pieces of our ideas—no matter how diluted or distorted—into every aspect of campus political life. This allowed us to construct a network that had considerable influence on the campus. I was not surprised when I received an invitation from the Catholic student organization, the Newman Club, to speak to them.

For the moment, we Communists were riding high. It wasn't that we were so good; we were the only ones who seriously struggled around a program of peace, jobs, and equal rights for all. We were the ones who picketed the dance halls and roller rinks that would not admit African Americans. We were the ones who leafleted and demonstrated against police brutality. We were the ones who organized demonstrations and protests against the increasing violations of academic freedom. We were in the front ranks against the fascist danger. We were the ones going to prison for our beliefs. Although the majority of the students did not agree with our final aim, we won their respect through our openness and activity.

The administration and the FBI were not sitting idly by watching this happen. First, a campus chapter of Americans for Democratic Action (ADA) was formed to become the center for Red-baiting. Second, and more dangerous, we were treated almost with deference on the campus.

The turning point for me came with an invitation to be initiated into one of the two "secret" honor societies on campus.

The Gray Friars was primarily an organization of graduating seniors who had made outstanding contributions to some aspect of campus life. I was perhaps the first sophomore and certainly the first African American to be invited to join. On one hand, I shared Mom's pride in what she considered an accomplishment "in spite of." On the other hand, I was a bit apprehensive. It was more than "beware the Greek bearing gifts." I hated the Black "leaders" who knowingly or unconsciously sold out for the honor of hobnobbing with big-shot white folks. I knew, no matter what the school's intention, I was on a greased skid and heading in that direction.

Over the months, Marion and I had grown close. Friday night was date night for us. After the usual relaxing small talk, I brought up the question of the Gray Friars. Marion listened quietly while I talked about my fears of being co-opted by the white liberals. She smiled and said, "Look, guy, you should be proud. You're opening doors for other Negro students. Not everybody is concerned about your being in the Party. There's nothing to worry about."

"I'm not worried. It's just that something is wrong when the people you are fighting start giving you honors. Either you're doing something they like or they see a way to disorient you."

"I think you owe it to the people coming behind you. You're smart enough not to fall into traps."

Few Uncle Toms began as sell-outs. Like everything else, becoming a Tom was a process. They began as talented, militant fighters for a just cause. The ruling class became aware of them and step-by-step convinced them that they could do more for their people within the system than fighting against it.

I had seen it happen with my father. A superb political opportunist, Pop learned to judge trends and join them before they matured. Thus, during the early days of the Depression he came close to the Communist Party. They saw him as a valuable asset and he enjoyed the deference they showed him. By 1939, he knew the inevitable war would end the Depression and with it any chance of the Communists succeeding. Overnight he found "principled" reasons to break relations with them. But he could not be neutral on any subject. If he wasn't pro-Communist, he would be anti-Communist. Anti-Communism paid off better than pro-Communism, and by the time he died in 1972, his living room wall held pictures taken with Richard Nixon, Ronald Reagan, and Nelson Rockefeller. He had secured a position on the Central Committee of the California Republican Party, and the huge public welfare building in the Watts neighborhood of Los Angeles is named after him. Not bad for a Missouri Black boy born in 1890. We knew that beyond the desertion of his family, beneath the betrayal of the principles he taught us, was his need to be respected by a society he actually despised. Deeper lay the longing to be respected and loved and admired by his sons. The Faustian bargain had gone terribly wrong. We looked contemptuously upon his individual achievements, convinced that he should have striven to rise with and not above his people. We knew that his anti-Communism was part of his deserting us as a family. The more he moved to the political right, the more we moved to the political left. Neither side knew where the ancient familial struggle ended and the political struggle began.

I knew the web that had ensnared Pop was being spun around me. The first step was to say that the path to social influence, prestige, and wealth was open to me. The second was to show me that path. The third would be to actually have it happen. The Gray Friars were the second step. I instinctively felt that should I get through this one, I would be trapped.

The tensions and apprehension deepened as the week dragged by. Late Saturday afternoon, a sleek new Buick pulled up in front of our rickety house on Fourth Avenue. I didn't want anyone coming up the steps and looking into the house, so I was outside waiting for them—my suit freshly pressed, shoes shined—ready to meet the Man.

I hardly knew the other four students in the car. They were seniors and didn't seem too happy that I was with them. After what seemed a terribly long time, the car pulled up to the stately front of the exclusive Interlaken Club.

Our neighbor Mr. Harris was a waiter at the club. We just happened to arrive at the same time. He was walking toward the waiters' entrance when he saw me. Our eyes met for a second and I could see the confusion and the question, "Nelson, what in the world are you doing here? You cannot go through the front door."

"Good evening, Mr. Harris." I walked over to him and extended my hand. The white guys nervously but politely waited for me. "Mr. Harris, I'm with the banquet here tonight. I guess I'm going to be initiated into the Gray Friars."

Mr. Harris grinned broadly. "Well, I sure got to congratulate you, son. You're the first colored man to walk through the front door of this club."

He meant it as a compliment, but it didn't sit well with me. I knew that to most Blacks the ultimate compliment was to be recognized as the first Black person to do this or that thing. I didn't like the idea. The first thought in my mind was, *So they finally found a Negro they approve of and are going to let him in. Why do they approve of me? I must be doing something wrong.* As I walked back to the group, the anger began to rise and I struggled to keep it from becoming open belligerency. The well-known reprint of a leaflet announcing a slave auction came to mind: "Twenty-nine prime negroes for sale." Well, somehow I'd have to let them know I wasn't for sale.

The country club was the most palatial place I'd ever seen or heard about. Here, politicians from all parties came together for golf and drinks and planning. Judges, prosecutors, and public defenders embraced like long-lost brothers. I'd heard about it, but I'd never been able to visualize the closeness of the upper class. I tried not to return the sidelong glances as the alumni and the invited city dignitaries began to arrive. I was relieved when the chaperone of our group motioned for us to assemble in the dining room.

Little paper friars in gray tunics stood on the dinner plates holding out our various names. Sitting down, I was terrified by the array of silverware that spread out from the plate like a bird in flight. I glanced furtively, intending to see how the rest used their silverware and follow their lead. Then I looked away. Getting caught would be the ultimate humiliation. Somehow, Mr. Harris understood my predicament and managed to be the one serving me. As he placed each of the seven courses before me, he would stealthily touch the proper knife, fork, or spoon with his little finger. It worked so well that the rest of the students were following my lead. They did not understand that a Black waiter in an exclusive country club necessarily knew more about table manners than most of the guests.

As the dinner wore on, eating gave way to small talk. It was clear that most of the older members knew the families of the students. I was left out of this informal bonding of the generations within the ruling class. I sensed more than saw the sidelong glances some of the alumni shot at me. I was sure they were thinking, *What the hell is that Black guy doing at a banquet of the Gray Friars?* I felt uncomfortably alone. I knew that what I said or did was going to affect the thinking of some influential people. I swallowed my militant pride and tried to discern the thin line between a dignified politeness and walking into the trap.

The chief of police sat directly across from me. It would be easier to out-stare a cat. I remembered one of his lieutenants once pulling me off a picket line and telling me, "I don't worry. Sooner or later we always catch up with people like you." The chief blandly returned my stare. I knew what he was thinking.

Discomfort began to give way to anger. Here was everything I hated and fought against. I had walked into their snare. I recalled an evening with an old family friend, John Herriford, who sat stirring a glass of Scotch and ice with his finger, his lower lip poked out in studied hostility, glaring over the rim of his thick glasses.

"You're going to be a Communist! A revolutionary? Hah! Jesus Christ, man! This white ruling class looks at a Negro revolutionary with—with amused contempt."

Here it was slapping me in the face—amused contempt. If I'd had a way home, I'd have walked out.

Short introductory speeches were made. My time came to be introduced. I stood up nodding as the chairman concluded, "And he has made such outstanding contributions to the social and political life of the university that he is the first sophomore to be initiated into the Gray Friars." I quietly thanked them for the opportunity to serve the university and sat down to the polite applause. I sat back thinking, *They've been buying and selling Black folks for so long, they figure we'll all sell for the price of a dinner and the applause from the very people we're supposed to be fighting.* I thought of Robeson and Du Bois giving up all their material wealth and social prestige in order to defend truth and principles. At that moment I was surer than ever that I would not desert them.

Glancing around the room again, I knew there were more here than my enemies. As our eyes met, Dean Edmund Williamson, who more than once risked his job in defense of academic freedom and the rights of minority students, smiled faintly. Deep down, I knew the committee that nominated me had not done so in order to entrap me. Almost everyone at the banquet wanted to quietly solve the "Negro problem" and secure world peace. It was more than individuals—good or bad. It was a system functioning blindly, ensnaring all who came within its reach.

The choices seemed clear: fight that system and probably be silenced, crushed, and destroyed by the FBI and the McCarthy gang, or join them and become the leader who's led by them. I was terrified of following in Pop's footsteps, but it seemed to be happening. Could I be more cagey and beat them at their own game? Could I use their forum to get my message across? Perhaps I could—but no one else had, not Robeson, not Du Bois. The system creates a special hell for Black leaders who betray them. Sitting there, I began to imagine what my life could be like in ten years: a nice house, a nice family, my name in the papers as a thoughtful leader of my people, and hating myself for betraying everything so many had fought so hard to defend. I might learn to like the accolades and the "good life" I was being offered. Again I thought of that patrol on Biak during the war when it was either pick up my rifle and advance or run away in terror. Again, I could not see any middle course. During that dinner, I decided to quit the university and learn a trade, where I'd be at least partially out of their grasp.

20

Telling Mom that I was going to quit the university was more difficult than when I told her I was joining the army. After the quiet, reasoned argument for at least thinking it over for a semester, she simply accepted it. Perhaps she knew the alternatives.

After putting my affairs in order at school, I went down to the Labor Temple and rejoined Local 544 of the Hodcarriers and Construction Laborers Union.

I missed the university. It had been my Shangri-la, a city of thirty thousand bright, inquisitive young people. I missed the hours of discussions in the coffee shops. I missed the library. It was there that I understood that the communist movement was more than a movement of the working class. It was the search for truth. In my early teens I'd asked the world, "Why am I, who never harmed anyone, mistreated, segregated, assigned an unequal place in a country that promises equality?" Everybody lied to me. Some thought they told the truth, but they lied. They wrote scores of books to propagate the lie, they fought wars to impose the lie. They created religions to sanctify the lie. In that library I learned the truth. When I entered that library I knew the facts that white society exploited, lynched, oppressed, and humiliated Black society. There I learned to distinguish between facts and truth. There I learned the truth that a system, not people, creates exploitation and oppression. No matter how hard Blacks and whites fight each other, the oppression will go on until they change the system. As I learned truth, I became a communist, for I could do nothing else. Truth—the ultimate subversion—cannot be killed, so the liars kill those who dare defend it. Truth demands that we stand beside Copernicus. I am terrified of tongs and fire, but more terrified of declaring the truth to be a lie. I had to leave the university. I could never explain to anyone the consequences of learning the truth.

As my friends and comrades graduated they had to make their choice—resign from the Party and sign a loyalty oath or never work at the profession they studied for. Aside from a professional agent that infiltrated our club, not one of the comrades turned informer.

Reentering the workforce was a difficult process. Two years had passed since I'd done any physical work. Construction labor paid well, but it was hard, unstable work. Work, meetings, and demonstrations took up my day. They also took a toll on my affair with Marion. We knew we were drifting apart. I no longer had time for the long, abstract discussions that were so much a part of our affair. I began to dislike and feel uncomfortable around most of her friends. My hands were rough and callused from work, and I'd quickly fallen back into the slang and earthy expressions of the Black construction laborer. I was becoming different from them. Despite their radical but cultured talk, I saw them becoming middle-class social workers and dragging her with them.

The struggle in the South intensified, and I toyed with the idea of going to Birmingham, where the struggle was the sharpest. I knew she could not be part of that. I was on the track of becoming a Party organizer. She could not be married to a Communist functionary and hold the job she was studying for. After our dates, these thoughts would force their way into my mind. I knew I was simply developing the rationale for breaking it off. The truth was, I didn't want to be married, didn't want any ties or any relationship that would be in the way as our tiny Party fought for its existence.

I didn't know how to tell her as our Friday night date drew to a close.

The political situation was more than a convenient excuse to end an affair. It was a desperate romantic idea, but I wanted to be free to move, to fight. I tried to tell her. She silenced me with a kiss and drew close.

As the electricity curled and flashed and synthesized, she whispered, "Look at me." I raised my head and kissed her mouth—a long, hungry, wet, lip-sucking kiss. She turned slightly from me—panting, at the verge of release, her silken voice calm and rational. "Look into my eyes."

"You're supposed to feel, not see," I whispered to her.

Afraid we would lose the moment, I raised my head and looked into the brown, limpid pools of desperate hope and love and passion.

Later, she lay silent in my arms. I felt the warmth of her tears dripping from her cheek onto my shoulder. She knew. It was over.

21

The idea hit me while I was in the hiring hall waiting for a job. Despite a body muscled and hardened by three and a half years in the infantry, I was sick of construction labor and knew I wouldn't be able to do it when I was fifty. I had to learn a trade. The Bricklayers Union, just one floor above the Laborers Union in the Labor Temple, seemed as sweet and far away as heaven. I decided on that one. There were no Black workers in the union of this elite group of the working class. In fact, in 1948 there were no unionized skilled Black workers in the entire construction industry in Minnesota. Craft unionism was much more complex than "Let's keep the colored people out." The first goal was to keep wages high by restricting the number of workers in the union. Second, union members wanted to pass the trade to their sons or relatives. This was achieved by giving apprenticeships only to those sponsored by union members. No one consciously had to fight for a lily-white union. If the union set up restrictions, they would doubly apply to African Americans since they had no connections within the union. It was part of the system.

I doubt that any Black worker had ever gotten up to that second-floor heaven or to any of those upper floors that held the offices of the construction trades' unions. It hit me that the Laborers Union was on the first floor, so no Black worker ever passed or was aware of the offices of the skilled trades.

Before my courage slipped from the sticking point, I left the laborers' hall and climbed the stairs. I stopped before the big door with the frosted glass and the bold businesslike black lettering that read, BRICKLAYERS, MASONS AND PLASTERERS' INTERNATIONAL UNION, LOCAL 2, MINNESOTA. At that point, being Black got the best of me. I was sure a white person would simply open the door and go in. I couldn't do it. I knocked. A slightly irritated voice ground out, "The door's open." I entered, pulling my sweat-stained laborer's cap off my head.

Rinehold Mangni, the bricklayers' business agent, looked up from his desk. The piercing greenish eyes behind the small round glasses, the lean, longish face, and the close-cropped iron-gray hair prepared the visitor for a curt no regardless of what was asked.

"What can I do for you?" He didn't sound too unpleasant.

"I want to take out an apprenticeship in the bricklayers' union."

Mangni smiled, reached into his desk, and handed me the union constitution, which he had opened to the preamble. "This union is open to white men of high moral caliber."

I fought back rage and after a few deep breaths said calmly, "Mr. Mangni, I'm none of these things, but I'm talking about the GI Bill of Rights. Either I get in an apprenticeship or I'll take you to court and put this union in my hip pocket."

Mangni flushed but lived up to his reputation as the American Federation of Labor's best negotiator. "You see your lawyer, and I'll see mine."

Three days later, I received a registered letter informing me that my application for initiation into the apprenticeship program had been approved. Swearing-in ceremonies were scheduled in one week.

I dressed carefully for the occasion, not too flashy, with a good working-class, going-to-union-meeting kind of pants, shirt, and tie. I knew I was going to get a hard time from those white union bricklayers. Their privileges depended on holding the color line. My future depended on breaking it. I was ready for the fight.

The meeting was well attended. I imagined that most of them had come out with the sole purpose of stopping me from joining the union. At the end of the agenda, it was time to swear in the twenty-six apprentices. We stood up before the membership and the president asked if there were objections to swearing in the new members. There was a moment's silence, and then a tipsy brickie got to his feet.

"Mr. Chairman, I want to ask that colored boy a question. Why are you wearing those red suspenders?"

I broke out in a light itchy sweat. Damn it. Why in the hell did I have to wear red suspenders? Trying to steel myself for the seemingly inevitable anti-Communist tirade, I answered, "To hold my pants up."

"Now, that boy's intelligent," the tipsy brickie said as he sat down. "Let him in the union."

There was some good-natured Scandinavian laughter, and the chairman called the meeting back to order.

The first few days on the job were pure hell. Laying brick requires muscles that most people never use. A brick weighs about six pounds, a trowel of mortar a bit more than six. We were expected to lay five hundred bricks per day. Six thousand pounds! Three tons of brick and mortar lifted and laid to the line in a stooped position was a guaranteed backache. Lime seeped into the tiny holes worn through the skin of my fingers by the rough brick. I would pour water on them trying to wash out the lime, which burned. An older bricklayer told me to go around the corner and pee on my fingers. I thought that was a disgusting way of putting down a Black guy. By the end of the day, in desperation, I tried it. It worked.

I would come home after work and lie down on the floor to straighten out my back, questioning the sense of learning to work that hard. Very often I stayed on that floor until it was time to go to work the next day. I was a living expression of the chain-gang blues line. "My head don't hurt bad as my back and side."

Over that first year, I learned to be a bricklayer. I had good teachers. Those who hated me because I was Black or Red or both pulled all the dirty tricks on me. They'd push the line out ever so little, so my wall would be out of plumb. Sometimes, if the foreman wasn't watching, they would double up on their half of the wall, finish the row, and then raise the line, forcing me to complete my half with my level instead of the line. Bricklayers called that "putting a man in the hole." It was a sure way to get a brick-layer fired. Then, if nothing else worked, a little pea gravel in my mortar would slow me down. There were other bricklayers—mostly older men—who taught me how to place the heel of my hand on a level brick and level the next one with my fingertips. They showed me how to feel plumb with the trowel, and how to "accidentally" cut the line when others forced me into a hole—then nobody could work for a few moments, giving me enough time to work my way out of the hole.

Thank God for the Black mason tenders. They took it as a matter of racial solidarity to see to it that my mortar was always tempered to just the right consistency and that bricks were always stacked in the most conve-nient places. My scaffold was always the cleanest. These little things made up for what I lacked in skill. Despite the joke that I'd never last, I kept up. One by one I made friends, first with the apprentices and then with most of the journeymen.

After a while, my back stopped aching. My arms, legs, and hands adapted to the work and became strong. There came the day when I real-ized that I was happy being a worker, building things that people need—happy to be young and strong, sweating in the sun, working with the gang, building a city.

The good-natured bantering between the trades hastened the day. We were especially haughty toward the carpenters—the wood butchers—who had to work almost as hard as bricklayers. At lunchtime there was no end to the talk of bricks and women. It was the common glue that held us to-gether. When the day was done and we assembled at the tavern for cold beer to wash down the day's dust, all divisions brought about by trades ended. Mason tenders joked and drank with electricians. Plasterers and tile setters, bricklayers and carpenters, plumbers and roofers laughed and lied and bragged until it was time to get home lest their wives should wonder why Jack would want to spend one extra moment with those rough men. Our cooperating on the job for eight hours a day instilled in most workers a sense of justice and fairness not to be found in any other class. I knew that if a just America was going to be created, it would be by them. I was happy driving home and seeing the finished buildings I'd worked on. It satisfied some visceral longing to contribute to society—a longing that arose with cities, nuclear families, and races. Most of all, I was happy that I was learning a trade that nobody could take from me. When the contractor needed bricklayers, you were hired, no matter what meeting you went to after work. When the job was done, you were laid off no matter how much he might like you. It made for a kind of equality not found in the professions.

22

If I had any questions about the direction of my life, they were answered by the Peekskill riots. For several years, Paul Robeson held concerts in a huge public park near Peekskill, a suburb of New York. This year, 1949, every reactionary force in the area converged to prevent Robeson from singing. Caught unaware by the violence of the mob, hundreds of members of trade unions, civil rights organizations, and groups influenced by the Party decided to not surrender to the violence of the fascist mobs. A call went out for young veterans and trade unionists to form a defensive perimeter around the park the following week to protect the concert. I volunteered to go to New York, but the request was turned down. The defenders had to pledge to be nonviolent. I grew up in the infantry and hesitated to take the pledge.

On the fourth of September, the concert, attended by twenty thousand people, was held in the park. The American Legion, the police, and hastily formed gangs of whites attacked the vulnerable convoy as it left the fairgrounds. Thousands of progressive people were injured as the mob attempted to kill Robeson. One footnote of Peekskill I have never forgotten was the role of the fairly large Jewish community. Unlike those from New York City, they lived there and had to face the townspeople the next day. Many of them were immigrants; some had served time in the concentration camps of Germany. As a community they came out in defense of free speech, stood fast, and paid for their convictions.

This fascist riot was applauded in Congress. Representative John Rankin, upheld by Speaker Sam Rayburn, repeatedly referred to Robeson as "that nigger." Peekskill was a significant moment in the accelerating drive toward fascism. I was sure it would mean the banning of the Party in the near future. I knew we would never disband, and began thinking in terms of life in the underground.

Things came to a head for my family when the state legislature held hearings on a bill to outlaw the Communist Party of Minnesota. Pop was chosen to represent and speak for the American Legion. My younger brother Ross was part of the Communist party delegation that came to testify against the bill. Pop took the podium in front of Governor Harold Stassen's henchmen and in his best rhetorical style preceded his remarks by shouting, "I have seen my seven sons swallowed in the bloody maw of Communism." He then went on to demand the outlawing of the Party. The press had a field day over the father-versus-son bit.

Mom saw the article and picture in the evening paper. Close to fainting, she closed her eyes for a moment. The quiet "My God" was her only comment. Slowly shaking her head, she looked over her brood and went back to making dinner. We paused for a moment, feeling very sorry for her. She would have to face the neighbors and relatives. We didn't give a damn what they thought. We went back to the chess game. We'd seen it all played out before with the rise of Hitler.

Through it all we remembered another Pop—this big man (actually he was only five foot eight) who'd taught us to fish, how to shoot, how to skin squirrels and rabbits. We remembered his ever-ready .38 pistol, which we knew would protect us from anything and anyone. We believed he'd use that pistol on anyone he couldn't whip. He pulled that gun on local bullies and on white men who thought they were better than Black people, and once, when a cop chased me into the house, he pulled his gun on the cop and ordered him off the property.

Although we never talked about it, we knew what had brought about the change in Pop. Fame was the spur that relentlessly raked and drove him. America took from him his full share of manhood, and he was determined to take it back. For him, nothing less than outstanding achievement—leading the pack—was acceptable. I fully understood this when I was on my last furlough before going overseas and into combat. He looked straight into my eyes and said, "Come back a hero, or on your shield." It was more than quoting a Greek father's charge to his warrior son.

Pop meant it—and it frightened me. I sensed he would rather see me killed in action than be a mediocre embarrassment to him.

In 1948, Pop left for California. It would be twenty years before we spoke to each other again.

Mom, though forbearing and tolerant, had a wide vindictive streak. Not many crossed her and got away with it. She was patient, and sometimes the payback was so subtle the offender was not aware that the score was evened. She didn't dwell on hurting the other person. Her goal was to even the score so she could feel good about herself. Pop had been dead for twelve years when Studs Terkel interviewed her for his bestselling book *Coming of Age*. At ninety-nine, she was the oldest person interviewed and had the longest interview in the book. There she finally settled her score with Pop. All the praise heaped on him as the "voice of moderation in Watts" or the fact that a huge Los Angeles County welfare building is named after him could not restore his good name after Mom told the world how he mortgaged the house and ran off to California with a woman fifteen years her junior.

23

The growing anti-Communist hysteria overshadowed our family turmoil. On August 3, 1948, J. Edgar Hoover of the FBI, Attorney General J. Howard McGrath, and President Truman created the semi-secret "Security Portfolio," allowing for the rounding up of up to twenty thousand "Communists" and holding them in camps without trial. The Internal Security Act—sponsored in part by Senator Hubert Humphrey, the "progressive" from Minnesota—allowed for preventative detention and the construction of thirty-five concentration camps. We looked to the future with a grim determination to fight to the very end.

People knock softly when they know you are asleep. It was that kind of knock—loud enough to irritate, not loud enough to awaken. I lay there a moment making sure it was a knock, then jolted awake. *Cops! No, they'd have kicked the door in.* Pulling on my pants as I slid off the bed, I ran as quietly as I could to the back door.

"Yeah?"

A tense, rasping whisper said, "It's Bob. Open up. I have to talk to you."

I turned the latch and pulled the door open. Bob Kelly, the labor secretary of the Minnesota Communist Party, stood quietly on the back steps. "Hey, Comrade Bob. C'mon in."

"No," he said, still whispering, "come away from the house. I have to talk to you."

Knowing they bugged our phones and houses, I closed the door softly and stepped out into the warm security of the backyard. "What's up, Comrade?"

Bob was never one to waste words. "It looks like Humphrey's preventive detention bill is going to pass. They are going to outlaw the Party. A reserve, underground apparatus has been created to guarantee the security of the organization. You've been selected as part of the cadre to go into hiding in case the bill passes." I sucked in the warm night air. *Jesus Christ, they're taking that final step. It's really happening! This is really war—what I joined up for.* The rush of adrenaline jarred me fully awake and alert.

"What do they want me to do, Bob?"

"You have to leave tonight. Get dressed and come with me."

"It'll take me a minute."

"We'll tell your folks later. It's important that we leave right away. We'll take care of everything on this end."

Mumbling an "OK," I tiptoed back into the room, dressed, crammed a few articles into a small satchel, stepped outside, and closed and locked the door.

Visions of storm troopers, Klansmen, and lynch mobs flashed through my mind as I settled back into the car seat. *It's the right thing to do. Freedom's a hard-bought thing. This is the revolution.*

Bob stopped a block from the train station. "You should walk from here. I don't want to bump into a cop who might recognize me." He handed me an envelope. "Here's the ticket. When you get to New York, go near but not to the information booth. Someone will meet you."

We shook hands and said good-bye. I walked to the station, hoping none of my friends would be on duty as a redcap or porter or aboard the train as a waiter. Bob had timed it so I would not have to wait for the train. Glancing around to be sure no one was watching, I walked swiftly through the station and boarded the train. It was nearly 2:00 A.M. and no one was paying any attention to anything other than getting comfortable. I chose a nearly empty car, slumped across two seats, and, despite the tension, fell asleep.

Twenty-six hours later, the train huffed its way into the New York station. The porter opened the doors and I followed the crowd into the big waiting area at Grand Central. Positioning myself some fifteen yards from the information booth, I looked over the fish school of humanity rushing by with no apparent purpose other than to move as fast as possible while reading a newspaper. After a few moments, I spotted him. The slender, swarthy-complexioned Jewish guy in his early thirties glanced over the people around the information booth. I didn't know him, but by his darting glances at the faces in the crowd, I knew he was my contact. His eyes swept over my face and on to the next young African American, shot back, and settled on mine. I half smiled. He glanced toward the phone booths along the wall and I turned to meet him there.

"Comrade Nelson? Glad to see you. Do you think you've been spotted or followed?"

"No, I watched all the way. Nobody has followed me."

"Okay. Here's a train ticket to Toledo. Get a bus there into Detroit. Here's some money for that. It looks more natural for a Negro to come in on a bus than a train. If someone is on to you, make sure you lose him in the station. This envelope has thirty bucks to get you started. Get a room, a new name. Get a social security number and a job. It wouldn't be safe to meet your contact in Detroit. You will meet him in Toledo. Next Saturday at one o'clock sharp walk past the front entrance of the Toledo library and a comrade will meet you. Be sure to be on time."

I made mental note of all he said. "If something happens, if I have to, whom shall I contact?"

"Comrade, you're going underground. We don't know who the agents are who have penetrated the Party. It takes time to weed them out. Under these circumstances we can't trust anybody. You are on your own. You know how important this assignment is. Under no circumstances should you contact the Party or any comrade. Don't keep books in your room. Don't keep a diary or write any letters. Don't make close friends or become involved with any women. The Party's existence might depend upon the reserve leadership. They have confidence in you and trust you."

I tried to pay complete attention, but my mind wandered back over the years when *underground* ceased to be a slave's word for the escape to freedom and became a revolutionary's word for confronting fascism against impossible odds. To slip into the underground demanded total commitment and discipline. I knew I was ready. I had taken the first step, and there was no turning back. I looked at this earnest young man. "I guess you were in the army. I was in the infantry. I'll dig in and hold until we start moving forward again."

He smiled. "Well, I was in the air force, but sometimes we had to hang on, too. You have to hurry to catch your train. Good luck, comrade."

It would be too obvious to shake hands. He turned and walked away. I stuffed the envelopes into my pocket, picked up my little satchel, and walked toward the flashing train light. The train pulled quietly out of the station. I felt a stab of pain as I cut the cord that bound me to family and comrades. The three-year-long surveillance by the FBI shattered, and I disappeared into the underground.

Detroit in 1949 was as close to a human beehive as a city can get. If the FBI had been in that bus station, they never would have spotted me. I was but a molecule of the humanity flowing into the city that summer.

The mechanization of southern agriculture, which would change America forever, was in full swing. The new cotton-picking machine, some thirty-five times more efficient than the sharecropper, turned their world upside down. All the legal and cultural superstructure of the South—its brutality, segregation, and lynch law—was developed to keep Blacks on the plantations working for next to nothing. Suddenly, sheriffs who patrolled the arrow-straight roads of the Delta to prevent Blacks from leaving the plantations changed their role. Now, they drove up to the shacks and with the age-old brutal vulgarity told the tenants, "You all be off this property by six in the morning—they gonna plow all this land under."

Southern country roads, littered with the pitiful belongings of the sharecroppers, became escape routes. Like raindrops, they flowed together to form the greatest concentrated migration in history. Drawing a line due north to the major cities, Black Mississippi headed for Chicago. Alabama aimed for Cleveland and Detroit.

We all looked alike—black and tan faces, little leather satchels, cloth caps and denim shirts. Most of the newcomers, met by friends or relatives, left the station secured and warmed by southern hugs and kisses. A few of us, on our own, looked around as if we could divine which way to go.

I had never been so alone. This was worse than the frightful loneliness of prewar hoboing. Then, broke and alone, I'd had a name, an identity, and the knowledge that somewhere there were friends and relatives and a home to return to. Taking the freight trains westward had been a rite of passage into socially conscious manhood. I had been one of millions who found themselves as they traveled the West looking for work. Now I was alone, a non-person. No name, identification, job, home, relatives, or friends. All the things that make a person a member of society I had relinquished to defend my Party and the African American liberation, socialism, peace, and security it stood for. I forced myself to remember that the members of the Central Committee had unflinchingly gone to prison for these ideals. I had no right to question duty. I was twenty-six, with three and a half years of wartime infantry discipline and two years of intellectual development at the university. I knew that if ever a warrior was ready for battle, I was. Desperately pushing back the melancholy and welled-up tears, I turned toward the entrance and walked into the seething streets of Detroit.

In 1949, the African American people were still, essentially, a community that spoke to one another and helped one another. I walked over to a group of young men who looked as if they belonged in Detroit. "How you all doing?"

"Fine. And you?"

"Just fine. Looky here, I just got in and got to find me a room. Where you think I should look?"

"I'll tell ya, fella, you can get a job here faster than you can find a room. Best bet is to walk down this street. This is Gratiot. Go all the way to a street called Hastings and ask around there."

I thanked them and started walking the ten blocks into Detroit's Black slums, affectionately called the Black Bottoms after the river bottoms they had known in the South. The barkeep in the tavern at Gratiot and Hastings sized me up for a moment and said, "Matter of fact, we just lost a tenant. We got a room upstairs. Ten bucks a week. You pay in advance."

That was a third of my money, but I had to have a place to sleep. I gave the bartender the ten-spot and one of his flunkies let me upstairs. The hallway smelled of stale beer and cigar smoke and rang with the hearty laughter of southern Black men drinking and telling tall tales.

The room's furniture was a broken chair and a bed the French settlers must have slept on. I turned to the guy who'd led me upstairs. "Look here, Friendly. I've got to get a job right away. Got any ideas?"

He looked me over for a moment and, perhaps feeling a bit of kinship with a Black fugitive, said, "If you looking for a job in auto, you got to go kiss the ass of them Uncle Toms at the Urban League or get some of them thievin'-ass preachers to take you to the white man."

I grinned at the common and irreverent reference to the preachers. The prestige of the churches was at an all-time low in America, and the northern mainstream Black churches in some cities faced extinction. I soon learned that many African Americans in Detroit mostly went to church to hear the preacher give a hint of the lottery number. Worker-preachers in storefront churches who brought their emotional services with them from rural Alabama filled the void. These churches were a gathering place for the poor and an adjunct of the spontaneous veteran-led civil rights movement. Sensing the danger to the social superstructure, the government found ways to fund the mainstream churches and the evangelical counteroffensive got under way. Their goal was not only to stabilize the church, but to urge it to become an important pillar of the anti-Communist crusade.

My guide finished mumbling something about the rotten deal that colored people get, even in Detroit. I nodded my agreement.

White people filled out applications to get jobs in the defense or auto industries. African Americans had to be vouched for by a Black man whom the white man trusted.

That sounded too complex. They would ask too many questions.

"Any other way to get work?"

"What most of the people do is take the bus up to Gratiot and Eight Mile Road. Contractors and people needin' help come up there."

The morning scene at Eight Mile and Gratiot had a duplicate in every city taking in the wave of southern immigrants. The area around the intersection was filled with men in work clothes standing around fires in oil drums, exchanging jokes or news from home. Here, the white boss would look them over and select those they thought most capable of doing the work they wanted done. The men correctly called it the slave market.

A pickup truck slowed down. The driver, a harried-looking, thin-faced white man, looked around from group to group and then stopped in front of the group I was standing with.

"Any of you men want to work?"

"Yes, suh!"

"Sure do."

One of the men looked around and said, "Do a dead man want a coffin?"

The white man didn't like the joking but, except for a condescending glance, ignored it and nodded to one of the men. "What can you do?"

"I can do anything."

"I can't use you. You over there." He nodded to me. I knew I should be specific.

"Carry hod, mix mortar. I did construction back home."

"Get in the truck."

The contractor hired three more men, including the jokester. After we settled down in the back of the pickup, the boss started for the construction site.

One of the men rolled his eyes, "Damn if this ain't just like a slave auction."

The jokester, humming and mimicking the white man, sang, "I come from Alabama with my niggah on my truck—"

We broke out into unrestrained laughter and then introduced ourselves.

"Everybody down home call me Joe Henry."

I almost panicked. I was next. I had to introduce myself and I didn't have a name. "My name's Nelson. David Nelson." Those were my first and middle names. I wouldn't forget those. The three nodded.

The next guy was a hard, tough-looking man in his middle thirties. A muscular, dark-skinned five foot eleven, a few small scars marked his face. "My name's Haywood. Haywood Patterson."

"Same as the Scottsboro Boy?" That was political. I wished I hadn't said it.

"Well, that's me. I don't talk about it and I don't want people to know it." He turned toward me. There was something lethal in his eyes and in his tone of voice. I had made a damned fool mistake. The year before, Patterson had escaped from prison in Alabama. He made it all the way to Detroit by simply approaching African Americans telling them who he was, confident that they would die rather than see a Scottsboro Boy returned to prison. Using his correct name probably brought him more security than danger.

"Sure." I glanced at him and turned away. The other man introduced himself and we settled back watching the fields and new construction until we swung into a lot where the workers were finishing up a big church.

My new boss was a roofing contractor. In a few moments he assigned work to each of the men and then turned to me. "You said you carry hod." I nodded. "Can't trust people going up the ladder with material. Most people don't know how to climb a ladder. Kill themselves or someone else. You be the ladder man and I'll add a dime to your wage."

We hauled up most of the work with a rope and pulley, but some things had to be hand-carried. It was all tough work. When I wasn't climbing the ladder, I was taking buckets of hot tar from the rope and pulley, carrying them to the roofers and poured while they mopped the tar and rolled the tarpaper. My eyes burned from the acrid tar smoke. Droplets of boiling tar smarted my face and hands. Small wonder roofers are known for their drinking—by the end of the day it seemed there was no other way to clear the throat and lungs of the taste and odor of tar. With the mopping completed, the really heavy work of pulling up the slate began. By the time the whistle blew to end the day, I was exhausted. The boss had to take us back to the bus line, and as we jumped from his truck he raised his hand and said, "Good night, fellows. I'll pick you up at the same place at seven o'clock sharp. Be there."

The truck pulled out and the jokester turned to us. "Now ain't that nice. 'Good night, fellows.' Last boss man I had down in Ala-boom-boom never did say a kind word to me. I'd say to him, 'Good mornin', boss.' He'd look like I'd cussed at him and say, 'Get yore mule.' When it got to be can't see, I'd say, 'Good night, boss.' He'd spit some tobacco and say, 'In the mornin'.' That's all that man ever said to me. Sure got some nice white folks in Detroit." We looked at him, shaking our heads. Jokester had a screw loose.

Thursday, the day before payday rolled around, I was into my last pennies and looked forward to a full week's pay. The boss handed out W-2 forms for us to fill out. I left the social security number blank. I had not had time to apply for a new number. The boss collected the slips, glanced over them, and turned to me. "You don't have a social security number?"

"Nobody got 'em down home, and I wasn't sure how to get one here."

The boss sucked in a lungful of air. "Damn it, I knew I should have checked this before. It's against the law to put you to work without a number. I'm going to have to take you down to the office."

After giving the foreman instructions, we got into the pickup and drove downtown to a temporary social security office set up to serve the wave of immigration into Detroit. Rows of desks stretched the breadth of the gym-size hall. The refugees from the plantations patiently stood in lines, whispering advice to one another as we shuffled forward. Finally, it was my turn.

"What's your name?"

"David Nelson."

"You ever had a social security number?"

"No, sir."

"You got any identification—passport? Driver's license? Birth certificate?"

"No, sir. My name and birthday are in the Bible down home. I can send for that."

The bureaucrat shook his head. Half in disgust and half in pity, he mumbled to himself, "You people down there must breed like jackrabbits in the brush. Half of you don't even have a birth certificate."

He paused for a moment looking at his papers. I thought about telling him how *his* people illegally withheld and pocketed thousands of dollars in social security payments in addition to the slave labor—or maybe I'd just go upside his head. I knew I wouldn't do either. I was a disciplined communist and had to avoid any trouble with the law.

"Well," he continued, "here's your social security number. Don't lose it and don't work without it."

I thanked the man, put the little card in my wallet, and went out to meet the boss. A big hurdle was past. I was a real person again with a name and identification.

On the way back to the job the boss glanced at me and said, "You're a pretty good worker. You seem to be too educated to stay a common laborer all your life. How'd you like to learn the roofer's trade? You work with the gang, but when you get caught up, I'll put you on the slate work. It's not hard to learn. I can't keep a good crew. These guys are drunk half the time. You stick with me and I'll get you in the union in a year or so."

Barred from apprenticeships by the craft unions' whites-only clause, half the Black craftsmen learned their trade by these arrangements. Doing the work bit by bit, far under scale and by close observation, they learned their trade. In that way the boss profited, as did the Black worker. The workers who went through a regular apprenticeship called this "stealing" the trade. However much they resented it, they found it preferable to allowing Blacks into the apprenticeship programs.

I didn't especially want to become a roofer. I didn't want anything that permanent, but it beat carrying those buckets of boiling tar. I thanked him. About forty-five years old, with a receding hairline and a perpetual harried look on his face, the boss wasn't a bad fellow. We drove back to the job in silence. I had a new name, identification, and a job that seemed steady. I looked forward to meeting with my contact and finding out what was happening with the Party.

The whistle blew, bringing Friday's work to an end. The boss handed me an envelope containing $60 for the week's work. I had never made so much money. I was whistling to myself in the construction shack as I pulled off the tar-stiffened coveralls and boots. Grinning, Haywood entered the shack saying, "The eagle done pooped a big one this week. Five straight days! I'll soon be caught up if the weather holds out." He turned to me, a soft boyish grin on his face, and said, "I suspect you gonna do some tom-cattin' tonight."

"Naw." I grinned back at him. "I got a family back home. I'm going to send them all the money."

"Yeah, I understand that," Haywood answered. "I've got to get me a room. I owe out most of this week. What say about sharing a room? Fifty-fifty." He must have sensed my apprehension because he went on, "Was you with the Labor Defense League or the Communists? How'd you know about Scottsboro?"

"Whole world knew about it."

"Yeah," Haywood chuckled. "When I was down at Atmore—the state farm—I used to get letters from white women all over the world: Sweden, England, Russia. Every time I get a letter the fuckin' guard set it up to have some motherfucker jump me. They'd only do it once. When you in prison, you can't let nobody whip you." A deadly caged-animal look came over his face. "Somebody fuck with me, I'm gonna steal his life." He looked at me and the boyish smile relaxed his face. " 'Course I wouldn't never do nothin' to you. I know you don't mean me no harm."

I only partly believed him. Earlier he had told me he hadn't trusted another person since his best friend stabbed and nearly killed him at the instigation of a guard.

The rapid change of personality disturbed me. I shuddered, thinking of the beatings and brutality he had endured in Alabama's prisons. He was the most intelligent and articulate of the Scottsboro Boys, and I felt sorry for him.

"Sure, Haywood. We can share. I'm on Gratiot and Hastings."

That night Haywood moved his suitcase of belongings into my room and we went downstairs to the tavern. While we were sipping the beer, Haywood turned toward me. Just then a man stepped to the bar beside him. Haywood suddenly turned against the man, switchblade knife open. "Motherfucker, don't crowd me—don't be pushing all up against me."

"What the hell's wrong with you, fella?" the man said in frightened confusion.

"Haywood," I said, trying to calm what seemed to me to be a dangerous situation, "he ain't done anything."

He half turned toward me, the knife aimed at my throat.

"I don't let nobody crowd me. That goes for you too, goddamn it."

The man moved away from Haywood. Half frightened and not wanting to provoke him further, I turned and faced the bar to finish my beer. I knew I had to get away from this man. Eventually he would do something to bring the cops, or in a fit of this prison-bred defensive anger he'd cut my throat.

The political consciousness of Black youth of my generation was defined by the Scottsboro case. In 1931, six Black youths looking for work were on a freight train in Alabama. They did not know one another. A group of white youths decided to throw the African Americans off the train. A fight ensued, which the Blacks won. The leader of the white gang told two prostitutes riding with them to accuse the Blacks of rape. The Black youths were arrested and after a kangaroo trial were sentenced to death. The NAACP was appealed to, but stated, "They have been tried and found guilty. They should be hanged." The Labor Defense League and the Communist Party came to their defense. The Scottsboro case became the banner of the international communist movement. We African American youth knew that if the Scottsboro boys were executed, we would all be in danger.

The judge and jury knew Haywood was innocent. When one of the women tried to recant the lie the police had forced her to tell, she was threatened with prison. He and the other five Black youths were convicted. For seventeen years, guards in Alabama's prisons kicked and beat them. Even some of the Black prisoners became goons paid to attack or kill them. Haywood finally escaped and came north—a shattered, paranoid, disoriented man whose days on the streets were numbered.

He was still asleep when I left the room Saturday morning. As I walked to the bus station, jumbled, disconnected thoughts floated through my head. *Mom must be worried sick. But I often disappeared. She'll understand. What if the country goes all the way fascist? What if this coalition of Dixiecrats and right-wing Republicans actually takes over? A Black person is really going to catch hell. They have the American fascist model in the South. What if I'm ac-*

tually called upon to give some sort of leadership to an underground move-ment? I hardly know anything. I made up my mind I would find some way to continue my study of Marxism. Despite my unshaken faith in the future, I knew nothing could be done in this country until the mass of white work-ers turned to the left. Rising wages, warmongering, anti-Black propaganda, and anti-Sovietism turned them to the right. Maybe we just would have to hide and wait—but God, that wasn't revolution.

Entering the bus station, I bought my ticket, got in the line, and caught the bus for Toledo, where I was to meet my contact. We arrived there before noon. That presented another problem. Black men were not permitted to simply hang around the library for an hour. A cop was sure to tell you to move on or else he'd run you in on some sort of suspicion. I couldn't just walk. If inadvertently I walked toward a white neighborhood, it would look suspicious and be asking for trouble. I discreetly asked a young white guy where the colored people lived and started walking in the direction he indi-cated. After half an hour I crossed the street and walked back.

When I returned to the library I saw a young white guy who looked like a student trying very hard to appear nonchalant while obviously looking for someone. I knew he was my contact but followed the agreed procedure. At exactly one o'clock, I crossed in front of the library, looked meaningfully at him, and turned to enter the library.

Our meeting in the reference room was short and to the point. Briefed by the local leadership on what to say or ask me, he spoke in clipped state-ments and generally acted the way some student would think an under-ground communist should act. There was a short summation of the political situation, consisting of the fight for peace in Korea, the struggle against the resurgent right wing in the unions, and the African American people's increasingly militant fight for civil rights. It all sounded good, but these were things I got from the daily papers. Away from the security of the Party's collective life, I had to make my own assessment, and I wanted to talk about that. I knew the Party was reeling under the blows of the FBI and the Justice Department. They couldn't and wouldn't catch a lyncher after you handed them the photographs along with names and addresses. Their efficiency lay in hounding people who tried to implement and not simply talk about democracy.

After making arrangements for the next meeting, I left. He remained, pretending to carry out some research.

I was uneasy about the meeting. My contact was not my idea of the stable proletarian capable of withstanding the stress of the time. I didn't like hiding outside the growing social struggle. During the war and the enemy occupation of their countries, the European and Asian communist underground, hidden from the police by the people, participated in their struggles and was accessible to them. Detroit was seething with scattered struggles against police brutality, discrimination, and the lack of housing. I was different from the Black upper-class so-called leaders. I lived down in the Black Bottoms and could unite that anger and those struggles, but this type of underground prevented me from doing so. I felt I was wasting my revolutionary time in this underground and, unable to discuss it with anyone, was becoming more and more frustrated. I constantly reminded myself that no soldier has the right to break ranks—especially under fire—because he disagrees with tactics. I tried to set aside my apprehensions. Not so with my contact.

After a month, he failed to show up for our meeting. The following week he again failed to show. I knew he'd joined the avalanche of disoriented, frightened, petty do-gooders fleeing our wounded Party for safety within the political arms of their "enemy."

I faced an impossible contradiction. My contact had obviously deserted the Party. The district office had no idea where I was, and I was under strict orders not to contact anyone under any circumstances. My first impulse was to go home and get back into activity. On the other hand, I was afraid this would look like deserting my post when things became difficult.

My total isolation was wearing on me. I had been in Detroit for six months and had no one to talk politics with. I hungered for books, knowing that without intellectual stimulation, I too would eventually become disoriented.

On schedule, I went again to the Toledo library. Again, my contact did not show up. I knew then for sure that he had quit. As I waited the agreed-upon ten minutes, I remembered the wonder-filled, heady hours I'd spent as a freshman in the library at the university as I conceptually grasped that humanity's knowledge of the world was in those books.

At that point I decided that neither the FBI nor the Party was going to keep me from those books. After a moment's hesitation I went into the library's reference room. The librarian, a young, heavyset woman, smiled a greeting, acknowledging that she had seen me before. I knew that librarians were under orders to report to the FBI the names and addresses of anyone who asked for Marxist books. The only ones able to get such literature were academics who needed it for anti-Communist propaganda. I knew that many of the librarians opposed this thought control and refused to cooperate. I decided to take the chance. The reference file on Marxism was empty except for a note instructing the user to get the file cards from the librarian. Feeling that I had the option of simply walking away if there were too many questions, I headed over to the librarian's desk.

"Good afternoon, miss. I am doing some research and I need a book that isn't in the reference file."

I noticed her glancing at my hands and knew that she knew those paws, callused and scarred by the slate and the boiling tar, were not the hands of a person who made his living writing.

"All right. We perhaps have it under another file. Could you give me the title and author?"

"*The German Ideology*, by Karl Marx."

She glanced at me for a split second and left to find the book. Returning, she looked into my eyes and said, "It's encouraging to see a working-class person doing such research."

My adrenaline spiked. *Working-class* was a communist buzzword. She hadn't asked for my name or for identification. She knew something.

"Thanks so much."

"You may do your research in that room, and it's important that you bring the book back to me when you finish. Don't give it to anyone else."

I smiled my thanks and went to the reading room. Sitting down, I slowly opened the book, thinking how gray and hollow is any liberty that is not firmly rooted in the liberty to know. How easily the American people, seduced with their new material possessions, gave up this essential liberty in hopes of securing the rest.

As closing time drew near, I finished the essay I was reading. My mind wandered, trying to grasp the complex philosophical formulations. The last sentence jolted me back to the printed page: "Philosophers have only interpreted the world differently; the point is to change it." I reread it. Here was the axe for America's frozen seas. Know it in order to change it! Thank God for books. I cheerfully said good night to the librarian and caught the evening bus to Detroit's Black Bottoms.

Knowing that I might be identified trying to use a library in Detroit, I never missed a Saturday afternoon in the Toledo library. Mostly I wanted to learn, but partly I was afraid to hang out on the streets. A Black man was always subject to arbitrary arrest by Detroit's cops. I never learned that librarian's name and she never asked mine. She risked her job, risked being blacklisted, but reinforced my belief that there are enough decent people in America to keep up the fight.

By the time we finished roofing the church, I was catching on to the trade. I spent less time carrying tar buckets and more with the slate gang. Sometimes the boss would send me and Haywood out to do a small repair job.

Working construction in the summer was almost fun. We Black laborers coalesced into a family. The jokes, laughter, and tall tales hastened the day's end, when we would have a beer. Friday evenings were our nights to howl, spending our money, pub crawling, "signifying" at one another, and enjoying Detroit's good times.

After a few weeks, I left the room on Gratiot and found one on Warren. It was a solid working-class area, and the warm, comfortable room in the neat rooming house was to be my home for the next five months. A few weeks later, Haywood missed work for three straight days. I went down to the Bottoms to make sure he wasn't deathly ill and uncared for. I stopped in the tavern to inquire about him. The bartender told me that Haywood had left after the Alabama state police had come around asking about him.

Walking back to the bus stop, I felt sad and angry. Can a judge or jury be accused of the destruction of a person's life? Can a society be put on trial? Somebody should be made to pay for Haywood—for all the Haywoods. No one would ever be brought to trial, no one would ever pay, and I became more determined to remain in my trench.

The days dragged on into weeks and the weeks into months. Irretrievably lost from everyone, I kept to myself in the rooming house. No mail. No visitors. No friends. I would catch myself looking longingly at the young women and their informal, laughing, singing, happy group, and I'd force myself to walk away from them. One evening as I went up the stairs to my room, I overheard two of the women talking about me.

"I don't know. I've done everything but lay down and yell at him."

"I don't think he's funny."

"Sure keeps to himself. Maybe he's a fugitive."

I backed out the front door and reentered, making enough noise to warn them. I hadn't realized how abnormally I acted. I began to carefully close the distance with my immediate neighbors.

The best part of the day was the breakfasts and suppers at the Southern, the little restaurant on the corner. I quickly became friendly with the two cheerful, buxom waitresses. They brought their smiling, charming ways with them from Alabama. Their "Well, hello there, Mr. Nelson" when I entered was a guarantee of good southern food served with an inquiry about the job and health. I always tipped them well, and they knew I liked them.

Winter rains reduced the construction week to two and three days. I was helpless as I began using up my savings from the summer. The old construction workers' joke about eating chicken all summer and feathers all winter again became a reality. As the rain turned to snow, I began to consciously pinch every penny and showed up for work no matter how threatening the weather.

Thanksgiving Day arrived when I was between a last paycheck and unemployment compensation. I simply didn't have enough money for a Thanksgiving dinner, yet I had to eat. By two o'clock I couldn't stand it any longer. I pulled on my overcoat and galoshes and trudged up to the Southern.

"Hello, Mr. Nelson! Where you been? You about to miss Thanksgiving!"

"Been really tied up, sugar. I'm going to eat dinner later. Just give me a bowl of beans and some cornbread for now and I'll come back later."

I sat for fifteen minutes listening to the hearty laughter. I tried to make sense out of the past nine months. As we used to say at the end of our club meetings, it was time to sum up. Why these nine months of longing for the embrace of a woman? I was indescribably lonely—a loneliness that renders all doctrine meaningless. I was twenty-six and longed to love and be loved. Why these nine months of hiding while the streets of America smoldered, awaiting the winds of change to burst forth the fire? How I wanted to be there! I couldn't be anywhere but where I was. It was my duty. I had long known there was some terrible god within me that overwhelmed all reason. It was a god that took over my consciousness in the discipline of the infantry. What veteran can ever forget the opening lines of the *Soldier's Handbook*, "The duty of the soldier . . ." Even before the war, before I created a sense of duty to the men in my platoon, I could see my mother's face, kindness covering her unbending will, telling me of my duty to uplift my people. Why me? Few others had such a sense of duty. Yet there have always been a few who deeply felt this sense of social duty and moved humanity forward. It was a rough time. I was doing the right thing. I knew I was doing it the wrong way.

Just as I was about to ask where was my bowl of beans, both waitresses came to my table with a tray laden with some of everything on the menu.

"Happy Thanksgiving, Mr. Nelson."

I didn't know what to say. There must have been tears in my eyes. One of them said softly, "Take your time eating, Mr. Nelson. You don't want to get indigestion."

I'll always love those southern women.

There was no possibility of my regaining contact with the Party in Detroit. Nearly broke, facing a frigid Detroit winter without work and tired of playing hide-and-seek with the FBI, I decided to go home. I packed my bag, said good-bye to my friends, and went to the bus station, where I purchased a ticket to Minneapolis.

Waiting for the bus, I sat apart from the crowd and tried to sum up my time in the underground. It seemed to have been so useless—yet every soldier knows that even if a skirmish seems useless, it is, or should be, part of a plan. We didn't seem to have a plan. I knew that in any war the army must not lose the initiative, must not become passive, simply responding to the enemy's initiative. We were isolated and passive. As difficult as the situation was, there was a lot of struggle going on in America and I knew we could regain that initiative. I consciously told myself I must not become demoralized. There was no other army to fight in.

The loudspeaker called for all aboard the express for Minneapolis. I picked up my little satchel and walked toward the open gate.

PART II

Cleveland, 1949

1

Nineteen forty-nine was a year of decision—for the world and for me. Rigidly blacklisted after the Detroit fiasco, I could not find work. I was ready to leave Minneapolis. When the Party asked that I transfer to Cleveland, a more important industrial area, I readily agreed.

As I packed my little satchel and tool bag, the struggle to end the old world of colonial dependence was fully joined. British forces bogged down in heavy fighting against the liberation armies in Burma faced a humiliating defeat. In China, the People's Liberation Army, led by Mao Zedong, advanced rapidly toward total victory. The battered Nationalist armies asked for peace talks if the People's Liberation Army would grant immunity for war criminals. In Iran, the shah outlawed the Tudeh (Communist) Party in hopes of calming the rising revolution. Tucked in the middle pages, the press reported on Nazi groups secretly re-forming in Germany. The *Chicago Tribune* headlined its investigation of Britain's use of Marshall Plan funds to expand and consolidate its African empire. The leaders of organized labor, shackled by anti-Communism, continued their halfhearted fight against the Taft-Hartley Act.

The forces of national liberation gained strength throughout the colonial world as the dark cloud of reaction and fascism consolidated and spread across the United States.

As thousands fled the Party, hoping to escape the spreading reach of McCarthy, I boarded the bus for Cleveland. I put aside the Detroit experience, the disorientation and disorganization of the Party; my thoughts, cradled in the doctrines of the infantry, were to go to this new front and grapple with the enemy.

As the bus passed over the bridge leading into downtown Cleveland, I looked down and over the industrial flats. I had never seen anything quite like it. A British journalist once described it as "hell with the lid off." Fire and smoke belched from the valley, almost hiding the sun. Little wooden houses and surrounding snowdrifts smudged and darkened by the residue from the steel mills, nestled along the rim of the valley. The Cuyahoga River, reduced to a lifeless chemical sewer for the industrial flats, had caught fire a short time back. It took the Cleveland Fire Department three days to put out the fire on the river. I wondered how anyone could live there.

The bus pulled into the station. Excited and happy, I stepped off. I'd left all the unhappiness behind in Minneapolis and was starting a new life as a cadre for the Party. From now on, it would be a life organized around the struggle for peace, for liberation and communism—the life I wanted.

I made my way from the bus into the terminal. I saw Sol right away and was glad it was he who'd come to meet me. We had built a warm and close relationship over the years in the Youth League and at Party meetings. After the bear hug greeting, I followed him to his car for the short ride to the Glenville section of Cleveland. Along the way he told me the youth section was holding a welcome party. Sol and his wife, Rachel, like most of the young people in the Party in Cleveland, were "colonizers." I don't know who made up that term, but it was unfortunately accurate. Answering chairman William Z. Foster's call to reestablish the Party in the working class, these young comrades had quit college to go live among the workers in the major industrial cities and bring them the message of communism.

In 1949, the Glenville section of Cleveland was in transition. Its mainly Jewish residents were moving into the suburbs, and the Black middle class and stable workers were moving in. Most of the white comrades lived in this area. It hadn't taken long before they retreated from the white ethnic communities into the African American community, where their idealism, if not their ideology, was welcome.

Sol opened the door, and I entered a room where some twenty or twenty-five young people were standing in small groups or milling around, soft drinks in hand. Sol raised his hand to get their attention and said, "This is Comrade Nelson."

Nodding to the smiles and welcomes, I said, "Glad to be here, comrades," and stepped forward to meet them.

This was as idealistic and decent a group as ever tried to bring a message to non-believers. Mainly Jewish and mostly from New York, they entered a working class that was enjoying a steadily rising standard of living. The militant traditions of these workers in their homelands—or in Cleveland— were no match for the virulent anti-Communism arising from the war against the Korean people, from the White House, from the powerful right wing of the trade unions and from Cleveland's omnipotent Catholic Church. There was no way for the comrades to influence the white section of Cleveland's working class, which was mainly Slavic, Irish, and Italian.

The Party, reeling from the arrests and deportations, considered the African American community their final line of defense. Under such conditions, African American cadres were indispensable. I understood why I was here.

One of the African American comrades stood to one side, chain-smoking Pall Malls. Glancing over the little gathering, now and again he would break out in a cherub-like smile that fit his small mouth. His closely cropped hair, slicked down by wearing a stocking cap the night before, glistened, and his round head seemed too small for his six-foot, 220-pound body. I couldn't tell if he was waiting because he thought he was too important to be part of the crowd or if he had something to tell me he didn't want the rest to hear.

Finally, with most of the introductions over and the group in the kitchen for snacks, he came over. "I'm Curtis Petitte. I'm a core maker at Alcoa and shop steward in the foundry. I consider myself the baddest motherfucker in the shop."

I smiled at him. I knew he was fishing—getting a glimpse at what kind of communist I was, a Goody Two-shoes or a street man who was a serious communist. I knew that was how he saw himself and wondered why he should feel it necessary to have these two faces.

"Nelson Peery, bricklayer, from Minnesota."

"What'd you come here for? Ain't no pussy in Minnesota?"

Taken a bit a back, I looked at him, then broke out laughing. "Plenty of that everywhere, man. The FBI starved me out. The Party wanted me to come here. I might as well come here as anywhere."

The cherubic grin was back. "You all right man, we together. I just wanted to make sure you ain't one of them Sa-ditty jokers from New York." Curtis's home was Cleveland, but he too was part of the group that left college to help stabilize the party in basic industry.

He nudged me and we joined the others in the kitchen. Curtis handed me a beer and introduced me to the few I'd missed.

Al and Heidi were from New England. Tall, with a receding hairline and a look of almost aloof intelligence, Al had given up a berth at a university to work in a steel mill. When he introduced me to Heidi, Curtis shot me a millisecond-long steely-eyed, Black-prisoner warning. She was blond and trim, with an athletic body—a good-looking woman. I didn't know what to watch out for, but found out after a few moments of discussion. An intelligent, well-educated comrade, she was clearly determined that neither her husband nor anyone else was going to ignore her and whatever she had to contribute to a conversation. This was the time when the modern woman's movement intellectually and ideologically was born. Working with even the most dedicated male communists, she had her hands full. The struggle for women's equality, in the Party and outside it, was moving from an ideological level to a practical one. I felt an immediate respect for this woman, since we African Americans were fighting the same sort of fight. Heidi then introduced me to her best friend, Judy, and Judy's husband, Ken. With thick black hair, a darker-than-olive complexion, green eyes, and a spontaneous smile revealing a perfect set of white teeth, Judy stepped forward and took my hand. I don't believe I'd ever seen such a beautiful young woman. I thought back to a conversation with a lecherous old comrade who'd told me, "If you've never been loved by a Belorussian Jewish communist woman, you've never been loved."

I glanced at Curtis. The cherubic smile was deeper than ever. I instantly knew he was after her and that I'd better stay away from what looked to me to be a dangerous game.

Ken, a nappy-haired, broad-faced, smiling Jewish communist, was totally obliterated by the charm and dazzling beauty of his comrade wife.

Vince Pieri was chairman of the Labor Youth League. A prematurely receding hairline made him appear older than his twenty-eight years. Of Italian decent, he had worked in a bank in Philadelphia before his assignment to the Cleveland area. As we were introduced I caught a flicker of a disturbing glint in his eyes, as if he was sizing me up in a hostile and aggressive manner. I have always been subjective about first impressions, and this one was uncomfortable. He took the cheroot from his mouth, warmly shook my hand, and welcomed me to the Cleveland organization.

When the gathering was over and Sol and his wife had gone to bed, I unfolded the blankets on the couch that was to be my home for the next several days. I sat there smoking for a while, thinking how different these people were from the comrades in Minnesota. This was the big time. Cleveland was one of the three industrial cities chosen by the Party for concentration. The other two cities were Detroit and Pittsburgh. We referred to them as "the iron triangle." I knew if we thought Cleveland important, so did the FBI. I did not want to think that one of those wonderful people I'd just met might be an agent or informer, yet I knew it was probably so. I could not shake off the feeling of apprehension, but finally drifted off to sleep.

2

During the next couple of days the weather broke enough for me to get down to the union hall and see what kind of work was available. Bricklayers Local 5, like most of the construction unions, had a few good and honest leaders who tried to keep the union straight, but cliques ran the show. These cliques were mostly ethnic. They saw to it that the best jobs circulated amongst themselves and they parceled the bull work out to the rest. There was a tremendous home-building boom underway. Parma and East Cleveland were rising out of the boondocks. There was plenty of bull work—building the basements or veneering the bungalows. Black bricklayers could get these jobs with or without the union.

The union supported two business agents. George King, an immigrant

Scot, was an honest person and it showed through. Jake Hamlin, from Virginia, a patronizing drunk, enjoyed dangling a few good jobs in front of the Black bricklayers in exchange for their bloc of votes at election.

I presented my card and asked about work. King had serious reservations about a two-year apprentice transferring under unexplained circumstance. He wanted some communication from the union in Minneapolis to make sure I wasn't a runaway apprentice before placing me on a job. I left the union hall and did what most Blacks looking for a job do—go to the local tavern and ask some questions.

I'd hardly gotten the word *bricklayer* out of my mouth when a guy put down his beer and asked if I wanted work. I assured him that I did and that I had my tools. He was a laborer but knew his boss needed bricklayers. We made arrangements to meet the next morning and he would drive me to his job. That was the best possible arrangement, since I didn't have a car and didn't know my way around the city.

Tom Snavely, owner of the Snavely Construction Company, was twenty-seven and just starting in business. Tall, slender, and intellectual-looking with horn-rimmed glasses, Tom looked as if he should be lecturing in some school rather than running a construction company. His father, one of the big contractors in the city, had died suddenly. Tom finished college and started learning the business from scratch as a "lumper," a contractor who takes only the bricklaying contracts. There were six Black bricklayers on the crew. Four of them were young men who had stolen the trade—that is, they did not go through a regular indentured apprenticeship but learned the essentials of the trade from another bricklayer off or on the job. They had the guts to get and lose jobs until they learned enough to pass the test and get a union card. Black bricklayers were willing to risk getting kicked out of the union to help a Black youth steal the trade, knowing the near impossibility of his getting an apprenticeship.

A white foreman, Carl, and Tom's younger brother, Jess, who was also an apprentice, completed the crew. Tom took mostly basements and veneers, and the work was hard. There was no steward, and few union rules were enforced. But it was work, and the $2 per hour was more than I'd ever earned.

The FBI had access to my social security number. After a week on the job, they quickly located me, and two agents came to the job. They talked to

Tom for a few moments and left. I started to bag up my tools, and Tom asked me where I was going.

"I know that was the FBI. They run me off every job I get."

"I don't know much about communism," Tom said. "I don't think I like it, but if the communists are trying to destroy democracy, I don't think we should help them. I hire bricklayers, not communists. The only reason I'll fire you is you don't do your job."

Over the next year the FBI confronted Tom several times. Even after his younger brother went to fight in Korea and Snavely Construction started to become a big company, he never changed his principled position. He was a decent guy. I respected him and I always gave him a good day's work.

After my first paycheck, I moved out of Sol and Rachel's living room and into a rented room off Woodlawn and Fifty-fifth Street. With a little money in my pocket and a growing urgency about meeting some of the women in the area, I began to integrate myself into the sprawling, over-crowded neighborhood.

3

Black Cleveland was pushing south toward the main thoroughfare, 105th Street. Juke joints and dance halls went with them, but the hub of Black nightlife was still centered on Fifty-fifth and Woodlawn. In those days, before the blues entered mainstream white America, wonderful talent came to the little nightclubs scattered along Woodlawn and down Fifty-fifth Street. Those who would later become rich and famous, such as Big Maybelle and Memphis Slim, drank and performed with local talent such as the ever-popular Sticks McGee.

A new stage in the consolidation of the African Americans as a people was forming. The unique root of our culture grew and developed within and because of the oppression and isolation in the rural South. The refugees brought that root with them into the Black ghettos across the country, strengthening the cultural unity and deepening the sense of identity that was so indispensable to the unfolding fight.

As rhythm and blues consolidated, a few whites, such as disk jockey Alan "Moondog" Freed, saw not only something of cultural importance emerging, but also a pot of gold. The concerts Freed promoted were packed. At one concert, with ten thousand Black music lovers expected, a nervous white city council alerted the National Guard. We used to bitterly joke that (not improbably) the white folks in Birmingham, Alabama, made it illegal for Black folks to laugh in public. What looked like trash barrels on every corner were, in fact, "laughing barrels." It wasn't much different in Cleveland, where if the Black people wanted to sing and dance, they had to do so under the bayonets of the National Guard.

Saturday nights, if I wasn't at a meeting, would find me on Woodlawn and Fifty-fifth with the gang of brickies, laborers, and carpenters, chucking Old Timers Ale and rolling to the good times.

When apprentices received their journeyman's card, it was traditional for them to quit their job and prove their worth on the market. I could have had a job for life, but I'd learned to be wary of security since it always brought dependency with it. I was afraid of the rough-and-tumble of working out of the hiring hall, but a certain freedom came with the tough times.

My life was a struggle to choose between the dependency of security and the perils of freedom. In my late teenage years I'd hoboed across the Great Plains, adrift in the bronzed sea of wheat and silk-tasseled golden corn. I left the freight train at the pinnacle of the Rocky Mountains and looked eastward across the rust-colored boulders of Colorado, the brown valleys, and on into green Nebraska and wondered if those who fought and toiled ever had a free moment to look upon and enjoy it. From the crest of the splendid Sierra Nevada I gazed down on the lumber camps and little farms where men and women grew gray and weathered, unheeding and blind to the beauty around them. I toiled in the fields from the Yakima to the orange groves of southern California. I lived at the terrifying edge of hunger, in fear of the array of city cops, county sheriffs, state police, and railroad detectives who hounded and harassed us. But I was free to know that beauty as I starved. I was free to move on. It was a terrible, murderous, addictive freedom.

Although I needed the security of a steady job, it conflicted with everything I wanted to do. With that job I would be immune to the threats of the

FBI. I would come to work every day. I would spend the rest of my life piling brick on brick. I loved Tom for offering me that security, but no, dear God, *no*. I had too much to do with life to allow that to stand in the way.

When I received my journeyman's card, I told Tom I was going to quit and go for myself. He smiled, shook my hand, and wished me well.

Shakespeare wrote that in the springtime a young man's fancy turns to thoughts of love. In fact, though, it happens in any season. As I stabilized financially, settled into a routine of meetings and political activity, my life became orderly. For the first time in months I could think about a personal life. Long ago I learned that when you are ready for something, it is ready for you.

I met Roberta, daughter of one of the men in our crew. An amalgam of every ethnic group in the hill country of Tennessee, she'd received the best that the Indians, Blacks, and Anglos had to offer. A fiercely independent, green-eyed, peach-colored beauty, she lived alone. At eighteen she knew exactly where she wanted to go and how to get there. Part of what attracted me to her was this stability. I did not understand that subconsciously I was looking for a relationship that would help me become stable, help end the fits of depression and drinking. Perhaps young people instinctively look for a mate with characteristics that they think will strengthen them. I didn't understand it, and neither did she. We were young, and within the year we danced and laughed and loved our way into marriage. We did not know what rocky, wrenching years lay ahead.

4

The sweltering summer of 1951 settled onto the Cedar-Central area of Cleveland. People sat on their porches fanning themselves, drinking beer, and cursing the weather. The kids, when they were able, cooled off beneath the spray of garden hoses. Prospect Park was at the edge of the spreading African American community. Black folks occupied one section, setting under the trees or tending to the barbecue. For years this had been their side of the park. Everything in Cleveland was divided and no one ever thought of why the division. At the other side of the park the white kids played in the big swimming pool, romped on the tennis courts, or lounged in the sunbathing area. They never gave a thought as to why no Black kids ever came to the pool or to that end of the park.

The winds of change were blowing across Cleveland, and one evening just as our club meeting was ending, Jimmy Jackson, an African American, said, "I want to add a point before we adjourn."

Vince Pieri nodded, and Jimmy went on.

"There is no segregation law in Cleveland, but this is one of the most segregated cities in the North. It will stay that way until we do something about it." Jimmy always got wound up when he spoke at meetings. The longer he spoke the more militant he became. "The colored people of this area don't have any way to get out of this heat. Prospect Park is just a few blocks from here, but people think they can't go into it. I think we should either hold a demonstration or mobilize people to go there and integrate that pool. We pay taxes like everybody else."

The African American comrades grinned and nodded approval. The white comrades appeared a bit apprehensive and looked to Vince for guidance. Vince glanced around the room and said, "I think it is a good idea—but for something this big, I think I should talk to the Party leadership before we begin."

We left the meeting enthused by the idea that we were going to fight for something that belonged to us. We believed there would probably be a fight, because the whites believed it belonged to them.

The Party agreed with the idea of integrating the pool, and the next day we set about writing and distributing leaflets calling upon the people to join us in asserting our right to swim in a publicly owned pool.

The African Americans of Cleveland were restless. Agitated by the growing struggles in the South, the favorable court decisions outlawing segregation in education, and above all by the increasingly militant African American press, they were becoming aware that they, too, had been denied what was rightfully theirs. The elements of a social struggle of historic importance were slowly falling into place.

That Saturday we assembled in Glenville at the home of one of the comrades for the short ride to Prospect Park. Most of the people who showed up were members or contacts of the Youth League. As usual, virtually none of those who enthusiastically read our leaflet and endorsed the fight showed up. As we divided up for rides I thought how history moves forward on the shoulders of such a few people. In France, 9 or 10 percent of the people actively fought the German occupation. About 7 percent actively collaborated with the Germans. The rest—the great majority— sullenly went about their lives until victory seemed possible. Only then did they join the fray. So it was with our fight. There were always 10 or 15 percent of African Americans who heroically challenged the Klan and the police—undaunted by the threat of lynching, beating, or jail. Ten percent grinned and collaborated with the Man and formed the official leadership of the African American people. The great majority in between chose to look straight ahead, feed their families, and stay out of trouble. Nonetheless, it was clear that a great movement challenging the system was getting under way. A broad section of the African American people began to feel they were fighting for what was legally and morally theirs. Deepening that sentiment was the way to arouse and ultimately radicalize the decisive but passive middle. The best way to accomplish this was through action.

Action has always escalated struggle. Both the Germans and the Allies thought they could terrorize their enemy into submission by bombing entire cities, but that only pulled the civilians actively into the war, arousing their hatred and stiffening their resistance. As the Germans advanced toward the inexperienced American army in North Africa, General George S. Patton screamed to his troops, "I want to see some dead lieutenants!" He knew that only an army that has shed blood could muster the hatred and determination that is necessary for them to be victorious. I didn't want a serious confrontation with the police or the whites in the park; we weren't ready for that. If it should happen, I knew the response would be hundreds if not thousands of people at the next demonstration.

With these thoughts in mind, our little caravan of five cars pulled into Prospect Park on the side that traditionally was for whites. The authorities had read our leaflets and six squad cars awaited us. As we pulled into the parking lot, the cops got out of their cars, clubs at the ready. We pretended to ignore them. Grouping together, we walked to the pool and undressed.

We had our swimming suits under our clothes so we wouldn't get separated in the bathhouses. As we approached the pool, the two lifeguards told us we would have to have our feet inspected and rinsed in a disinfectant. It appeared that everyone else had done it, so we lined up. After the foot inspection, we turned to the pool as a group. As if by some signal, all the whites exited the pool as we dove in.

There were plenty of pools for the whites to use, and I never again saw them in Prospect Park. It was hardly integration, but a tiny victory was won. More than a few people in Cedar-Central knew what happened and warmly greeted the comrades on the next leaflet distribution.

Our little contribution to the struggle made the front page of the generally passive Black Newspaper, the *Cleveland Call and Post.* It wasn't much of a struggle, but it added to the thousands of minor struggles for equality that took place that day. It was part of a growing and irresistible movement for freedom.

5

The Harlem Negro Labor Council, supported by various Negro Labor Councils around the country, issued a call to establish the National Negro Labor Council. The call reflected the growing self-consciousness of the Black worker. Politically it reflected Paul Robeson's developing view that in order to fight for equality, the African American people must proceed from a base of Black power. Some of the white comrades cringed at the idea as if it replaced the Party's traditional "Black and white! Unite and fight!" I reminded a few of them that they did not oppose progressive Jews or Italians uniting in order to fight for a broader class unity.

Led by the International Union of Mine, Mill, and Smelter Workers (Mine Mill), the leftist unions swung in behind the idea. Terrified of anything that smelled of independent African American activity, the center and right-wing unions screamed "dual unionism" and made sure their ethnic bases were protected.

•   •   •

The founding convention of the National Negro Labor Council, held October 27, 1951, in Cincinnati, was a turning point in my life. After the convention was called to order, two white men spoke. The mayor of Cincinnati warmly welcomed the convention and left. The next speaker was Morris Travis, the president of Mine Mill. The union was deep in a campaign to organize the South. That meant organizing the Black workers. It was practically the only union doing so. Travis, walking the picket line with the Black workers in Birmingham, Alabama, was singled out for attack by the cops. During the beating, one of the cops jabbed his billy club into Travis's eye, blinding it. Travis, a black patch over his eye, walked to the podium to a thunderous ovation. After a short congratulatory speech, he left the stage. As we stood to applaud I saw my younger brother Al. After the hugs and backslapping he told me he was a delegate from the Construction Laborers Union, Local 544.

Never before and never again would I see so many articulate, militant, dedicated working-class Black men and women gathered together in the cause of their freedom. It was something new. This was the first organized national expression of Black worker independence from the compromised Black upper class. Their sense of mission, of destiny, charged the air like electricity.

Plans were made for a founding convention to be held in Cleveland the next year. Paul Robeson sang and talked, smiling encouragement to all of us. We delegates left shaking each other's callused hands, embracing with the love of comrades and promising to meet again in Cleveland.

6

Winter settled upon Cleveland. The work slowed down and groups of idle bricklayers hung out at the hiring hall, playing cards and hoping against hope that a call for men would come in. I was one of the lucky ones. The project I worked on was nearing completion, but there was still several more months' work to be done.

The men were working in absolute silence save for the call to raise the guide line when the last man was finished. All the noise was coming from Louie De Marco, the foreman. We all knew that the next day—a week before Christmas—there would be a big layoff. Working bent over the wall, each man had a little pile of snow on his back. Our feet felt like blocks of wood and our hands were stiff and cold in the wet canvas gloves. By three-thirty it was getting dark and the cold, damp wind was rising from the lake, adding to the misery.

Hoping to stave off the layoff slip and make it through the holidays, the men sped up a little and did their best work as Louie walked by singing, "He's making a list and checking it twice." The man next to me muttered, "I'd like to bend my level over that bastard's head."

It was no surprise that just before the whistle blew on Friday evening, Louie walked the scaffold handing out two pay envelopes to all the Black bricklayers and a few of the whites. It would be another bleak Christmas for most of the men.

Some of the white guys openly wondered why the Black bricklayers were so unprepared for winter. They never understood that, being the last hired and the first fired, the Black bricklayers spent their summer wages paying last winter's bills and never caught up.

At that time, an African American bricklayer was, economically, almost part of the Black upper class. Most of them cherished the hope that someday they would go into the contracting business. Some had learned their trade at the various agricultural and mechanical schools that the southern states passed off as colleges for African Americans. Those who graduated from A&M schools had a solid foundation in basic engineering and architecture and could go into contracting if they could get the money and backing from a white man. This glimmer of hope, plus the high hourly wage, made the Black bricklayers the most conservative section of the Black workers.

The average white who hated Black communists hated them because they were Black as well as Red. The aspiring Black middle class loathed the Black communist because his existence gave the white man a rationale to hold them back. I didn't get along with many of the Black bricklayers. The few who felt a responsibility for the African American people defended me.

The guys who stole the trade were close to me because they knew I would defend them on the union floor.

7

I went to Curtis Petitte's house often. A Party member for over three years, Curtis still had one foot in the street life of the Black slum. Friday nights he went to bed early, slept most of Saturday, and then ran a poker game until Sunday morning. When I only half jokingly questioned him about the morality of a Communist running a gambling den, he answered that without the extra income he could not provide for his brothers and mother. I never mentioned it again.

His two boisterous younger brothers kept the house full of their high school friends—male and female. The front door did not lock and the general lived-in disorder of the house made me feel at home. Curtis's mother soon accepted me as one of the family, and I called her "Ma" along with the rest of her sons.

No one paid any attention to me as I sipped a beer and watched Curtis making notes for the union meeting. His lips moved slightly as he wrote down and memorized his talk. It would seem to come off spontaneously, off the top of his head, leaving the impression of a brilliant, dedicated union man. He was carefully laying the groundwork to run for shop committeeman, a step away from and the foundation for running for president of the union.

I was beginning to understand my complex comrade. It wasn't that he wanted to be union president. He wanted to prove to himself that he could do it. He wanted to prove it to the white workers who attacked and Redbaited him. He wanted to prove it to the Black workers who doubted that any Black man could do it. He had to prove to himself that he was a leader. Then I realized this was why he strove so hard to make out with every woman around him. He wasn't interested in proving to them he was a man; he had a constant need to prove it to himself. It seemed all so unnecessary.

He was a big, husky, articulate, educated person, a good dancer, and a committed communist. I took another slug of the beer. I could not avoid the conclusion that if you think you are inferior, all the victories in the world will not change that opinion. Somehow I knew that my comrade was going to strive and smoke and drink and fuck himself to death before he was sixty. I felt a little sad about it all. I finished my beer and rose to leave.

"Later on, man."

"Easy, baby," Curtis replied without looking up. I closed the door and left.

8

Roberta went to work every day. I went when the weather permitted. I could almost feel the resentment when I would pick her up at her job. As the pressures against the marriage increased, living in one room was becoming unbearable. When the weather broke that spring and work became a little more stable, we went hunting for any kind of an apartment. I felt that my political work required me to stay in the working-class areas, but apart from that restriction, anything would do. We finally found one on the corner of Thirty-eighth and Quincy, the heart of the ghetto. Although it was a violent and dangerous area, Roberta and I never felt that we were in danger. After getting a few men jobs on construction, I became well known and had many friends in the area. Southern-like, they referred to me as "Mr. Nelson," and I could not make them change it.

Monday morning I left the apartment as usual for the job. Approaching the car, I saw that the rear window was rolled down a little. The first thing I thought of was the battery—but people who steal batteries don't bother to roll down windows. I approached the car and glanced in. A young man was asleep in the rear seat. I opened the door and shook him gently.

"Hey, man. What you doing in my car?"

The man, about twenty years old, opened his eyes, rubbed, them and asked, "You Mr. Peery?"

"Yeah, but what you doing sleeping in my car?"

"I got in from Anniston a few days ago. I was looking for a job. Folks told me you might be able to get me a job. I was afraid I'd miss you, so I slept in the car."

Southern folks! Anybody else might have shot him. He climbed out of the car. A husky, personable young man eager to work, he made a favorable impression on me.

"Maybe I can help. Where do you live?"

"When I get a job, I can get a room somewhere. I don't have a place right now."

I was sure he hadn't eaten breakfast, but there was no time for that.

"Well, if you want to take the chance, get in the car and I'll ask my boss."

I told the foreman that Tyrone was my nephew and needed a job. He was hired and enthusiastically went to work.

Ty was a good worker, and by the end of the day his job was secure. He had no money and no place to live. The wife didn't object too much when I put up a cot in the kitchen, and he stayed with us until he made a paycheck. When he left, his genuine, heartfelt thanks and promises to return the favor were touching. Over the next year and a half I taught him the fundamentals of bricklaying. When he was caught up with his work and the foreman wasn't around I'd give him a trowel and he'd work the line with the rest of the men. Ty left the company after he felt he could hold a job as bricklayer with the contractors who were throwing up the basements and veneers out in the boondocks. It would be several years before I saw him again.

9

Sitting at the big kitchen table, Curtis and I were into our favorite beer-time discussion: trying to figure out what the Party was going to do against the increasing attacks, and jokingly fantasizing about the women in the Youth League. A loud knock on the door interrupted us.

"Come on in, man," Curtis shouted without getting up.

A middle-aged Black guy slowly opened the door, stuck his head in, smiled, and then entered the room.

"How ya doin', Welby? What's the happenins'?" Curtis' personality changed in a split second from the communist discussing politics to the signifying jive artist that was his street face.

"I'm doin' fine, man. Look here, I wanted to come by and drop this bread on you." He handed Curtis an envelope containing money.

"Hey, Welby, you could have waited till I saw you at the shop." Curtis glanced into the envelope, then stuffed the money into his pocket.

"I wants to thank you man, you saved my life," Welby said, pulling a pint of whiskey from his jacket pocket. "Thought you might like a little taste."

Curtis twisted the cap off the bottle and shoved it toward Welby.

"Thanks, man. Here, have a sip."

"Thanks, Curtis. I got to get back. The old gal's still low sick. I don't want to leave her alone." Welby grinned, nodded to me, and left the room.

Curtis, anticipating my question, said, "I make a few loans at the shop. Most of the guys charge seventy-five percent. I go for thirty-five percent."

"Thirty-five percent! Christ, Curtis, that's usury."

"Usury? Those fuckin' words don't mean nothin' down here. Man's wife is sick. He got no collateral and the banks ain't gonna lend him nothin'. The white sharks in the plant charge him a hundred percent. The colored sharks charge him seventy-five percent. I charge him thirty-five percent. That barely covers the loss from the cats that split town on me. I'm doing him a favor and he knows it. So he brings me a bottle to say thanks and I know I got a cat that is going to work hard for me in the next election." Curtis glanced at me for a moment and, sensing that I was trying to adjust communist morality to the reality of the slums, added, "That's life in the big city, man."

Taking a sip of whiskey and a good drink of beer, I looked at this complex comrade across the table from me. The jive artist and the street hustler were minor sides of his personality. At union picnics or other gatherings of men and women from Alcoa I would listen carefully as he sauntered amongst the groups talking politics, preaching socialism. The few times I heard him speak publicly he was a textbook communist, basing his program on class struggle and African American rights. Probably we got along so well because he was my mirror image. Amongst white people, including the white comrades, he was the calm, calculating Black unionist. He would never ask them questions except in a rhetorical manner that allowed him to answer his own question. Amongst Black people, Curtis presented himself as the leader of the street, someone who was a communist because it was the only way for the African American people to achieve freedom. He felt this would override any ideological considerations.

Curtis's nickname was "the Front." "Fronting off" preceded his most serious discussions. This charade would begin by challenging or belittling whoever or whatever he was up against. After humiliating his opponent and putting him thoroughly on the defensive, he would state his superior qualifications. The coup de grâce consisted of a cock-of-the-walk strut and contemptuous advice to "wake up and see." Part of the "front" was the hundred-dollar bill wrapped around a few singles and a big wad of toilet paper.

10

At that time about 15 percent of the Party membership (i.e., 10,500 members) was Black. The FBI never understood the reason for the fierce loyalty of the working-class African American comrades to the Party. It lay in the fact that the FBI refused to prosecute known lynchers and murderers. They often withheld information from the few lawmen who wanted to carry out such prosecutions. This was common knowledge. On the other hand, even the conservative Blacks gave the Party credit for consistently defending the African American people. Therefore, in the minds of many Black comrades, disloyalty to the Party was disloyalty to African American people.

One day it occurred to me how few *communists* I had ever met. There were thousands of Party members, but few communists. There were hundreds of highly developed Marxists, but few communists. The average Black communist was in the Party to fight against Jim Crow and all the results of white supremacy. The trade unionists were there to fight against the economic exploitation of the class. The women were fighting for equality and liberation; the young comrades were fighting against the draft, for access to education and jobs. Some comrades were academics, won over by the logic and idealism of Marx and Engels. It seemed that few deeply understood that *communism* was an economic term, not a political one. Few were communists in the sense of fighting for a new society—communism in its historical sense. Few were fighting to create the conditions for the people to move forward to the next stage of development as human beings. Deep down, I knew this lack of historical purpose on the part of not only most of the members but also most of the leaders would make it impossible for the Party to withstand the external and internal blows that were shattering our organization.

When someone's objective understanding of historical necessity becomes connected to his or her subjective sense of personal responsibility, that person becomes a communist. I often thought back to how during the war in the Solomons, a semiliterate southern country preacher who'd dedicated his life to "saving" his fellow soldiers brought this understanding to me.

Josh was a jackleg preacher in Company A of the 369th Infantry. We were never close friends, but from time to time I attended the little group of soldiers he preached to, rather than go to the official church services that upheld the army and the Constitution. One Sunday evening after he finished leading the men in their last beautiful spiritual and said his last prayer, Josh called to me, "Sergeant, let me ask you a question."

"Sure, Josh, what is it?"

"Well, I see you come to our prayer meetings, but you don't hardly ever really join in. You a Christian? You been saved?"

I didn't know how to answer him. I couldn't tell him I mostly came to hear the spirituals.

"I been baptized."

"That don't make you no Christian. That means you been saved. You ain't a Christian if you ain't had a burning."

I knew what he meant. I had seen soldiers suddenly fall into the clutch of religion during his preaching, seen them joyously dancing through the jungle with their eyes closed, seen them cry like children when the spirit gripped them, heard them confess their sins and cry to the Lord for forgiveness—seen them "get religion." Getting a burning was the correct description. I agreed with Josh that you're not really anything until you get a burning. It could come suddenly, while Josh was preaching, or it could come slowly, with books and the thoughts they generate. Or it could come with an event. When a soldier gives his life to save his comrades it's because he had a burning. He understood how unimportant he was compared to his comrades, their mission, and the war. Great people in history became great after they had a burning and could no longer simply carry on their work because they thought it the right thing to do; rather, they did it because they had no choice.

I never thought that becoming a communist was the same as becoming a Christian. I knew, though, that signing a Party card or fighting to win a strike or sitting through a study class on *Capital* didn't make one a communist. It took a special kind of burning. The burning came to me as I realized how profound Hegel's statement that men make their history was. I deeply and emotionally understood that through cooperation we can create the conditions to raise humanity out of the swamp of exploitation and war and ignorance forever. I got that burning when I believed we could create a new humanity, when I understood that I was indispensable to making it happen. When I knew I marched in the footsteps of Martin Luther and Paul Robeson and the legions of humanity who had changed the world because they could do nothing else, then I had had my burning and could never turn back.

11

The growing unity and strength of the world's colored nations in the United Nations presented the embattled African Americans with a new forum in their fight for justice. The National Negro Congress petitioned the United Nations to hear their demand for freedom. The U.S. delegation to the United Nations blocked the petition. A year later the NAACP presented its petition. Again, the U.S. delegation prevented it from coming to the floor of the UN.

In 1951, the Civil Rights Congress (CRC) called on all its members to participate in gathering signatures to support its petition, "We Charge Genocide," to the United Nations. What few spare hours I had were spent in the very successful door-to-door signature campaign.

The Civil Rights Congress bypassed the General Assembly, where the U.S. delegation could block them, and went directly to the United Nations Commission on Human Rights in Geneva, Switzerland, with its petition. The petition was an international sensation. The colored peoples of the Southern and Eastern hemispheres as well as the socialist world applauded and popularized the document. The U.S. State Department's embassies around the world demanded that the government do something to counter the effect of the petition. When William Patterson, head of the CRC, went to Paris to present the petition to the United Nations Assembly, the government made its move: upon Patterson's return to the United States, his passport was seized. Image-wise, it was perhaps the worst thing they could have done. The petition was in the hands of tens of millions, and once again "the Negro question" derailed the government's propaganda.

African America's most respected intellectual, eighty-four-year-old W.E.B. Du Bois, was arrested in 1951 for the treasonous act of speaking for peace. Our grayed, frail leader stood erect and defiant as he was shackled, frisked like a common criminal, and led to jail. As usual, the Black establishment either was silent or actively prevented the mobilization of the Black masses in Du Bois' defense. As during the days of slavery, the Black driver, the Black whip hand, did the dirty work. The commanding white hand of the master remained clean. We Black comrades gritted our teeth, donated what we had, cursed the bastards, and continued to march until Du Bois and his four co-defendants were eventually acquitted.

12

Job-wise, Cleveland was the best location in the nation. Between the booming construction industry and the insatiable demand for labor in the steel mills and factories, there were jobs for just about everyone. That wasn't true when it came to housing for the expanding African American population.

Every day, two "Cleveland Specials"—nonstop buses from Birmingham, Alabama—dumped their cargo of Black refugees into Cleveland's overcrowded slum. With every busload, the housing shortage tightened. Those who were buying homes in the ghetto got their crumbs from the bonanza. Living and dining rooms were converted to sleeping quarters; even large closets were rented out. Smart people watched the obituary column to see if anyone in the ghetto died and perhaps left an empty apartment.

Roberta and I got lucky. We qualified for a small apartment in a rehabilitated building on Seventy-first and Central. I was glad to leave the grimy heart of the ghetto. Having money to afford a decent apartment made living in a cramped, bed bug- and roach-infested, decaying building unbearable.

The tension and frustration grew by the day. There was nowhere for the African Americans to go. Roughly from Twelfth Street to Eighty-fifth and from Cedar to Broadway was the solid-Black core area.

Against sometimes violent resistance, the Black neighborhood sporadically crept south and east. Redlining by the banks made it almost impossible for African Americans to purchase a home through a reputable broker. Those who were financially able to buy a house were caught between the redlining and the blockbusters.

The real estate blockbusters were making a fortune around 105th Street by secretly buying a home in an adjacent white—almost always Jewish—neighborhood and then moving a Black family in. In a matter of weeks the whites fled, selling out to the real estate speculators for any price they could get. They left thanking the white speculators for helping sell their house—and cursing and hating the Blacks for ruining "their" neighborhood. The houses would then be sold to African Americans for many times more than what was paid for them.

The ghetto pressed against the city center to the north and could not expand. To make matters worse, the city cleared a swath from Fifteenth to Twenty-third Streets to make sure the ghetto could not expand northward. Later, they ran a freeway through this area. We called this empty space "no-man's-land." An iron ring of Cleveland's white workers flanked the ghetto to the east and west. Walking their streets, let alone moving into their neighborhoods, could mean a beating and sometimes a killing by thugs or police.

By 1951, Cleveland was bursting at the seams. The Blacks were not the only immigrants. The mechanization of southern agriculture uprooted millions of sharecropping whites. These displaced persons tended to go straight north to an industrial city. Cleveland along with Chicago and Detroit were their natural destinations. The mechanization of the mines sent hundreds of thousands from the hill country, especially West Virginia, into Cleveland. Competing with the African Americans for jobs and housing, they understood their strategic weapon was their white skin. They banded together and used it to the maximum.

During World War II, the labor shortage for the mills forced the labor recruiters to look beyond the continental United States for workers. They turned to Puerto Rico. At that time Puerto Ricans were not treated as United States citizens and immigration was difficult. A government committee screened and selected workers in Puerto Rico for the mills in Elyria and Cleveland. This committee knew the revolutionary history of the Blacks in Puerto Rico. They knew of the relatively democratic relations between the light- and dark-skinned people on the island. They wanted none of that transported into the United States. Those selected were of the lightest skin color, and after being in the United States a few days, they learned what the Italians and Irish had learned before them: if you don't want to be treated as a Black, don't associate with them. If you want to prove your loyalty to and join the white race, the quickest way is to join the racist street thugs. The Appalachians and Puerto Ricans did this with a vengeance.

The steady influx of Black immigrants, along with well-paying jobs, made it inevitable that some of the braver—mostly veterans—would cross Carnegie to inquire about an occasional apartment for rent. One was murdered and his body dumped in an alley between Carnegie and Euclid.

We Black workers were furious and set about planning to retaliate. It was difficult. They could kill any African American to get their message across. Their tactic was to kill one and scare a thousand. It made no difference to them who that Black was. I had to keep reminding the group that there were decent people over there and we could not indiscriminately take our revenge.

The tavern on Seventy-first and Central was our schoolroom, our headquarters for a hundred freedom plots that died a-birthing. It was our hideout from failing marriages. I went there often, and our conversations would drift from our personal problems to those we had as a group. We could meet informally to discuss how we could retaliate against the increasing brutality by the whites. We talked about setting a trap, having ten of us hidden in cars and sending one person into their neighborhood. When the whites attacked him, we could take care of them quickly and get back to the safety of our ghetto.

From the day the first slaves landed on these shores, the principal weakness in their resistance has been the Black informer. A close second has been the Black "leaders" appointed by the white rulers and desiring nothing more than to be applauded by and close to them. So even before God got the news, the police were aware of our plotting. As usual, the NAACP leaders did their duty, coming down into the slum to warn us of falling into the clutches of the communists by instigating violence. The militancy simmered down. Frustrations were finally drowned in beer and the lament, "We're crabs in the barrel—pulling one another down and nobody getting out."

It was Tuesday evening and the tavern itself seemed to resonate with the feelings of every Black in Cleveland: subdued but exuding a sullen, threatening air. I closed the door behind me, waved to Harry the bartender, and headed for my usual booth—the only one near a window. Billie Holiday had just begun singing from the jukebox. The patrons sat silently as the mournful lyrics of "Strange Fruit" settled into their consciousness. There was no need to speak of the hurt and the anger. There was no use saying what everyone knew and felt. The African Americans in Cleveland's ghetto were at the end of our rope. We weren't going to take it anymore. The time had come when life was not as important as the right to life.

Limpy threw the door open with such force it slammed against the wall. He stood in the doorway for a moment gasping for breath, his game leg jutting awkwardly to the side.

"What's the matter, Limpy?" The bartender's voice was tense but soothing and low. Limpy glanced around along the bar and then over to the tables. Lady Day dug at us: *Blood on the leaves and blood on the roots. Black bodies swinging . . .* were we men or cowards?

"They done killed another colored man," Limpy shouted.

"Where?"

"What happened?"

"Over on Carnegie—dragged him into the alley an' beat him to death with a garbage can!"

The choking, shocked silence spurred the adrenaline, boiled the blood, and sent it shooting to the heart and brain, tensing the muscles—eager for battle! Most of the men were already pushing back their chairs, turning on their barstools, anticipating the battle cry, "Let's go! Let's get those mother-fuckers!" Nobody knew or cared who shouted it.

I had not heard or felt that since the war. I was jostled and pushed running for the door. By the time we reached Seventy-first Street and turned the corner toward Cedar Avenue I realized it was not my M1 rifle I was holding at high port but the two-by-four used to secure the door at the bar. The people living along Seventy-first Street heard of the murder. The people along Cedar heard of it. Standing on their porches, in their yards, and along the sidewalks, they anxiously waited to vent their years of pent-up fury. As we reached Cedar Avenue, I could see that our army had almost doubled to thirty warriors. As it grew in size, it grew in militancy. We ran across Cedar Avenue, with the near silence of battle-hardened infantry.

Approaching Carnegie Avenue, we could see the Puerto Ricans and Appalachian whites standing in scattered groups. Some still held clubs and what I later discovered were lengths of garden hose filled with sand, which had been used in the murder. We felt, sensed, and believed only one thing: they were laughing about killing another nigger. We charged across Carnegie. *Faster! Don't let 'em get away!* The enemy, seeing us rolling across the boulevard, paused in a moment of confusion.

Branded into my subconscious as deep as my army serial number: *Your mission is to close with the enemy and destroy him with your primary weapons—rifle, bayonet, and grenade.* As in combat, the last vestige of civilization fell to the gutter and I ran faster, cursed louder—driven by the battle cry, "Get 'em—get 'em. Kill the motherfuckers!" Muffled, confused shouts and curses erupted on one side, an expanding roar of "Kill the motherfuckers!" on the other. Some turned to meet us with fists and clubs. Our first wave overwhelmed them. The rest turned to run.

Panic, hate-filled battle cries. Bodies tumbled under fists and clubs, tripped over picket fences. Those who brought up the rear of our group were still running, leaping over the fallen lest the more fleet-footed of the enemy get away. The two-by-four thudded against an arm, a shoulder, a head. I heard the snarling, hate-filled curse and realized it came from me. I turned and swung again at the white or tan face before me.

The scream of sirens—cops!

"Get back, men!"

No one had to explain what Cleveland's cops would do if they caught us. Ganging up, we knocked down the few that still stood and fought.

Disengage!

We ran back across Carnegie and scattered through the alleys behind Cedar. The cops would think twice about going into that labyrinth. Suddenly, it was over. A few of us made our way through the alleys back to the tavern. The cops cruised Seventy-first, up and down Cedar and Central, flashing their spotlights, throwing bewildered boys and men against the walls, searching them for weapons, cursing, threatening, interrogating.

Back at the bar, we spoke in whispers. Most of the men had prudently gone home. Those who returned to the bar nursed swollen and bruised knuckles. My hand trembled as I drank the beer, half expecting the cops to break down the door and come in shooting. Nothing happened. After an hour, I felt safe and left. Roberta would be asleep. She would go to work in the morning. I would go to the union hall and be told no work had come in and I would come back to the tavern. Everything seemed to wear against the marriage. Climbing the stairs to the apartment, I thought back to the fight and how much I hated "them." They wanted to show the ruling class they could be trusted. *Kill a nigger and prove you're a good American! How the hell are we going to unite? The stupid motherfuckers!* There were no longer classes or national groups or imperialism. There was only "them"— the white and tan faces of those who would drive us back into slavery for the privilege of a job in the steel mill. Jesus, I hated them.

I sat down at the kitchen table staring at the wall, my thoughts going back six years to the last time I'd said those words.

During the spring of 1945, our division had left the tiny island of Emiru for Indonesia. The Indonesian island of Morotai was to be the staging area for the invasion of the Philippines and Borneo.

Thousands of troops converged on the island. Aussies and New Zealanders fresh from the African campaign, a few French, Javanese, and Dutch soldiers—stragglers from their defeated armies—joined Black troops from Dutch Guyana and staged for the invasion of Borneo. An assortment of American infantry and support units staged for Leyte.

My segregated, all-Black Ninety-third Division was assigned the task of finishing off the Japanese stragglers on Morotai and securing the island against the forty-five thousand Imperial troops bottled up on the island of Halmahara, twelve miles away.

Over the past year we had been totally isolated from white American troops, and I had forgotten how hatefully vicious they could be when it came to dealing with us. The Australian government was as racist as any on earth, but their troops, having had a tiny taste of British imperialism, from time to time felt a bit of sympathy for the underdog. They would raise the question of why there existed such brutality against and segregation of the Black soldiers. For most white Americans, however, it was more important to defend this brutality than defeat Hitler and Tojo. They lost no time filling the Aussies' heads with the lies and slander that for three centuries has been the rationale and excuse for slavery, lynching, and segregation. Many of the Allied troops became convinced that we were a race of lazy rapists and could be controlled only by force.

From time to time groups of Aussies or New Zealanders would come to our area to sell trinkets or trade their excellent beer for our cigarettes. After the usual "Good night, mate" greeting (which seemed odd to us, since for us that meant good-bye) and a few exchanges made, the talk turned to race. "The Yanks all say that you rape white women unless they control you. Is that true, mate?" Then would come hours of discussion, giving them copies of Black newspapers and magazines and generally trying to make them understand something that defied explanation. After one such session, an Australian soldier gave me his home address and, shaking my hand, said, "Be careful, mate. They hate you."

I could not explain to him that slowly the forbearance of a defenseless people was also turning to hate.

The Thirty-first, the all-white Dixie Division, had taken the island, and its commanding general was island commander. Consequently, Dixie Division military police patrolled the roads and were in command outside of our immediate regimental area. Everything the cops did in Dixie, their military police did on Morotai. We suddenly found ourselves back under the rule of racist cops. The island roads became dangerous traps for us. Our men were stopped and arrested for the slightest reason, such as wearing a mixed uniform, even though we were in a combat zone. More often they were stopped to be humiliated and threatened because they were Black and in a uniform that posed the ultimate threat of equality. With good reason, I was becoming afraid of these Dixie Division bastards, and there is no hatred so all-consuming as the kind that arises from fear.

After supper was served and my work was finished I watched as a white soldier left the road and walked toward me. *What the heck is this guy doing?* I wondered. Then I saw the Dixie Division shoulder patch and thought, *This cat got to be nuts coming here!*

There was nothing special about him. He was medium in almost everything: five foot eight or nine, his sandy-colored hair parted to the side, emphasizing the lean face and greenish eyes. He approached me.

"Evening, Sergeant. Got a minute?" The voice was New England.

"Sure. What can I do for you?"

"You can see I'm in the Thirty-first. But I'm not from the South."

"I can see that, too."

"My name is William Berry. I'm from Maine, a small town, East Fryberg, Maine. I don't suppose you've heard of it."

I admitted I hadn't, and he went on.

"Before I was drafted, I never saw a colored man, and you're the first one I ever talked to." He paused for a moment, waiting for me to speak or perhaps to collect his thoughts. "In the division they talk terrible about colored people. Call them terrible names."

I almost smiled as he continued.

"They don't like me either. Had my share of fights with them. Some of them are OK. Anyway, I finally made up my mind to talk to a colored man because I don't believe the things they say about you. God made us all." William Berry was out of breath.

I introduced myself and shook hands, and we sat together on the coconut log that served as the platoon meeting place. It would have been easier to explain race and racial history and racial economics to a visitor from Mars.

Berry listened quietly, his hands clasped, fingers interlocked, staring at the ground. I gave him the latest editions of the Black press. As he read, he would say to himself, "My God, I didn't know these things happened."

As curfew time drew near, we shook hands, exchanged addresses, and promised, as soldiers do, to get in touch. I watched him walking away thinking, *There goes the American. Generous, decent, and so damned dumb that all his good qualities are blocked.*

My mind came back to Cleveland and the fight we had had. I couldn't hate William Berry, just as I couldn't hate America. I knew we would have to fight them before we could unite with them. How could a white person not know what had happened and was happening to the African American people? But then, the African Americans didn't know what was happening to the Indians. I began to see it more clearly. It wasn't that they or we didn't care. We were isolated from one another and invisible. We were going to have to make these people pay attention to us. But we'd have to pay attention to others, too. Man! Building working-class unity in America was going to be one hell of a job. I opened a beer to calm down before going to bed.

I did not and could not have known at the time that two white revolutionaries from the mines of Appalachia were risking their lives over on Chester Avenue. Trying to calm the situation, they explained to their brethren how the landlords were using them and how their only salvation was to unite with the African Americans and fight for housing and jobs for all. I would meet them years after in the fight to rebuild the revolutionary movement. Nor could I have known that Piri Thomas and his friends on those mean streets of New York were trying to convince their Puerto Rican comrades that they had to stop fighting and killing the Blacks for the very white man who oppressed their homeland.

I knew, and anyone who read the Black press knew, that these spontaneous outbursts were happening all over the country. The official revolutionary movement, guided by a beautiful ideology rather than a set of ugly facts, was more and more isolated and impotent as the scattered groups and individuals in the streets struggled for ways to come together in the fight for equality. Mainly led by working-class veterans with no place to retreat, they were writing a new chapter in the struggle of the African American people.

13

As members fled in increasing numbers, the Party attempted to fill the gaps by concentrating its work. The day came in the winter of 1952 when I was asked to take a job in the steel mills in order to maintain a presence there. I didn't like the idea of going from the bricklayer's wage of $3 an hour to the steelworker's $1.50, but I hadn't come to Cleveland to make money. Construction work was slack, so it wasn't a sacrifice.

The Jones and Laughton Steel Corporation was one of the mills packed into the industrial flats. They advertised for all the various crafts along with a big sign for common labor. Since I had worked rebuilding their furnaces, I thought I might get a job as a bricklayer and stay in the mill. At the employment office I was handed a short form to fill out stamped "Labor Gang." I mentioned to the clerk that I had some experience with firebrick. He offhandedly said, "If you want to work, fill out the form." It was clear that the company was supporting the union demand that the hearth and all skilled work be done by whites. Black workers were restricted to the labor gang. Since I was there for a purpose, I filled out the form. Along with the rest of the Black men applying for work, I was herded into a small assembly room. After everyone was seated, the white man, assuming that none of the Blacks had ever held a job in industry, gave a short lecture about the necessity of coming to work every day. "If your wife is sick, the best way to care for her is to report to work on time. If you don't have carfare, give yourself time to walk to work. If you are sick, get to work on time and let the company doctor take care of you." We filled out W-2 forms and were given slips showing the location of the labor gang lockers and the shifts we were assigned to.

I went to work that Sunday afternoon as a car knocker. The freight gondolas loaded with ore or coke stopped above huge hoppers, the sides were unlatched, and the cargo was emptied into the hoppers to be dropped into the furnace. There was always frozen ore or coke stuck in the corners that had to be dislodged with shovels or pikes. The union reserved this dirty, hard, and dangerous work for its Black members.

Construction trains its workers to work eight hours a day, and very often I would find myself working while others were standing or wandering around the yard. Not wanting to distance myself from the crew, I tried to follow their lead. At the end of the week, the boss called me to follow him. As we entered the furnace area he turned to me and said, "You see those people? They don't know how to work. I've been watching you. You seem to be a good worker. I'm going to give you a chance on the furnace. It'll mean a raise to a dollar sixty-five an hour."

I didn't want to leave the gang, as I was just beginning to make contact with a few of the more socially conscious guys, but I was anxious to get away from the hard, filthy work. I thanked the boss, and he turned me over to a wiry, dark-skinned guy who was to give me instructions regarding my new job. With the boss out of earshot, he took off his plastic helmet and said, "My name is Rufus—but everybody call me Gator-tail cause I come from the Sea Islands."

I introduced myself, and after shaking hands he continued, "You a third helper on the furnace. That is to say, you a cinder snapper. There's the keeper of the furnace. He's the big shot. Then there's the second helper; he takes care of the iron run. They white people—they don't let no colored man have those jobs. The third helper cleans the slag run. That's where all the work is and that's where we are."

Gator-tail went on to explain how the keeper taps into the furnace, allowing the slag and iron to run out. The iron, being heavy, stayed in its trench, flowed into a huge kettle on the railroad, and was taken to the hearth for refining. The slag ran into a chemical pit, producing a huge cloud of gut-wrenching, stinking steam. The slag was light and tended to overflow its trench and run all over the furnace area. The cinder snapper, using the long steel rods, shovels, and rakes, kept the slag flowing in place.

When time came to tap the furnace I was given a heavy asbestos cloak, asbestos gloves, asbestos covering for my shoes, and a plastic helmet. Gaiter-tail gave me a final warning,

"Sometimes there's a bad tap. The coal and iron and all that shit gets mixed up and it blows out the hole like a goddamn volcano. You got to always watch. If you see the pour ain't right, you got to get behind one of the steel beams till it calms down—otherwise you might get burned to death."

I looked up at the furnace. The dust-covered, conical four-story steel mountain seemed alive and threatening. It was a volcano. I could hear the growling and rumbling in its guts as the iron ore melted and settled at the bottom.

I was more than a bit apprehensive as the skinny little Hungarian who was keeper of the furnace pushed the drill up to the furnace tap and started the motor. The tap went well and I worked beside Gator-tail pushing the slag, filling in holes when it broke through the ditch. In the battle to keep the slag moving, my poker melted from ten to five feet and my face became drenched with sweat while a solid sheath of ice and snow formed on my back. By the end of the run I was exhausted, but I knew the tasks of the cinder snapper.

During the following weeks I learned some other things from Gator-tail. I learned how to get paid for a week each month without working. In the furnace the shift changes every week. For one week a month Gator-tail would report to work for the eleven P.M. to seven A.M. shift, but that didn't shift didn't pour until six A.M. My shift would then be from seven to three with a pour at two P.M. To get the week off, Gator-tail would check in at eleven and then go home. I would get to the furnace at five-thirty A.M., clean the slag run after his pour, and then punch out his time card at six. That way I worked nine hours with two pours. Gator-tail got paid for standing on the corner swinging his gold pimp chain like he didn't have to work. The following week the change in shifts did not allow us to carry on the scam. The week after that it would be my turn to check in and go home. Gator-tail would have two pours. I don't know if the bosses knew of our little trick. Perhaps they didn't care so long as the work got done.

I tried to keep contact with the few progressive-thinking people on the labor gang while listening to the men at the furnace to see if there was any radical thought amongst them. The years of second-class citizenship had left their mark. People tend to accept what they cannot change. Yet conditions change. The growing freedom struggle in the South affected the Black laborers since so many of them had only recently left the area. They began to question their position in the union and in the mill. I thought the time had come to get some literature in their hands.

With the help of a few of the older comrades working at Republic Steel, I drafted a leaflet condemning the collusion between the union and the company in keeping the Black worker restricted to the labor gang. I tried to tie this to the necessary functioning of the capitalist system and signed it the Communist Party.

Wrapping the fifty leaflets in a newspaper, I walked past the unsuspecting guard at the gate. After cleaning the slag run and while the rest of the workers were at their jobs, I walked over to the labor gang locker room and pushed a carefully folded leaflet into each locker. The leaflet was the talk of the whole gang, and there was no doubt that management had gotten a copy as well. I went about my work as if nothing had happened, but the looks and remarks by some on the labor gang as well as from the furnace crew left no doubt that I was the prime suspect. The ethnic whites on the furnace crew were bitterly anti-Communist but class-conscious enough to keep their suspicions to themselves.

It was almost impossible for a serious communist to hide. In 1951 America, if you spoke out for equal rights for the African American people, you were a Communist. If you murmured anything about women's equality, you were a Communist. If you spoke for peace (and were not wearing the cloth), you were a Communist. The intellectually independent African American was a Communist. Because I lived my convictions and never hid my thoughts, the people I worked with would have assumed I was a communist, even if I hadn't been.

•   •   •

I finally got my introduction to the hazards of working on the furnace. One day the tap started badly, with chunks of burning coal shooting from the tap hole into the furnace area. Sure something terrible was about to happen, I moved behind the nearest steel beam. The keeper could not continue the drill. He began trying to plug the tap hole with clay in order to begin again. At that moment all hell broke lose. The immense pressure within the furnace blew out the plug. An explosion of white-hot coke and iron from the tap hole followed a deafening roar from within the furnace. I felt the hot coke smashing against the beam like the explosion of phosphorous shells during the war. The slag and iron shot out, clogging the ditch and spreading out over the furnace area. Small fires erupted wherever the molten iron touched coal dust or anything flammable. Without being told, I knew it was imperative that the slag and iron run be cleared before the molten iron set the railroad track ablaze or, worse yet, I would be surrounded by the stuff and unable to get to safety. As the fiery barrage subsided I left the safety of the beam, leaped across the burning puddles, and grabbed my ten-foot poker. One side of my brain was telling me, *Why kill yourself? It isn't your steel mill.* But the discipline of the worker won out and I rammed my poker against the hardening lumps of slag blocking the runway. The battle went on for over an hour. Finally the furnace was plugged and I set about cleaning up the horrendous mess of slag and pig iron. I went home that night utterly exhausted and not at all sure that I wanted to stay in the mill.

My weekly leaflets were probably having some effect, because the guard at the entrance gate was paying closer attention to me as I entered and left the plant. I continued to stuff leaflets in the lockers every week. I was sure management was aware of it and would try to stop it without making a martyr of me. But first they had to catch me with the leaflets. I would come to work with the daily paper rolled up under my arm. The guard would make me unroll it. He would look into my lunch pail and inside my jacket. I learned from stories of the French underground and tied the leaflets around my legs. I was never caught.

14

We were so involved in the never-ending political work that we had very little time for social life. The club's monthly social was a chance to relax and talk of trivia. I asked Roberta if she would like to come to the social. With a smile she declined, reminding me that a working woman had to use weekends to prepare for the next week's work. She kept our social life private, although she did not object to my going alone to Party socials. I felt it was important to be there since they were the only interracial social gatherings held in the segregated city.

This one was held in Glenville. I arrived late, and after paying my pledge, I took a beer from the cooler and settled into a corner chair to catch my breath. As my eyes adjusted to the subdued lights I glanced over the group. Curtis was looking at Judy. Vince was looking at Curtis. Slow, sensuous music began, and a few couples took to the dance floor. Curtis rose and with his best cherub smile nodded to Judy. She was already moving toward him. As they approached each other, touched hands, and glided onto the dance floor, a scene from my childhood flashed into my mind.

I was about fourteen years old when I accompanied my father and our neighbor, Mr. Mason, as they took his cow to be mated with Mr. Sorensen's bull. It was the middle of the Depression, and Mason didn't want to pay to have her mated. The cow was in such heat that she could hardly give milk, so he had to give in to the demands of Mother Nature. As we neared Sorensen's farm the cow and the bull smelled each other. With a bellow, the cow tore the rope from Mr. Mason's hand and smashed through a fence. The bull, also bellowing, tore down the fence of his corral, met the cow in the cornfield, and mounted her. I was a bit frightened by the bellowing and the primeval clashing of tons of lusting flesh.

Mason turned to Pop and said, "Maybe the kid shouldn't see this."

"No," Pop said, "let him see it. Maybe he'll learn how to act. There are people out there just like them two."

Now I glanced over at Ken. He seemed too involved with the discussion he was carrying on, or perhaps thought it was male supremacy even to look to see whom his gorgeous wife was dancing with. I smiled to myself and reached for my Old Timers Ale.

Summer passed building East Cleveland out of the boondocks, with meetings, picket lines, and demonstrations. Ken and Al received their "greetings" from the draft board. As the time for them to report for duty came near, the club held a good-bye party. It was a quiet and sober affair. Judy and Heidi clung to their husbands, and the comrades huddled in little groups talking to one another. I tried to say a few words to cheer them up but finally settled back, sipping my beer and thinking what a terrible thing to be drafted to fight a war one is fighting against.

15

In a trial that remains unsettled, Julius and Ethel Rosenberg were convicted of conspiring to commit espionage for the Soviet Union. They were condemned to death and the execution date was set for June 19, 1953. On that day, the Party and its youth league joined millions around the world in one final effort to save their lives.

Vince, as chair of the Youth League, was giving out the assignments. He looked at me for a second and said, "Comrades Nelson and Abe are assigned to leaflet Ninth and Prospect."

I looked around at the other comrades; most obviously did not have the slightest understanding of what was at stake. Abe understood, and for a moment he flushed and then turned ashen white. They didn't like Jews in that area either.

"Comrade Vince, you know damned well that that is an Italian shopping area where no Negro can go."

"Are you afraid to go there?"

"It's not a question of being afraid. It's a question of how are we going to mobilize the largest number of people possible to try to save the Rosenbergs. No Negro is going to mobilize anything in that area."

"If you go against the decision, you're going to get expelled."

I knew he had already raised the question of my expulsion with the National Office in New York, and Leon Wofsy, the national chairman, had given him the go ahead signal if it could be done legally. The enemy within the Party had the tactic of expelling the African American comrades one by one so no concerted fight could be made. I had the responsibility of staying in the Party in order to carry on the fight.

"I'll carry out the decision, but you're responsible for whatever happens."

Vince looked at Abe. He shrugged and didn't answer.

Saturday, June 19, 1953. The *Cleveland Plain Dealer* headlined the demand that the Rosenbergs be put to death as scheduled. There was little time. The executions were scheduled for three o'clock and the distribution was scheduled for ten in the morning. It was going to be a dangerous day. The press and the Catholic Church, despite the fact that the Pope had begged for clemency, agitated Cleveland's large, influential, working-class Italian community with daily anti-Communism and concentrated on demanding the Rosenbergs be put to death.

I met Abe at Ninth and Euclid, which catered mainly to African American shoppers. He had the leaflets. I glanced over one of them. The leaflet urged people to call the White House and demand that the executions not be carried out. The Communist Party had signed the leaflets. We divided the leaflets and started walking toward Prospect Avenue. It was only one block, but in segregated Cleveland, socially Prospect was miles from Euclid.

Abe was silent. I knew he was frightened, and I didn't want him to know that I was at least apprehensive. An empty storefront was on one of the corners. I chose that corner and stood with my back to the entrance. That way, if anything happened, no one could get behind me.

I started handing out the leaflets. Those who took them seemed shocked and angered that a real live Communist would come to their shopping district and boldly pass out a leaflet. The backward glares as they hurried away were warning enough to get ready.

In a few moments three young toughs, perhaps in their late twenties, approached me. "What ya handin' out?" one of them said to me.

I didn't reply but gave him a leaflet. I saw four more coming. One was a big, rough-looking man in his thirties, his scowl exuding danger. I backed up just a bit into the store entrance.

Emboldened by the reinforcements, the guy crumpled the leaflet. "You handin' out this Communist shit?"

I glared back. "If you don't want it, don't read it."

The big guy elbowed his way in front of me. "You can't pass that crap out here. Gimme them goddamn leaflets!"

"I got a right to pass 'em out. If you don't like it, too bad."

From the corner of my eye I saw Abe running across the street and down Prospect Avenue. I knew I was in for a fight, and anger was overcoming any fear of the seven of them. I tried to think out a battle plan. The glass walls of the storefront entrance converged, narrowing the entrance until they joined the door frame. I backed up deeper into the areaway until there was room for only two of them to be in front of me.

"Either gimme those fuckin' papers or I'll knock 'em outa your hand and kick your ass."

The crowd had grown from seven into a mob. They were cursing and shouting—urging one another to start the fight. Looking the big guy in the eyes, I held the leaflets out with my right hand under them, counting on them believing their own crap about a Black man with a knife.

"You touch my leaflets, you ain't gonna touch nothin' else."

The big bastard moved a step toward me, and my battle brain took control. *He'll knock the leaflets with his left and cross-punch with his right. When he pulls back to punch, he'll be off balance. Grab him and slam him into the plate glass—push him against the broken glass. Try to get a piece of the plate glass and stab whoever else I can before they close in.*

We stood glaring at each other. He was a bit afraid that one move on his part would mean a knife in his guts. I knew that his eyes would shift for a second if he intended to knock the leaflets out of my hand and punch me. When I got the sense that he was about to make his move, I shifted my weight to grab him.

"Break it up! Stand back. FBI! Break it up!"

Two men holding their gold badges and guns up in front of them parted the crowd. One of them grabbed my arm. "What the hell are you doing, Peery? Trying to start a riot?"

Walking between them to the waiting car, I didn't answer.

As we pulled away from the mob, one of the agents turned to me. "My name is Fred Anderson. I just transferred up from the Chattanooga office. You're damned lucky we came by."

"Well, I never thought I'd be glad to see the FBI. Thanks."

Something didn't jive. These guys just happened to come along, and now they were talking to me like a long-lost buddy?

"I'd like to ask you a question. Why are you wasting your life? These people you're associated with aren't serious."

"*I'm* serious. I think I'd be wasting my life if I went along with all this . . ."

"You've got to admit that things are getting better. I have the feeling that before long they are going to get a lot better. You can contribute to that."

Suddenly, it was clear. The whole thing was a setup. They'd set up a situation where I'd be dependent on them, willing to listen to them—maybe even become a cog in their network inside the Party. For Christ's sake! Vince, I realized, had to be an FBI agent or an informer. But whom could I report it to? Another informer? Perhaps J. Edgar Hoover had been telling the truth for the first time—the FBI had gained control of the Party. I was shaken by the inescapable conclusion.

"I think I am contributing to it. Look, I really thank you gentlemen for what you've done, I don't want to appear ungrateful, but I don't want to talk to you about the Party."

"OK, it's your life. When you find out that we're telling you the truth, come and talk to us. No one will know."

They pulled over at Ninth and Euclid. I thanked them as politely as I could and got out of the car.

The Rosenbergs were executed that afternoon despite the worldwide protests.

16

The southern civil rights movement, led by Dr. Martin Luther King Jr., aimed to secure for Blacks the civil rights granted by the Constitution. The freedom movement was much broader. In the North that movement was more localized and aimed toward securing equal rights, especially in employment and housing.

The National Negro Labor Council (NNLC) was one of the most important organizations leading this fight. Its purpose originally was to unite the scattered Black trade unionists to fight for their rights in the unions and in the factory. Inspired by Paul Robeson's call for "Black power" and led by working-class Black Communists, the NNLC moved out of the factories into the Black working-class neighborhoods.

In 1953, the Cleveland National Negro Labor Council attempted to negotiate with Sears, Roebuck about the company's refusal to hire Black workers. The management of Sears refused to meet with them. The NNLC then made plans to demonstrate and picket the huge Sears store at Eighty-sixth and Carnegie, which bordered the Black neighborhood. The NNLC flooded the ghetto with leaflets explaining the coming demonstration and calling for the neighborhood to come out en masse to demand their rights. The Cleveland police and its Red Squad, notorious for their hatred of the Black population, prepared to contain if not prevent the demonstration.

Preparing myself for the worst, I clocked out of work early and left for the demonstration.

"Jesus Christ," I mumbled to myself. "I'm gonna be late again."

I swung the old Studebaker into an empty space on Eighty-sixth, slammed the door, and ran for the corner of Carnegie.

"Goddamn—lookit that!"

There were more than three thousand people in front of the Sears building already. They stood bunched together, talking and sensing their strength. The west side of Carnegie Avenue was bumper-to-bumper police cars. The cops stood in squads, fondling their clubs, occasionally sliding a gloved hand to touch the butt of a pistol.

Ethel Goodman was half walking and half running up and down the line, raincoat and red dress flopping in the breeze, wide-brimmed floppy black hat askew, finger pushing at her glasses, which kept sliding partway down her nose. Originally an itinerant Pentecostal preacher in Birmingham, Alabama, Ethel had found it a short journey into the National Negro

Labor Council and into the CP. She was preaching for a new God now. Her southern Black church-born simplicity endeared her to the Council. At the meetings she would take the floor to discuss some point and would end up walking the aisle, preaching the gospel of struggle. She had to become president of the NNLC. Only thus was she prevented from using up half the meeting time fighting whoever was president.

Down Eighty-sixth Street, toward Euclid Avenue, the white people—mostly from the Appalachian South—stood on their porches watching with apprehension as the crowd of African Americans grew from three thousand to four thousand.

The light changed, and I headed for the parking lot to report to Bert Washington, the state chairman of the NNLC.

With my first step off the curb, I almost bumped into a little fascist bastard named John Ungvary, though I didn't recognize him at first. As I turned to avoid colliding with him, my elbow hit the pistol in his underarm holster. I started to say, "Excuse me," but cut it short as I realized who it was. He pushed his felt hat back from his beady, close-set eyes. His hooked nose always had a shiny spot of snot on the end, and the crisp Cleveland autumn made it worse. Ungvary was a caricature of a Hungarian Nazi trying to mimic an American detective—trench coat, felt hat, facial bones covered by what looked like old dough with reddish blotches, and the power of being head of Cleveland's Red Squad.

He always looked at Black people with contemptuous hatred. But this was special. His eyes were saying, *You damned nigger Communist—don't you bump me.* That slit in his face barely moved as he said, "Watch where the hell you're going."

Three huge Black guys in brown leather jackets, their foundry-scarred hands beginning to double into fists, started across the street. I gave them the high sign to be cool.

"*You* bumped into *me.*"

"You want some more trouble with me?"

There had been trouble last week. Ungvary had had me picked up and grilled by the Red Squad for two hours. They hadn't charged me or hurt me. It was as if they wanted me to know that when the shit went down, they were the cat and I was the mouse, and there was no way to escape from their claws.

"I don't give a goddamn—do what you want to do."

A couple of cops, clubs at the ready, were moving toward us. Bert had seen what was happening and was almost running across Carnegie.

"I ain't fuckin' with you. We got a permit. I ain't got to take no shit off you."

"I'll disperse this god dammed demonstration, you fuck with me."

"What's the problem, Detective Ungvary?" Bert intervened. His balding head bare, glasses hanging at the end of his nose, he bent his tall, lanky frame to speak down to this professional anti-Communist.

Ungvary chewed his dead cigar at the other end of what served as a mouth.

"Washington, this boy bumped me on purpose."

"I saw what happened. Neither one of you was watching—you bumped each other. Do you want an apology? Is that it? Apologize, Nels, and let's get to work."

*Apologize! I'll break that hunkey's fuckin' jaw.**

"Sorry." I spat out the apology.

Bert put his arm around me and guided me across the street. The two cops moved closer to Ungvary, glaring at me, etching my face in their memory for future reference.

"Listen, fella," Bert half whispered, "we've got some real problems." He glanced at the growing crowd that was milling around in little groups, darting glances of hate at the cops. "There's already over four thousand people here and more coming."

Bert stopped for a moment to work up a half grin when I said, "That doesn't seem to be a problem to me—the more the merrier."

"The other part," Bert went on, "is that I got a special delivery from

---

*The term *hunkey* (or *honky*) originated during the struggle against the Fugitive Slave Act. The pro-slavery group hunkered down despite appeals to reason. The abolitionists referred to them as "hunkers." The transition to *hunkey* and then *honky* did not take long.

New York a couple of hours ago. The Party is ordering us out of the Labor Council."

Every Party member was aware that something was going down in New York. The Party had seemed to be without direction for the past several months. We didn't dare mention it, but we very well understood that it was precisely the paralysis of the CP headquarters in New York that gave us the freedom to break out into the Black workers of Cleveland.

We twisted our way through the crowd and into the parking lot where the comrades were waiting. Bert picked up where he had left off. "I'm not sure what is going on—but it's serious. I just received a special-delivery letter from New York. There has been a Central Committee decision that Party forces are to pull out of the Labor Council. People I trust in New York tell me that some sort of deal has been struck with the government around bringing the second string of leadership to trial. I'm telling you this in the strictest confidence. You have a right to know whatever I'm told. I don't necessarily believe all of it, but something's happened."

"Damned right something's happening," Curtis Petitte said. Thirty years old, he had just been elected chief shop steward at the Alcoa local. He was part of—and had campaigned to—the Black majority at the plant. They were the production workers. He proved how the white union administration had constantly sold out the production workers in order to get wage increases for the skilled trades, which were almost entirely white. It had been a bitter, racially acrimonious struggle. On top of his having to fight most of the white workers in the plant, the State Committee of the Party had censured him for appealing to Black Nationalism. Curt was in no mood to hear anything about a Marxism that didn't deal with the immediate needs of the Black workers. If something bad was happening in the Party, he would understand it as a trade union struggle on a higher level—a case of white leaders protecting themselves at the expense of the Blacks.

"Comrades"—Bert always had a nasal slur when he said it—"whatever we decide to do will be for the Party. We can't do anything without the Party. Let me tell you what I was told. First, it seems that a representative from the Justice Department met with a representative from the Party and they worked out a deal on further indictments. It looks like the government has already gotten what it was after. The deal is no more indictments. Now, in return, the Party has to withdraw from the National Negro Labor Council and liquidate the Party in the South and in Puerto Rico."

Curtis broke in, "The real deal is what I said before. The fuckin' government ain't afraid of a bunch of middle-class whites. They ain't going to persecute 'em. They're afraid of what's out there." He jerked his head toward the crowd in front of Sears. "They gonna persecute *them*."

"What are they proposing, Bert—that we walk away from all that over there, just abandon them?" I asked.

Bert said, "So far it's only rumor. I'll keep you informed."

I glanced toward the main entrance doors of the Sears building. The men and women from the NNLC who were in charge of the demonstration had begun to line the people up six abreast. They covered the wide sidewalk from the curb to the edge of the Sears building. The lines stretched along the block from Eighty-sixth to Eighty-fifth along Carnegie, an eighth of a mile. The demonstrators were getting restless. The leadership, sensing the growing tensions with the cops, decided the best thing to do was march.

Sam Gaston, who grew up in Epps, Alabama, had learned to lead a march during the three and a half years he was the guide for Company A, 369th Infantry. He must have been thinking of those days. His placard was raised as if it were the company banner with the curved sword imposed over the big letter *A* and the number *369*. He turned the placard toward the traffic on Carnegie and shouted out its message: "Don't buy where you can't work—boycott Sears!"

Sam stepped off with a military thirty-inch step, and the demonstration began to move like an expanding giant accordion. The leading ranks had turned the corner at Eighty-sixth and were marching toward Euclid before the rear ranks could step forward.

I pulled at Bert's arm and tilted my head toward the Sears entrance. The doors swung open and three white men in suits stepped out. A group of cops moved forward to protect them. The demonstrators slowed down to protect Ethel.

"Oh, shit," Bert muttered. Half trotting, he excused his way through the column and up to where Ethel seemed to be having a stand-off with the three men and the cops. The four of us followed. We knew that if anything happened, Bert and not Ethel would be the target. One of the white men who seemed to be in charge of the others and appeared to be the manager was trying to speak to Ethel.

"Miss Goodman—"

"Well, ain't that nice! It's Miss Goodman now, huh? Yesterday it was 'you people.' "

"Miss Goodman—" There was a studied firmness in his voice. He drew himself up to his full five feet seven inches to become the father or teacher addressing a stubborn and unpredictable child. "I want to settle this. If you will send this crowd home, we can talk this out."

Ethel grinned and used both hands to adjust her glasses. She glanced over the sea of black, brown, and tan faces that were turned toward her. The telepathy that underlay Black communication in America over the centuries came through. "We've got this white bastard where the hair is short. Don't let go!" We all knew that grin. Ethel was going to act the fool now that she had the upper hand.

"So, you want to talk." She dipped a curtsy. "Yesterday I asked you to talk and you told me to walk."

Curtis was grinning. He liked that rhyming jive of the colored disk jockeys. "So now we walkin' and you want to start talkin'."

Those close enough to hear broke out into unrestrained laughter. They turned and mimicked Ethel to those who could not hear. There were no laughing barrels on Carnegie Avenue. The men and women laughed the throaty, gutsy laughter that was still rooted in the earth of Alabama and Mississippi. The guffaws rolled through the crowd. The tension-relieving, fun-poking laughter of Black folk filled the air and made the white folks on the porches lean forward to hear.

The cops muttered racial slurs under their breath to one another. One young African American woman, free for the day from her job at the laundry, narrowed her eyes at the cops. "Ain't no one person gonna be hasslin' with you now. You bad, huh? If you feel froggish, jump! Jar the ground!" One of the parade marshals moved to her side and whispered, "Don't provoke the motherfuckers. Don't give them no excuse."

Everyone knew that 150 armed cops were no match for 5,000 working-class Blacks. Not when they had smelled the sweet aroma of power. Not when they'd had the taste of strength that unity puts in the mouths of those who have been helpless.

"Miss Goodman." The big-shot white man had come down off his high horse. "If you'll step into my office, our lawyer is there and we are prepared to draw up an agreement."

Ethel was about the same height as her antagonist. She glared into his eyes for a few seconds and then spoke with slow and measured words.

"I'm from Alabama, mister. I know what it means to be dragged into a room full of white men to come to some agreement. You ain't dealing with me. You dealing with all of us. These folk came here to walk, 'cause we're sick and tired of your little nickel-slick games and the way you all been treatin' us." She looked from one set of brown eyes to the next. The message was clear. Alabama preaching grew hot in her blood. She shot a glance at the white man and raised her voice to the crowd. "We walkin', man. You want to talk, get your little shyster lawyer down here and we'll talk while we walk." She raised her floppy hat as a banner and shouted to the crowd, "Let's walk! Let's walk like men-o'-war!"

Ethel shouted out the agreements as they were made. The Negro Labor Council, in consultation with the Urban League, would select twelve high school graduates to be trained as clerks, ten to be trained as office personnel, and five to be trained as building maintenance personnel. Next year another twenty-seven would be selected. After that, all employment applications would be processed without regard to race.

Sam Gaston raised his placard as high as his six-foot-two-inch frame and gangling arms could stretch. The roaring response of the crowd rose like a cresting tidal wave. The spontaneous *"Yeahhhh"* rolled over Sam's placard and down Carnegie Avenue and Eighty-sixth Street. Motorists on Euclid pulled to the curb to see what was happening. The roar rolled over to Cedar Avenue. The Black folk who couldn't or wouldn't come to the demonstration opened their windows and slid from under the cars and sucked in the yell of victory. Most of them pulled at their aprons or wiped their hands of the oil and grease and started running toward the big Sears store where Joshua in a red dress and a floppy black hat had blown the ram's horn and the walls of Jericho—those damnable walls of segregation and discrimination, those goddamned walls made from the muck of history, from the blood of the slaughtered, from the hot, hopeless tears of the slave, from the mountain of gold that grew with the sale of sweat and agony in the form of cotton and sugar and pig iron—cracked. We heard it. The cops and the Black people and the white people heard it. Cleveland paused and trembled as a new day was birthing.

17

In 1953 we faced another serious threat to our existence: the government began to levy fines against the Party. In an attempt to safeguard its resources, the most trusted comrades were given the Party's treasury for safekeeping. The communist vision brings out everything noble in a person, and the very worst emerges if that vision is lost. Many of these trusted comrades, deciding the cause was lost, took the money and ran. Some were afraid or ashamed to go where there was a Party organization. They discovered a lovely little university town along Interstate 40 in New Mexico. It was a joke that Albuquerque was colonized by ex-Communists with Party money. Others fled from New York, Cleveland, and Chicago to Los Angeles. Pretending to maintain a semblance of morality, they practically started the coin laundry business on the West Coast. It was a moneymaker that didn't exploit labor. Others, more brazen, opened up automobile and motor home agencies and went into the construction business in their hometowns.

The Party's vision attracted the very best of people. But the Party was more than its vision. It was an organization of real people—people who were influential in unions and organizations. They were people with connections, people who could open doors and break paths. Many were attracted to the Party for this reason. The Party was a social as well as political organization. At its meetings and social gatherings men and women met and sometimes carried on affairs. Very often, in the process of rejecting bourgeois morality, communists appeared to have no morality at all. Along with the most idealistic, the Party attracted every kind of opportunist as well. The FBI understood this and took advantage of it.

The strongest rampart of the Party was its historic work with and for African American liberation. The FBI understood that this was also their least defensible point. It was a point of penetration into the Party, and some of the most destructive FBI work was done through Black informers. The Party's desperate struggle against white chauvinism (which in later years was termed racism) created the political atmosphere for white agents within the Party to protect and advance the Black informer. The FBI approached many militant African Americans and almost all Black comrades with a carrot and a stick. They were offered money as well as job security if they would become informers. At the same time they were threatened with or faced exposure and blacklisting if they did not cooperate. The vast majority refused. A few became informers. Most informers were simply opportunists or political degenerates. They were easy to spot. We Black comrades were always on guard against any infiltration from this direction. We seldom talked about it, but we knew that the struggle against white chauvinism had blinded many of the white comrades to any danger coming from this direction.

At a statewide conference on "Negro work" I was introduced to a new member, Comrade William Cummins from Toledo. We shook hands, and I was happy to see a Black United Auto Workers (UAW) worker join the Party. His callused hands and cheap clothing set him apart from the many middle-class Blacks who were attending. During the convention he did not seem to pay much attention or participate other than hold grinning conversations with most of the women delegates. I also noticed how several of the white comrades from Toledo took Cummins around, making sure he met the right people and generally presenting him as an outstanding, militant leader of the Black workers in the Toledo area. That raised a red flag for me. One of the Party leaders once half-jokingly said that a twelve-year-old Black youth had a better understanding of the state than most of our college graduates. He was right. We all understood that one of the principal methods of control by the white man was to pick a leader of the African American struggle and present him as a militant danger to the status quo. I wasn't the only one to take notice. Bert Washington, a veteran Black comrade named Admiral Kilpatrick, and Curtis Petitte all mentioned to me that this guy didn't seem for real. I decided to keep an eye on him.

The usual social gathering followed the convention, and Bill Cummins found a place to contribute. He was a good dancer and was on the floor doing his thing with every record. Few African American comrades did much dancing at these gatherings. I couldn't, but most of them simply wouldn't for fear of reinforcing stereotypes. It was a different story when a comrade showed up at a neighborhood party. There was no need for a dignified front and they wholeheartedly blended in with their neighbors.

When the Party ended, I noticed Cummins leaving with the wife of one of the district officers. I didn't mention it to anyone. Was he here as a serious communist, his affairs developed naturally from associations, or was he looking for affairs and using the Party for that purpose?

Two months later Cummins came back to Cleveland to attend a conference on work in the UAW. This time he was decked out in a new suit and driving a new green Oldsmobile.

Not bad for a worker in an auto parts factory, I thought, *but the FBI has plenty of money.* I was now convinced that Cummins was an agent.

The Black comrades of Cleveland took pride in their position as the cutting edge of the Party. At its conferences and meetings they worked hard at making contributions. Cummins did not speak often at such meetings. When he did speak it was an embarrassing, transparently coached statement.

During the meeting I noticed that one of the white Cleveland comrades, Harry Forrest, had become very close with Cummins. It didn't ring any bells with me. A jovial, outgoing person, Forrest went out of his way to be friends with the African American comrades. At the end of the meeting, Forrest took the floor to propose Cummins for a vacant seat on the industrial commission. The motion was passed without discussion. This position would put him in touch with our industrial cadre throughout the Midwest. I decided to take my concerns to the state leadership.

I arrived at the Party office at the wrong time. A meeting was just concluding. Forrest greeted me, and the district organizer asked what it was I wanted. I had hoped to speak to him privately, but decided to go ahead.

"Well, comrades, I have some questions to raise concerning Comrade Cummins from Toledo." Forrest's eyes narrowed, and the district organizer nodded for me to continue. "Something is not right with that guy. He joins the Party and then suddenly shows up with a new car. He makes few contributions to discussions, and in general Negro comrades distrust him. I thought I should raise this with you."

Forrest's eyes narrowed slightly. He glanced at the district organizer and said, "I haven't heard any questions from any of the comrades about Comrade Bill. He is leading the struggle in Toledo."

I knew at once I had made a mistake. One after another, they challenged my motives in bringing up the question. Even Joe Black, a hero of the Spanish Civil War and a comrade I respected and trusted, raised the stump of the arm he'd lost in combat in Spain and said, "Comrade, we are under fire from all directions. The last thing we need is a witch-hunt based on generalities. Perhaps you are a little envious of the role Bill is playing."

It all became so clear to me. Forrest was protecting Cummins, and the others joined in for fear of being labeled "white chauvinists."

I mumbled something about simply answering the call for the comrades to be vigilant, and left the building.

When the so-called second string of Party leaders was brought to trial in 1953, one of the chief stool pigeons was William Cummins. His blatant lying would have been simple enough to disprove, but the prosecution informed the defense that Cummins would expose his affairs with some of the women defendants and the wives of others if he was challenged. Forrest testified for the government and was then whisked to Fairbanks, Alaska, where he was given the job of business agent for the construction laborers' local. I was glad Curtis had had an affair with his wife.

It was all so clear. It was not simply that the FBI had agents within the Party—they had a whole network. One grouping protected the other. It was also clear that the FBI could not destroy the Party except by relying on doctrine-blinded comrades, by relying on twisted ideas that passed as theory.

The "struggle against white chauvinism" was a desperate effort to prevent the disintegration of the Party over the African American question. It was the ideological side of the fight for equality and class unity. It was a relatively simple moral decision to say that lynching and discrimination is wrong and to join an organization to fight against it. It was quite another thing to cleanse one's mind of the stereotypes, the race jokes, and the sewage of American social history that created the pervasive cobweb of white supremacy. Even the most dedicated white leaders were from time to time criticized for falling back into the thinking that has dominated America since its beginning. Decades later this struggle would provide a good part of the ideological foundation for the fight against racism. However, at that time the FBI converted it into one of its principal weapons. Accusing a white comrade of white chauvinism, or getting some Black informer to do so, was akin to a political lynching. Even those who understood what was going on dared not defend the accused for fear of becoming part of the crime. The flip side of the coin was always there. Any charge of white chauvinism on the part of a serious African American comrade inevitably ended in a debate over Black nationalism. For the honest Party members, the struggle against white chauvinism became a lose-lose situation.

18

The cold drizzle heralded the onslaught of the winter of 1953. We sat in the bricklayers' shack watching the drizzle wash away our workday. It was already eleven, and the sky was still darkening in the west. The foreman, looking at the sky and at his watch said, "I guess we might as well call it a day. See you guys tomorrow morning."

The men shoved their tool bags under the bench, got out of their overalls and mumbling about the weather filed out of the shack. We Black guys left in a group for the restaurant. We didn't want to go home to chores or to a wife who might quietly say that a job that depends on the weather isn't much of a job. I could visualize Roberta at work, glancing out the window, thinking that by now we had left the job and probably I was heading for a tavern while she had to work. The intensifying arguments about work shielded the reality that the marriage was falling apart. It was clear that we did not want the same things. Her agenda in life was simple and transparent—a decent home, an orderly life, the financial preparations for old age. I was becoming more deeply involved in the struggle as the FBI made my life more and more unstable. We never spoke of it and covered the widening gulf with petty arguments.

We both knew the marriage was over. We did not discuss it, we simply drifted in our separate currents, maintaining a shell of a marriage long after the content was gone.

The other men and I jostled our way into the restaurant and crowded into a booth. The waitress was new. Slender and in her mid-twenties, her Swiss-chocolate-colored skin brightened her large and expressive eyes. Half smiling and barely shaking her head in response to the sidelong leers, she brought us our coffee, grits and gravy, scrambled eggs, and biscuits. We finished our brunch, sheepishly left a bigger-than-average tip, and went to our respective automobiles.

I hadn't seen Curtis in quite a while. Sure he would be home preparing for his second shift at Alcoa, I headed for the big rambling house on Kinsman where the door was never locked. I gave the usual three raps and pushed against the door. It was locked. As I turned to leave, Curtis opened the door a crack.

"Hey, Curtis. If this is a bad time, I'll see you later."

"C'mon in. You my man."

Judy—Ken's wife—was seated at the big kitchen table, her face flushed, her green eyes asking me to understand.

My "Hi, Judy" was as nonchalant as possible.

"Hi, Comrade Nelson." Barely looking up, she twisted her glass between her hands and shifted her eyes to the checkered tablecloth. A terribly sad expression deadened her beautiful face.

"Sorry to barge in like this, Curtis. I was just driving by and—"

"Fuck it man, you at home. Judy and I were just discussing something."

I didn't want to be part of it, so I said, "I really got to go. I'll see you tomorrow."

"Have a taste." He reached behind a stack of folded towels and pulled out a bottle of whiskey. I swallowed the shot, nodded to Judy, and left.

I knew what was happening. Even before Ken left for the army it was clear that Judy's need to be constantly reassured that she was loved would open the door for an affair. Now, with Ken gone, she was torn between her need for love—not just sex, but love—and the Party's garbled sense of proletarian morality. I hoped, for all our sakes, she wouldn't do anything stupid.

Criticism and self-criticism are necessary for any serious person's development. In order to understand why things didn't work as planned, one must critically examine the idea and the way it was carried out. If error is found, one must ask oneself: *How did I contribute to this error?* In this way both the process and the individual are strengthened. Sadly, the Party reduced this to the level of ideology. If there was error, it was the result of a shallow ideology. To guarantee that such ideological weakness was overcome, the offending comrade was assigned a "control task." A control task carried out satisfactorily was considered proof of ideological rectification and the matter was shelved.

Judy, overwhelmed with guilt and the ideological consequences of the affair, went to Vince with a confession and a self-criticism. It was what he had been waiting for. Vince wrote both Curtis and Judy up for expulsion from the Party. However, Curtis belonged to the all-Black Cedar-Central club and had to be tried there. Admiral Kilpatrick, a veteran communist worker, was chairman of the club, and we all knew Kil's attitude concerning anything sexual.

While Kil had been in the Soviet Union, attending the Lenin Institute, sexual relations were guided by the "glass of water" theory. Essentially, that theory proposed that sexual desires, being natural, were no different from thirst. If one is thirsty, one gets a glass of water and attaches no particular importance to it. Seemingly, few people discussed Engels's thesis that the combining of sex and love lays the foundations for a new and equal relationship between men and women. The reality was that eleven million Russian men died in World War I and millions more died in the counter-revolution and the endless wars forced on the Soviet Union during the 1920s and 1930s. There must have been an overwhelming number of women without men.

The "glass of water" theory not only belittled the teachings of the church but also complemented the exploding movement for women's liberation. Soviet women were no longer tied to kitchen, church, and children. They could have sex when and with whom they chose—and, if

needed, abortions on demand. It must have seemed to be no more important than (and just as necessary as) a glass of water.

Kil never relinquished this view of sex. The Party ideologues were constantly bringing someone up for criticism regarding "misconduct" around
sex, and Kil would light into them for their attitudes. Some of the comrades might have hated him, but they kept it to themselves. After all, Kil had
been a political commissioner in the Spanish Civil War, and he was a graduate from the Lenin Institute and "the leading Negro comrade." So Kil held
to his "glass of water" theory, and I rather envied him for his time in Russia.

The Cedar-Central club held its meeting within a few days. The district
organizer was the only white person there. He must have felt terribly out of
place as a white man coming to a Black club to ask for the expulsion of an
active Black male comrade for having an affair with a white female comrade. Curtis refused to come to the meeting, using union business as an excuse. After the district organizer read the charges, I glanced over at Kil. He
was glowering at the organizer. As soon as he finished reading, Kil lit into
him. Ample quotes from Lenin flavored with droplets of contemptuous
saliva shot from Kil's mouth. He ranted for ten minutes without stopping.
Finally, taking a deep breath, he said quietly, "Comrades, I propose that this
trash be stricken from the agenda."

A few other comrades joined in asking what was wrong with consen-
sual sex, adding they were not in the movement to uphold capitalist law or
segregation. The organizer mumbled a few words about proletarian
morality and left the meeting. The African American comrades shook their
heads in disbelief. Jailed and blacklisted, they had little time for talk about
what amounted to a glass of water.

19

Nineteen fifty-three was a high-water mark for McCarthyism. The FBI
launched an investigation into the possible Communist affiliations of
newly elected Senator Barry Goldwater when it was revealed that he was
"backed by a large percentage of Negroes" in his campaign. World-

renowned artist Georgia O'Keeffe came under FBI scrutiny when they dug up the fact that she had committed the disloyal act of voting for Henry Wallace's Progressive Party in 1948. That year the FBI opened a file on Malcolm X. They even turned their guns on Groucho Marx, perhaps thinking they had hit a jackpot because of his "suspicious" name—people were investigated, slandered, and ruined on flimsier grounds. They did find that he had supported and given money to the defense of the Scottsboro Boys.

The world knew of such high-profile cases. As in war, people know of the generals—they know nothing of the foot soldiers whose daily sacrifice and sense of duty determined the victory. In the Black slums of America's industrial cities, we were the foot soldiers and knew it.

"Come on in," Curtis yelled, responding to my knock. I pushed the door open and entered the old, dilapidated duplex.

"What's going on, man?"

"The rent. How ya doin'? Want a taste?" He was already bringing a beer from the refrigerator.

I sat down at the kitchen table and opened the bottle.

"That chicken-shit Vince came by the house and left a note that I've been transferred to the club in East Cleveland."

"What do you think that means?"

"It means they're going to expel us all. They're breaking up the Cedar-Central club, scattering us out where they can deal with us one by one."

He took another beer from the refrigerator and sat down across from me. He opened it slowly and took a long drink, organizing his thoughts.

"I don't know. I don't know what happens next. I know the Party is through. The whites are runnin' scared and they're expelling all the Blacks. Guess J. Edgar Hoover is right. They finally got control of the Party."

"It's rough, Curtis, but that's the class struggle. There has to be some way to save the Party or create one that's not controlled by the FBI."

"I don't know, man. I was thinking about it last night. I joined the Party at Wilberforce, right after I got married. Then the Party asked for people to go into basic industry. I figured, well, we got the most to gain; we should be ready to sacrifice the most. Winnie quit me, took the kid. I still thought it was the right thing to do. I'm chief shop steward now, and probably can make president next year. I represent something. These fuckin' comrades that're going to expel us represent nothing. They're all running back to New York and back to school. I have to stay in the trade union movement now."

"I know they want to expel us, but I didn't think this was the time. We're moving ahead with the work here."

"That's why. They want the work to go in the other direction. Man, face it. The Party is dropping the Negro question as a national question, and now they got to drop the Negroes. Clara, the organizational secretary of the youth league, told me that the order came from New York to expel you. Leon Wofsy [national chairman of the Labor Youth League] wants your ass."

"I don't understand why."

"You understand. White folks get their heads together and decide what to do with Black folk. Nothin' new about that. That fuckin' Wofsy will end up a psychiatrist or professor while you're still living in these slums and humping those bricks."

"How does Clara know all this shit?" I asked.

"Man, you know who she's fuckin'," Curtis replied.

"Not outside of you."

Curtis grinned. "She fuckin' the district organizer. He tells her everything to impress her, and then she tells me everything to impress me. Wonder how the FBI got control? That's why I know it's all over. Fuck 'em."

It didn't seem possible that the Party was actually disintegrating that fast. "It's just like battle, Curtis. They made a breakthrough and now they're trying to exploit it. They're throwing in everything they've got. If we could only get the Party to take a stand, we could still win."

"It's life in the big city, baby boy. The deck's stacked. I ain't gonna quit and I ain't gonna give them the pleasure of throwing me out."

"If I'm out, they're going to have to throw me out. I haven't been paying rent in the Party. It's my Party. I helped build it. I'm going to fight for the Party. This is the class struggle inside the Party, man," I said.

"They know you're going to fight. That's why they transferred you to the East Cleveland Club. The Cedar-Central Club isn't going to expel any Negro. Comrade Mr. Charlie will," Curtis said with a slight shake of his head.

"I told you I wrote Meridel LeSueur about all this. I got a letter from her yesterday telling me to see Gus Hall [the Ohio state organizer and later longtime head of the Communist Party] about it. I can't tell her that our homeboy would rather talk to a white FBI agent that will agree with him rather than a Black communist who don't."

"You better wake up and see, baby boy. One thing I learned in the union is that people talk about principles. They don't fight for them. Money, prestige, women, they fight for that—but not principles. Principles are the excuse to do what they want to do for other reasons," Curtis said, reaching for his beer.

"The CPUSA was never known for its revolutionaries, that's for sure, but there are principled people in the Party—white and Black. They're disoriented," I said.

"Get your ass expelled and see how many of your principled white comrades take a position."

"I know." I finished the beer. There was little left to say. "I got to split, Curtis. I'm going to run by Bert's and tell him about the transfer."

It was only a short drive from the slum on Kinsman to Bert Washington's comfortable working-class home in Glenville. He opened the door as I walked up toward the porch.

"How you doing, Comrade?" That was Bert's standard opening to people he liked. He really wanted to know.

"I'm not sure, Bert. That's why I came by."

I sat down on one of the porch chairs while Bert went for coffee. When we were comfortable he smiled at me. "Want to talk about it?"

"Yes. I mainly wanted to bring you up to date. You know I've had some run-ins against the Party leadership, here and in New York." In New York I'd found out that Harold Johnson, head of the party's National Education Committee, was living in one of the apartment buildings that faced Gramarcy Park and thus had a key to the locked park, which didn't allow Blacks, and so I'd brought charges against him. Nothing ever came of it, but it gave me the name of a troublemaker. "And I've had run-ins with the district organizer and a few other big shots. Well, after they transferred me to youth work I've been fighting it out with the national office of the Labor Youth League. Since Vince was transferred here, we've been fighting. I didn't think that I'd be doing a service to the Party to let them carry on their rotten chauvinism without a fight. About a month ago Vince asked the National for permission to expel me. The Cedar-Central Club wouldn't do it. He tried again, but Rosie Ward, the Black guy who's the organizational director of the Youth League, blocked it. Yesterday, Vince came by the house and left a note that I have been transferred to the East Cleveland Club."

Bert clicked his tongue. "The cops are liable to shoot you on the way to the club meeting."

"I think that they realize they aren't able to fight us head-on in the Negro Labor Council or as a group of comrades. I think they are going to scatter us out among white comrades who don't know us, then expel us one by one. That way there's no scandal and no organized resistance."

"You may be right. I received a letter from my friends in New York. Their information is that the Party is going to issue a directive summarily expelling all comrades who do not withdraw from the Negro Labor Council by this Friday."

"What are you going to do, Bert?"

"I'm going to do the same thing you're going to do. I can't lead four hundred Black workers up against the police and then leave them there. I'm going to have to go down with them." Bert pushed his glasses up into place. He was such a gentle, intellectual person to be involved in such a dirty game. He was proof that there are principled people in the world. "We have to have the Party. None of us counts for much without it."

"Bert, do you think that it's un-Marxist to have a Negro Communist Party?"

"I used to. The Labor Council straightened me out on a lot of theoretical propositions that I'd taken for granted. One, the working class isn't united and probably never will be. It's not wrong to have white leadership in the Party; it's that they are either petty bourgeois or from the highly paid section of the working class. It's incidental that they are white."

"Yeah, that's kind of what I was thinking. There are some white comrades who understand that very well."

"There are plenty of white comrades who understand. The problem is they lose their privileges when they fight too hard against the system."

I set the cup aside. "Guess I'd better go, Bert. Does the Party know about the meeting tonight?"

"Oh, yes. I was careful to tell them. We're not a faction. We're meeting to see how to implement the directive. Whatever we say is going to be reported to the Party leadership—and the FBI."

A family man who had an intellectual bent, Bert managed to create a home, raise two children, and develop himself into one of the country's leading practical yet intellectual and widely read Marxists. Bert had graduated from Oberlin College in 1925. There wasn't much future for a Black graduate with a liberal arts degree. He had intended to go on with his education, perhaps to medical school, but took a job in the post office. He joined the Communist Party in 1933. Bert was the chief organizer of the National Postal Alliance, the segregated African American union for postal employees in Cleveland. As with most unions, the Blacks either had their own locals or wished they did. A job at the post office was about as good as it got for the Black worker. Partially protected by Federal regulations and given a good pension on retirement, the better-educated African Americans gravitated toward the post office. It was the largest single employer of African Americans in the country, and they actually were better off with their own locals. Bert held the post of chairman of the "colored" local until 1951. He was fired from the post office as one of the first targets of the House Un-American Activities Committee.

The cadre assigned to the Negro Labor Council began arriving at the United Electrical, Radio, and Machine Workers hall early. I felt a wave of melancholy wash over me as they quietly took their seats, whispering to one another and lighting their cigarettes. I knew this was the end of our relationship. We had been so close. Been through so many struggles—not simply as comrades, but as Black communists—the conscious, cutting edge of the movement. There was such a deep, comradely love between us.

Bert pushed his glasses into place and prepared to call the meeting to order. I was conscious of the influence he had had on me. He was so different from Admiral Kilpatrick. Where Kil held a fierce loyalty to the Party, Bert's commitment was to the revolution.

"Comrades"—Bert always spoke softly when he was very serious—"I asked you all to come to this meeting so we can agree on how to disband the collective. I think it must be done in such a way as to protect the non-Party cadre who are on the firing line."

Ethel raised her hand. Bert acknowledged her. "Comrade Bert, maybe I'm confused, but it looks to me that not only is the Un-American Committee zeroing in on us, but we've become the sacrificial lambs for the Party leadership. What right have they to order us out of the Council and disband the organization with out so much as a by-your-leave?"

Bert replied, "You heard the district organizer last night. I can't answer for him. As far as I'm concerned, it's a violation of internal legality for the national office to order us out of a mass organization without consulting us. More than that, I think it's the worst white chauvinism to dump the Negro workers after we've managed to expose them all to the FBI."

I could feel Kil fidgeting, torn between his disciplined outlook of not creating a faction and yet not supporting a decision he believed illegal from a leadership he hated. Kil took another drag on his pipe and raised his hand. "Comrade Chairman, I think we should stick to the business at hand."

"Comrade Kil," Ethel interrupted, "you know as well as I do what happened. The white folks got their heads together, and as usual we're the ones that are going to pay. Who's going to protect those workers now that the Party has made a decision to sacrifice the Council?"

Curtis stood up. We didn't call him "the Front" for nothing. He assumed his best trade union stance, speaking softly at first so everyone would be quiet and strain to hear him, but I know that by the time he reached his conclusion he'd be shouting. "Comrade Chairman, comrades, three years ago, one thousand ninety-five days ago, the Party grouped us together and told us of the decision to throw all available forces into the formation of the Council. When I asked the Alcoa local to support this effort, the right wing attacked me and the Council as dual unionists. I defeated them and got the resolution passed. Two years later we forced the mayor of Cincinnati to address our convention. We forced the NAACP to shift to the left. We are on our way to becoming the biggest, most militant fighter for the rights of the Negro workers in the country. We brought the mighty Sears, Roebuck to their knees. We now have a membership here in

Cleveland of over four hundred, bigger than the Party membership. Does that sound like an organization that has completed its tasks? That's the shit that the district organizer handed us last night. No, comrades!" Curtis stepped into the aisle, raising his voice. "We haven't completed our tasks. They have completed theirs. Now they tell me to desert the workers we led into the battle. The Party taught me to tell the capitalists to go to hell. I learned the lesson well. I'm stickin' with the workers, and anybody who opposed them can go to hell."

Ethel and a few others wanted to applaud, but knew they shouldn't. Kil asked for and took the floor. "Comrades, Lenin says that anyone can be a revolutionary during a revolution. It takes a special type of person to be a revolutionary during the period of reaction. Basing himself on Lenin's words, Stalin taught us all that we Bolsheviks are people of a special mold. There were four thousand workers in front of Sears. There are only eighteen of us here. It proves Comrade Lenin's point. The Party is in serious danger, comrades. We have been in danger before. During the Palmer raids they almost broke us. When Earl Browder dissolved the Party we almost disintegrated. Now, the leading comrades are indicted or in prison. I do not agree with the decision. I am a Party member and a revolutionary. I urge all of you comrades to carry out the decision while we struggle to change it. This is the communist way of inner Party struggle."

We all looked at the floor or at our hands. We knew Kil was right. We also knew that right or wrong wasn't the issue. The issue was whether we would disband and leave four hundred Black workers without the protection of the Negro Labor Council.

After several more-subdued speakers, Bert took the floor. "Comrades," he said softly, "we all love and need our Party. I understand everything the comrades have said and disagree with none. This is one of those moments when a person must follow their conscience or their training. I followed my conscience when I joined the Party. I am following my conscience when I say I cannot follow the directive. I am not going to resign from the Party and I'll fight against expulsion. Defending the Party has to mean defending the class. When defending the class contradicts defending the Party, then something is seriously wrong." Bert, choked up, excused himself and sat down.

The meeting dissolved. There was no motion to adjourn. Ethel, picking up her coat and floppy hat, tiptoed to the door. By ones and twos the other comrades left the hall. Something indescribably sad was happening. That which had nourished us over the difficult years was consuming us. Curtis's eyes met mine. We might as well leave together. I knew the battle for the Party was lost.

A few weeks later Bert Washington, the best-known and most respected African American Communist in Ohio, was expelled from the Party because he refused to leave the Negro Labor Council. A year later he died from a heart attack. Those of us closest to him knew he simply withered away when all he lived for was taken from him in such a cowardly way.

Ethel Goodman, adrift after resigning from the Party, finally went back to Birmingham and her church. There she would give leadership to the wave of freedom struggles that broke out a decade later.

Jimmy Wells, one of the local cadre of the NNLC, was the best example of the African American working class comrade. Intelligent though uneducated, he knew that the daily and unending abuse from white society was rooted in the capitalist system. He knew there was no capitalism in the Soviet Union and believed there was no racial discrimination there either. The bigger and mightier the Soviet Union, the better he liked it. He turned a deaf ear to McCarthy's anti-Communist ranting. His logic was if they didn't begin in Cleveland, they could not be serious about bringing democracy to the Soviet Union. With proletarian firmness, he did not flinch when the FBI told his employer he was a Communist. He was fired and placed on the blacklist, never to hold a job again. Like Kil and other blacklisted comrades, he scraped up money for a beat-up truck and turned to "scuffling," the lowest form of hustling—picking up scrap iron and steel, cleaning basements and garages, working from dawn to dark. Jimmy never turned back and never complained. For him, this was part of the class struggle. So long as the Party was his Party and it was fighting back, no burden was too great to bear.

The liquidation of the Negro Labor Council and the slow disintegration of the Party drained his lifeblood, however, and Jimmy became less and less vocal about the struggle. Without the NNLC there was no organization to stabilize him and give him the essential sense of purpose. A month after the dissolving of the Negro Labor Council it occurred to me that I hadn't seen Jimmy in over a week. I asked other comrades about him. They hadn't seen him either. I never saw Jimmy Wells again. This unknown, unappreciated, indispensable foot soldier of the revolution became a casualty when he lost faith in his Party and its leadership.

20

The following night, March 5, 1953, was anticlimactic. Driving through the forbidden streets of East Cleveland, I didn't have much fighting spirit left. I was tired, sleepless, and crushed by the disintegration of everything I had fought for and believed in. A bit afraid of East Cleveland's notorious cops finding me wandering through their neighborhood, I carefully noted each street number. I pulled over at the address I'd been given and knocked on the door. Art, paunchy and well dressed, a rebel against the good life he wallowed in, opened the door a few inches. The meeting was in progress.

"What do you want?"

I saw a few people I knew, professionals and a few workers—all white. I felt drained and weak. "What the hell you mean, 'What do I want?' I've been assigned to this club and I'm coming to the meeting."

"You've been expelled."

"You don't fuckin' expel me from my Party without a trial. I'm coming to my meeting."

"If you don't leave this property at once, I'll call the police."

I couldn't get the needed adrenaline to punch him. I started to call him a white motherfucker, for want of a better curse. In the split second before the words left my mouth, I thought of the comrades in Germany and Alabama and South Africa—the heroic men and women who had given meaning to my life. Then I realized the door was shut. Angry, defeated, and a bit afraid he might call the police, I left the porch.

By the time I got to Buckeye Road I realized I was heading for Curtis' house. At Woodland I stopped for the light as the deliveryman was putting the extra of the *Plain Dealer* on the stand. The headline blared, "JOSEPH STALIN DEAD." I handed the man a dime and folded the paper so I couldn't read it. I thought back to those terrible days in October 1942 when the fascist armies were everywhere on the offensive. The Germans had reached the Volga, and only a tiny force of the Soviet Red Army stood between world victory and defeat. The *New York Times* editorial grimly stated, "The future of civilization rests on the tips of Red Army bayonets." Back then it was "Uncle Joe"—but after ten years of Cold War and anti-Communist propaganda, few remembered.

I turned at Kinsman and parked in front of the old shack. I didn't bother to knock. Curtis was sitting in the one easy chair, beer in hand, half watching television. He turned toward me. "You look like hell. They kick you out?"

"Yeah. That ain't the reason. Stalin's dead."

I opened the paper, reading the communiqué with him. Curtis gave a long, noisy sigh. "Got a stroke at seventy-five—at least he don't have to live to see what's happening over here. Here today, gone tomorrow. That's life in the big city, baby boy."

"I guess it's just that it's happening all at once."

"Well, no matter what happened, I got to get up and go to work at four-thirty. Stick around if you want to."

Curtis must have felt real sorry for me, because with one hand he reached behind the stack of towels and handed me the fifth of Kentucky Tavern, and with the other hand he slid a beer in front of me. "Fuck 'em. Them motherfuckers don't represent anything. I'll talk to you tomorrow."

Curtis closed his bedroom door and I continued to read the bulletins concerning Stalin's death. Winston Churchill said, "Stalin inherited the Russia of the wooden plow and left it a nuclear superpower." Other world leaders spoke of Stalin and the war. I put the paper aside and reached for the bottle of Kentucky Tavern.

I slugged down a quarter glass of whiskey and doused the fire with the cool, soothing, bubbling beer. As the warm tingling sensation spread, I relaxed for the first time in three days.

How the hell had it all happened? Everything had seemed so right— the comrades, the struggle. There isn't a beginning to anything, but it'd

been a long journey from Fort Huachuca through the war and the movement. Another slug of the whiskey, another gulp of the beer, and I leaned
back remembering—almost enjoying the hurt of seeing and sensing the
passion of those years.

I spoke to my younger brother Norman and decided that since the Party
wasn't going to say anything about Stalin, we should. That evening we con-
stituted ourselves as the Negro Peoples Memorial Committee and composed a leaflet. We pointed out that Stalin had been the only head of state
to call upon the people of the world to help stop the lynching and brutality
against African Americans. We pointed out that his ideas about the development of nations led to an understanding of the causes of African American oppression and how to fight it. Since we had no equipment to print
the leaflet, we went down to the Party's office just before closing time. The
few people there knew of my expulsion but were willing to help us. We ran
off the leaflet and at two o'clock the next morning went out to finish our
task. With the help of a can of condensed milk, we pasted the leaflets on the
bank, other buildings, and bus stops at Fifty-fifth and Woodlawn, the center of Cleveland's African American community.

At 4:00 A.M. I passed the corner on my way to the mill. A group of police and detectives from the Red Squad as well as FBI agents were trying to
scrape the leaflets off the windows and walls. Condensed milk does its job
well. Several years would pass before the remains of that leaflet finally
washed away.

Anti-Communist propagandists make quite a thing of an expulsion
from the Party. They like to equate it to excommunication from a church.
This is an inaccurate parallel. The communist joins the Party because he
has a vision of a new society without the hatreds and exploitation. Achieving this vision becomes the center of his life. He cannot achieve it alone,
but only in concert with his comrades. Expulsion from the Party is so destructive because he can no longer struggle for the most important thing in
his life. The reactions of the expellees are varied. Some, confused and hurt,
turn and attack the Party for wounding them. The FBI well understands
this and recruits them on the basis of revenge. They are sent back into the
Party with the most destructive results. Some return to their former,

mostly upper-class lives and try to begin again. Some, buoyed with the knowledge they received in the Party, go back to school or enter the union movement on an anti-Communist basis. I decided right away that nothing could be done without a serious Communist Party and transferred all my hurt and anger to achieving this.

I was determined to maintain my position as a revolutionary. I tried to create an organization of the good people who were leaving the Party, disgusted with its sudden and decisive swing to the right. I tried to set up study circles, but after a few meetings they fell apart. Without an organization one cannot organize. It was clear that without funds and an experienced cadre I could not accomplish my goal. Little by little I gave up. Curtis and the gang that hung out at his house became my crutch.

I had been in the steel mill for almost three months—just a few days short of the required time to have union protection for the job—when the boss called me over and handed me two paychecks. Surprised I had lasted that long, there was nothing I could legally do about getting fired. I cashed the checks, bought a bottle of whiskey, and went home to get my tools in order and prepared to get back on the scaffold.

21

In 1935 workers began in an organized manner to resist the terrible wage and working conditions brought on by the Depression. The American Federation of Labor would not unionize the industrial workers. The workers formed unions in the individual shops apart from the AFL and engulfed the country in a wave of wildcat strikes. The employers resisted with every legal and illegal weapon at their disposal. The more enlightened employers understood that they could not meet this upsurge head-on and defeat it. They needed some way to hold the workers legally responsible for carrying out a contract as to the quantity and quality of work. This could not be done through bargaining with disconnected local semi-underground groups. They needed a stable union to sign a legal contract and discipline the workers to abide by that contract.

President Roosevelt moved to accommodate this need through the National Labor Relations Act. The workers needed the union, but so did the employers. A few years later, John L. Lewis, then head of the Congress of Industrial Organizations, would boast that "a CIO contract is the best guarantee against a wildcat strike."

I only partially understood what this labor history held for the deepening struggle of the African American people. I did know that while we were dancing and boozing it up, the Man was meeting and planning how to apply those lessons to a growing spontaneous movement they could no longer ignore.

By 1954 the thousands of local protests and demonstrations against racial oppression had undercut the credibility of the United States in its Cold War with the Soviet Union. The nation's more enlightened leaders and especially the State Department constantly pressured the government to do something about this growing and often violent movement. There was little the government could do. It could not deal with hundreds of scattered individuals or small groups.

Beginning with the days of slavery, the white power structure, be it plantation or political, has always appointed a "head Negro" to speak for the mass of Blacks, should the whites find it necessary to listen to them. After slavery, this pattern continued. There was no way for the government to control this mass, growing rebelliousness without consolidating a leadership corps with which they could deal.

On December 1, 1955, Rosa Parks took her famous bus seat in Montgomery, Alabama. (When Fannie Lou Hamer tried this in Mississippi she was beaten half to death and crippled for life.) Parks's arrest and the ensuing Montgomery bus boycott made the nation's headlines and captured the imagination of millions striving for equality. The Montgomery Improvement Association was formed, and gravity shifted from a thousand scattered local struggles led by veterans to one center led by ministers. Shortly thereafter the Southern Christian Leadership Conference (SCLC) was formed, and it became clear to local people that this was the organization that the power structure preferred to deal with. It became the official movement. Eclipsed by the SCLC, local people continued the local struggles.

We admired the bravery and determination of the African American people of Montgomery in carrying out the boycott. We stood absolutely opposed to limiting our struggle to nonviolent protests. It was more than rejecting the idea that we should accept the beatings by the racists. We were unwilling to give up any tactic, especially when we knew Cold War politics made it difficult for the government to ignore a fighting resistance on our part. We also knew nothing was possible without the support of the white liberals and they would never support anything but a nonviolent, controlled, and limited struggle. Nat Turner is deep in the conscious of white America, whether they have heard of him or not. The fear of "Negroes with guns" has consistently been deeper than the fear of an external enemy. The deep and broadening support for nonviolent tactics compelled us to face the fundamentals of Black-white relations.

Comprising one-tenth of the nation's population and scattered across the county in vulnerable enclaves, we knew that despite our defiance and heroism we could only get what white America was willing to give us. The question of how to make them willing to give us our rights split the movement and made it even weaker. The right wing believed, as they had from the days of slavery, that we had to work quietly within the system, relying on the "decent white folks" to convince the rest. The militants believed they had to rely on and exacerbate social and political divisions within white America. They knew our moments of progress came when one or the other side needed our strength and were willing to make compromises. The Civil War and the wars that followed were their guidelines. The revolutionaries believed the struggle for democracy was an international expression of the class struggle. We, the most working-class section of American society, could not fight simply as African Americans; we had to develop tactics reflecting the fact that we were working-class African Americans. This meant solidarity with workers everywhere and relying on them to support us. This made us political, and we found ourselves confronting not just "white folks" but also the government.

22

One of the worst years for Cleveland's bricklayers was 1957. Working conditions deteriorated along with the relations between the men and the contractors. May 1 was at hand. Still known as strike day in the building trades, it was a hangover from the big strike for the eight-hour day in 1886. It was the final day of negotiations with the contractors. Work was slow, and we knew we couldn't win any wage increases this year.

It was not uncommon to see a bricklayer pour a cup of coffee from his thermos while the line was being raised and sighted, but there was never enough time for him to take more than a sip. We wanted a coffee break. Every other trade had it. The only demand we presented to the contractors was a ten-minute break for coffee at ten o'clock. The contractors said no.

The union meeting was packed when the negotiation team reported back. The men sat silent for a moment, not believing the slap in the face that we had received. A young brickie whom I had never seen at meetings asked for the floor and said calmly, "If those bastards won't even give us a coffee break, I think it's time to strike."

A roar of approval filled the hall. The business agent warned that a strike now, with such unemployment, would be difficult to win. Still, the men wouldn't hear of anything but strike. The vote was taken and carried by a huge majority. I left the union meeting full of apprehension about the coming months.

We struck from the first of May until the first of September, when the contractors finally agreed to give us the coffee break. During the strike some work had gone on, and when we were called back to the jobs we let the bosses know that we couldn't lay union brick on top of scab brick and that they had to tear down all the work that had been done during the strike. They weren't going to let us get away with that, so they locked us out from the first of September to the first of May. We lost a whole year of work. We won our coffee break, but relations with the contractors were never again the same.

Luckily, I wasn't working when the strike began, so I received all six months of unemployment compensation. The day came when I picked up my last check and knew something had to give, and soon. Roberta's salary was not enough to cover our expenses, and the threatening disaster only increased the tension in the house.

My friend L.T. was in worse shape than I was, but he had connections. He found out they were advertising for bricklayers in a little town along the lakefront in New York State. Five of us piled into his Chrysler and headed for Dunkirk. They were desperate for men to finish a big electrical generator plant before the worst of the winter set in. We were all immediately hired.

Dunkirk was unbelievable. The next stop to the north was Canada, yet it was as if this little town was in Mississippi. It was completely segregated. At that time, it was an agricultural center. Black and Puerto Rican migrant workers provided the labor for the farms and packing sheds. A few stayed after the harvest to work in the agriculture-related industries. Total segregation was part of the control of this labor.

The only place we could stay was a fleabag hotel that charged more money than the decent places we couldn't get into. I never learned to accept segregation, but driving back to Cleveland at night was too much. I took one of their rooms.

A combination lounge, diner, and tavern were on the ground floor of "our" hotel. It was the only place the Puerto Ricans and Blacks could go for a drink and to relax. Relaxing in a tavern full of men was next to impossible. It was difficult for a migrant worker to bring his wife or girlfriend with him, and few young women of color lived in the town. There were a few beat-down prostitutes who hung out there, but that just emphasized the fact that the colored section of Dunkirk was filled with lonely men.

Across the street a clean, friendly-looking tavern was the recreation center for the whites. We were envious and a bit angry watching the couples go in for a drink or a dance. Music blared from the dance floor, taunting us. Nobody had to tell us not to try to go there. We knew.

It was almost dark on Thursday when the four-thirty whistle blew, ending the workday. One of the brickies yelped, "This is the brick I been looking for all day. If I'd'a found it at eight-thirty, we would all be home by now." We were too cold and too tired to joke. One more day and we would make the trip back to Cleveland, pay some of the bills, and get ready to do it all over again.

It was a cold damp night. A layer of wet snow and sleet covered yesterday's ice, making walking difficult and driving almost impossible. I inched my old Hudson along the dark road from the power plant toward town. The headlights picked up a couple waving their arms for me to stop. I was afraid of hitchhikers, especially white ones, but I couldn't leave anyone on such a deserted road to freeze.

"Need a lift?"

"Yeah, we skidded off the road and then I killed the battery trying to get back on. Are you going to Dunkirk?"

"Yeah. Get in."

They introduced themselves. Jeb and Sharon had known each other since high school, a few years back. In school they had talked about getting married, but neither ever had a steady job nor enough money. I listened to them chatter about the hard times.

When I could take my eyes off the road for a moment I'd glance at Sharon, who was sitting beside me, or Jeb, crowded against the door. Maybe twenty-one or twenty-two, he looked like he'd seen too many James Dean movies. The few pimples didn't detract from the rebellious tilt of his cap or the fuzzy Elvis Presley pork-chop sideburns—a countrified white-folks version of a hep cat.

Sharon was a farm girl with a ruddy face and shoulder-length brown hair parted in the middle. Most people around there were of German descent, and I thought she probably was, too. She was pretty—not beautiful, but pretty and wholesome. My roots were in the small town and the farm, and I liked scrubbed, healthy, full-breasted country women. She was trying to be a hep cat too, or she wouldn't be with him. I stopped daydreaming and pulled up in front of the hotel.

They got out. Jeb had a five-dollar bill in his hand. "Thanks a lot, mister. You really saved our lives."

"I didn't go out of my way. You don't owe me anything."

Jeb hesitated for a moment, decided not to try again, and said, "Well, at least have a drink on us."

That sounded good to me. I was chilled to the bone, and the fingers on my left hand seemed fossilized to the width of a brick. I turned to go to my tavern and he turned to go to his.

"Let's go over there. It's a little nicer," he said.

I allowed that that was true but told them I couldn't get served over there.

"I grew up in this town. You're with me. Nobody is going to say anything."

I gave in and, walking between them, crossed the street. Jeb held the door for me, and as I walked in, every head turned in either amazement or hostility. Jeb entered, placed his hand on my shoulder, and guided me to the bar. Most of the patrons went back to their dancing or drinking. A few continued to glare, not quite sure what to do.

The bartender, a few years older than me, smiled a hello to Jeb and Sharon. "What will it be?"

"Hi, Kurt! Beer for us, and give my friend what he wants. He saved us. Car went out and he brought us in."

Kurt turned toward me, holding the welcoming smile.

"Nasty night. What will you have?" He glanced at the top shelf as he reached for a water glass. That disturbed me. I instinctively thought of the bars where they threw away the shot glasses after a Black person drank from them. I took the hint about the top shelf and asked for Jack Daniel's. As he opened and poured, I tried to sum him up. *Clean-cut country boy, given to smiling, sure isn't hostile like the rest of these motherfuckers.*

"Say when."

The glass was already half full. "That's plenty."

"Ice?"

"Please."

He filled the glass with ice and partly leaned over the bar as he gently pushed the glass to me. "You a veteran?"

I needed a long gasp of air behind the swig of straight whiskey. The alcohol warmed my insides.

"Yeah, infantry. I served in the Pacific."

"I was in the infantry, too. Normandy, the Bulge—all the way. I was raised around here and didn't know much when I went into the army. By the time the war ended, I believed in those things they said we were fighting for. I believe in democracy. I lost a lot of buddies at Bastogne fighting for it whether they understood it or not. After Bastogne, I began to realize what a rotten deal the colored people get. Especially the soldiers. They worked twenty hours a day to keep us fighting. Some of them fought right along-side us, and they still got a rotten deal. It wasn't fair. It wasn't democracy. I didn't like it and said so."

I took another big drink and waited for him to continue—I knew he was telling me something. He reached into his wallet and pulled out a pic-ture of the typical family of the 1950's—a pretty woman standing against a new car and holding a cute little girl.

"Your family?"

"Yeah. They mean the world and all to me. There isn't much work in this town, and this is the best job I can get. If I give you another drink, I ain't going to have this job. I really don't know what to do. If I lose this job over giving you a drink, I won't be able to look my family in the face. If I refuse to serve you, I won't be able to look myself in the face. You decide."

I finished the drink.

"Thanks, pal. I think I'd better leave." I thought he felt worse than I did. "We can change all this shit if we try. Someday—" *Fuck,* I thought, *this ain't the time or place for communist propaganda.* Kurt looked like he was about to cry. I turned and walked toward the door suddenly aware of the chunks of frozen mortar that spilled from the cuffs of my work-stained coveralls. I opened the door, disregarding the hostile glares.

Jeb and Sharon went out with me. "Hey, fella. I didn't understand they would treat you like this. I'm sorry," Jeb offered.

"I'm so embarrassed," Sharon said, taking my arm. "You've been so good to us."

If I didn't smile, I was going to cry over these two young Americans. It was sad. They daily participated in and strengthened the segregation with-out even knowing it. I smiled at them and told them it would be best if they went back. Jeb shook my hand and Sharon looked at me, eyes filling with tears, "I wish I could make it up to you."

"It's all right. You didn't do it and I'm not blaming you."

They turned and walked slowly through the sleet back toward their tavern. I turned and entered mine. The bricklayers, laborers, and farm workers were drinking, laughing, half listening to the jukebox alternately playing Puerto Rican music or Chuck Berry's rock and roll. Unlike in Cleveland, the Puerto Ricans here were colonized farm workers. They were treated as such and saw no difference between themselves and the African American workers.

I ate supper at the bar, where you could get collard greens and pork chops or *arroz con pollo*.

The evening wore on with the crude jokes and bragging of the bricklayers. If they weren't talking about some woman's hindquarters, they were bragging about how many bricks they could lay. Boring as all hell. The hour hand crept around to almost ten—my bedtime. The dry heat, the bourbon, and a few beers had knocked me out. I got up from the frayed easy chair. "I'm gonna sack out. See you all in the morning."

I opened the door to the hallway that led to the staircase and saw her. I didn't know how long she had been there.

"Sharon! Hi. What are you doing here? Where's Jeb?"

"He had to go away. I don't have any way to get home. . . ."

Something didn't seem right. It was too good to be true. Just to make sure, I said, "Can I drive you home?"

She fixed her gaze on me. "Besides, I don't want to be by myself."

Suddenly the booze and the beer settled in my groin. She did look lonesome and a little unsure of things. I didn't want the other guys to see her. I took her arm and guided her up the stairway to my room. I was glad the army was still with me. The bed was made, the room not too scruffy. She threw her coat across the only chair and looked up to me.

"I never did it with anybody but Jeb," she said, and almost mechanically stepped forward to embrace me. I guided her to the bed, sat down beside her, and held her. It took a little while to reassure and relax her. It was worth it.

Later, she lay beside me, head on my shoulder. "I want to get out of Dunkirk. Will you want to take me back to Cleveland with you?"

"I'd like to—but I can't."

She looked into my eyes for a moment, then, resigned to that reality, kissed my chest, turned, shoved her cold rump against my belly and fell asleep. I smiled to myself. There are some good people in Dunkirk.

I lay there half asleep thinking how much my life had changed. Since the expulsion from the Party I never spent time talking or socializing with white people anymore. I'd begun to see them as just that—white people. No longer individuals with ideals and dreams and problems, but "white people" whose sole purpose was to keep us down. Sharon had fallen into a deep sleep, her full breasts rising and falling with the regular breathing. Why had she come here? Was she lonely? Was it a moment of passion? Was it that she suddenly wanted me? Was she trying to find a way out of this burg? Did she see in me the possibility of changing her life, of finding some decent future? Or was it that she saw and understood the hurt of segregation and humiliation and was trying to make up for it the only way she knew how—with her body? Perhaps a woman isolated in a farm town has no voice but her body. I was glad she'd come to me. Spiritually and physically I needed to lie close to and hold a woman. I was drifting from job to job, from woman to woman, without vision or purpose. By nature I was not a drifter and that night I resolved that I was going to break with all this, get some direction and somehow get back into the struggle.

When the job in Dunkirk finished, the rest of the crew went back to Cleveland and their families. I had no reason to go back and knew I would not find work there. Instead I picked up the *Dodge Report*, a construction journal, to see where the big jobs were. Although work was slack in most of the country, there was an advertisement for bricklayers for the big army base going up in Huntsville, Alabama.

I felt a bit ambivalent about going to Huntsville. I knew the FBI would get word of my whereabouts as soon as I made a paycheck. A few years before, the Alabama state legislature had passed a law giving a mandatory forty years on the chain gang to any Communist entering or living in Alabama. The Supreme Court's overturning that law didn't change the minds of the Alabama cops, judges, or wardens. Still, there was work there. The army had let out contracts for seven eleven-story buildings, and Huntsville was short of men. I decided to go. But I knew a job was going on at the prison in Columbus, Ohio, and thought I'd try to get a week or two of work there before going on to Huntsville.

The Hudson purred along the highway approaching Columbus. The roadway was a bit slick from the rain and snow. I slowed down as I approached a group of some forty men walking along the side of the road. They were prisoners, all of them Black. I drove slowly past them, nodding sympathetically should one of them raise his head and glance at me. Around the curve a truck loaded with cement blocks had slid partly off the road. I was sure that he was heading for the job I was looking for and pulled over to ask directions. The group of prisoners approached, the men slugging along, heads down, exhausted—appearing as their great-grandparents must have appeared as a coffle of slaves returning from the fields.

The truck driver held up his hand, signaling to the gang boss, "Hey, fella! Do me a favor. When you get in, tell somebody I slid in the ditch. Tell 'em to send out a tow truck."

"You goin' to the prison?"

"Yeah."

"You don't need no tow truck." The boss was a caricature of a Nazi SS officer: tall, lean, a narrow face with thin lips that hardly moved as he spoke. "These niggas will get ya out." The driver, a startled look on his face, turned and climbed into the cab. I glared at the gang boss, thinking of the .32 special in my glove compartment. The boss glanced past me as if I were not there.

"All right! You all get ahold of that truck—we gonna get it back on the road."

The prisoners spread out around the truck. The driver gunned the motor, the rear wheels spun. The truck barely moved. The prison guards cursed, threatening the men, then suddenly began to jab them with the broomstick-sized cudgels they carried. That provoked groans of pain, with some of the prisoners trying to protect their heads with their arms. The wheels spun. The men, grunting with the effort, slipping in the mud, inched the loaded truck onto the roadway. The driver thanked the head guard and turned to me with an "I didn't do it" look in his eyes before easing the truck down the road.

The guard yelled for the men to fall in, and they resumed their age-old shuffle toward the prison.

I'd never seriously wanted to kill a person before. During the war I didn't feel any particular emotion trying to kill the enemy. That was like killing rats or roaches—it was something you did. But I *wanted* to kill those guards. Two of them had shotguns. I had a little .32. I knew even if I was lucky, the state of Ohio would replace them the next day. The age-old frustrations overwhelmed me. *What good is one sacrifice? I'm worth more than they are. We need organization, not sacrifice. I have to hang on until someday a revolutionary movement is reborn.*

I swung the Hudson to the opposite side of the road, passing the prisoners. Thinking it best not to stop, I turned south, heading for Kentucky.

As I was leaving Carbon, Kentucky, I noticed a police car following me. I carefully kept my speed five miles below the limit, praying with each breath that I'd clear the city limits without being pulled over. As I cleared the town, the cop switched on the red light and I pulled over. I got out of the car, hoping he'd take that as a sign of surrender. I knew cops in Kentucky and Tennessee enjoyed giving people from Ohio a hard time. In the Civil War, Ohio regiments were among the most ideological for freedom, and the slave states never forgave them.

The cop—fat, ruddy, threatening—got out of the car, billy club in his right hand. "Where you goin', boy?"

"I'm going to Alabama. Huntsville."

"That your home?"

"No. I'm going to work."

The cop narrowed his eyes, "You speak to me, you say 'sir.' "

I looked at him without answering.

"An' when you talk to me, come out from under that hat." He deliberately placed the tip of his club under the bill of my white bricklayer's hat and flipped it to the ground. My first impulse was to pick it up. I immediately got the sense that if I bent down he was going to hit me. I looked past him, knowing with all the instinct bred from three centuries of slavery that if I irritated this white bastard any more, I was going to jail or be killed. "What kind of work you do?"

"I'm a bricklayer."

"Ooh. That's why you got that nice car. It yours?"

I knew he was waiting for the correct answer.

"Yes, sir. It's mine. Do you need the registration?"

His face relaxed. The proper relationship was established.

"I don't need it, son. Down here a colored man who's a bricklayer keeps a nice car. Hudson. Fast car. You watch your speed. What's your name?"

"Nelson Peery."

"Mine's Willie Nab. You got to obey the law down here. Them that's written and them that ain't."

I couldn't muster another "Yes, sir," so I didn't answer. The cop turned and waddled back to the patrol car. I picked up my hat and walked to my car. I knew he was thinking that a little more humiliation would make his lesson clear. Instinct told me to wait until he pulled away. I pretended to look at the map until he left.

Even though the job at Huntsville was on an army base, I knew I wasn't going to take much more of what I'd seen in the last few days. The *Dodge Report* listed another big job, an Air Force base, opening up in Emerado, North Dakota. Although it was still in America and still Jim Crowed, I was sure it beat Alabama. I turned the Hudson north. My family had scattered away from Minneapolis, so there was no reason to stop there. I drove on into North Dakota.

I was only one of five thousand construction workers who piled into Emerado, a little village of eight hundred native-born souls. I was hired immediately and put on work laying tile indoors. That was good because winter was already setting in.

Food was scarce and lodging impossible. For the first few nights I slept in the car and lived off sandwiches. The third day one of the local men I befriended introduced me to a little old lady and man who ran a chicken farm. They had converted an old coop into a hut with a little kerosene stove, heater, and cot. Now they needed a tenant. I quickly agreed to the ten bucks per week and set up housekeeping.

The work was steady, and I again sent money home to Roberta to pay my share of the bills. With little to do after work, I fell into the habit of helping my elderly landlords with the chores around the farm. They repaid me with pails of fresh but fertile eggs—I never got used to that little red eye and the network of red veins spreading octopus-like across the frying pan. Later came roast chicken, baked chicken, boiled chicken, fried chicken—

God knows what some of the recipes were. They adopted me, but I wasn't sure if it was to my advantage.

The days grew shorter and the cold crept down from Canada into our bones. I awoke one morning and could barely force the door open against the huge drift of snow. I was snowbound for two days and probably would have died had not the old couple came out to make sure I survived the first "little snow."

When I finally got back to the job I told the boss I was going to quit and head south to Minneapolis. Desperate for bricklayers, he offered me straight time—I would be paid whether I could make it to work or not. It was tempting, but apart from the fear of freezing to death, how does a young man sit alone in a chicken coop in Emerado during the long bitterly cold night that North Dakotans call "winter"?

After a few days the roads were clear. I shook hands with the boss and took my pay. I hugged those two wonderful old people who'd treated me like their son and headed off to Fargo and then southeast across Minnesota, not stopping until I was in the relative safety of Minneapolis. Winter was closing in there, too, and there would be little work until spring. I had to keep moving, even though there was no place to go. Reluctantly, I swung the Hudson back onto the highway and headed for Cleveland.

23

By 1958 the world communist movement had slid into its mortal crisis. Khrushchev's attack against Stalin in 1956 split a world movement used to blindly following the leader. This was followed by his "goulash communism" speech, wherein he declared the Soviet people had given enough to the world movement and it was time for them to enjoy a little goulash. Militant communists around the world correctly took these speeches to mean that the Communist Party of the Soviet Union was willing to drop its support of the revolutionary movements throughout the world if the United States and NATO would back off.

The effect on the American Communist Party was catastrophic. Hundreds of militant comrades, declaring that Khrushchev had destroyed socialism, quit the Party. I never would have left the CP just because I disagreed with some of its projections or disliked some of its leaders, any more than I would have deserted my platoon because I hated George Patton or because Douglas MacArthur had referred to us as a "bunch of niggers."

Hundreds, sensing an opportunity to get out of the line of fire, publicly denounced the Party, stating they had been fooled and lied to by the leadership. Others, declaring their intentions to defend the Party, came together as informal groupings. A nationally known comrade led each of these groups. Spontaneously, the Party began to break up into the factions that once had formed its base. I thought that somebody should do something, but I no longer belonged to the Party and there was nothing I could do.

The Provisional Organizing Committee to Reconstitute a Marxist-Leninist Communist Party in the United States of America (POC) had been one of the major caucuses within the Communist Party at its sixteenth national convention in 1958. At the convention, the Party confirmed its turn to the right. The POC declared a policy of "disengagement" and as a body walked out. The POC was the most working-class of any of the caucuses and held some of the most developed practical leaders of the movement. Harry Haywood, veteran African American Communist and the author of *Negro Liberation*, and Joe Dougher, a former military commander of the Lincoln Brigade, which fought in the Spanish Civil War, were elected co-chairs. Armando Roman, former chair of the Queens County Party Committee, was elected general secretary of the POC.

When I returned to Cleveland, Jimmy Jackson and Admiral Kilpatrick met with me. They were already in the POC and invited me to join. I was happy to see Kil elected as part of the leading committee. It seemed to me that the POC included the most respected working-class leaders of the Party, but the unity did not last long. In October 1958 a conference was called to resolve the deepening ideological and theoretical division in the POC. The meeting ended in a split, and Harry Haywood led most of the white comrades out of the conference. Suddenly the POC was an organization composed almost entirely of African American and Puerto Rican workers and without a chair or executive committee. Armando, being the only remaining elected official, finally got up from his chair and walked to the podium. Looking through his thick glasses, he said softly, "I don't see nothin' here but niggers and spics. Do you think we can build a Communist Party?"

The room fell into a shocked silence. Then suddenly applause and cheers broke that silence. Something wonderfully new was happening. White intellectuals who "understood" Marxism and "were on our side" had always led us. But they'd walked out with Harry Haywood, and suddenly we were on our own. I looked around the room. There were three or four white comrades; the rest were Black and Puerto Rican workers. We knew we were the proletariat Marx had spoken of—longshoremen, bricklayers, carpenters, sailors, stock clerks, factory workers, and janitors. It was a moment of euphoria. We were the workers and we were going to build *our* Communist Party.

I then knew how the slaves must have felt at emancipation: no money, no jobs, little knowledge, no place to live, no anything—but freedom. How sweet it was.

The year 1958 drew to a painful close. It was clear that the FBI was pressuring the union to deny me work. Hunting jobs on my own no longer paid off. Contractors either were afraid to hire me or were themselves so anti-Communist they wouldn't.

The holidays came and went unnoticed. I was suddenly facing the possibility of losing the house if I didn't get some stable employment. There was none for me. I had applications in all over the city with no response. Finally I realized I had hit bottom and needed money for the immediate expenses of food and transportation. I did not mention it to Roberta, but the day came when I lined up at Manpower and took a job shoveling snow for 75 cents per hour. It was a long way from the $3.85 the brickies were making when they could find work.

The unusually heavy snowfall in December and early January had been bulldozed into huge, ugly, soot-smeared mounds in the vacant lots and school parking areas. Luckily, I was assigned to a team of men shoveling snow into trucks at the elementary school a few blocks from our house. My first day was the beginning of a January thaw. The salt-packed layers of snow had begun to turn to a freezing slush. The cold Canadian wind blew off the lake into our faces, and the men turned their backs and lowered their heads as they lined up to have the African American foreman assign us to the four waiting trucks.

The day dragged on shoveling the heavy mounds of snow and slush. After four o'clock the wind off the lake turned cold and I felt sorry for those who were in worse shape than me, without adequate coats and shoes, but still wallowed in my own misery. My marriage, torn apart by all the political pressure and economic instability, was clearly at an end. I had fallen into relying on a shot of whiskey as an antidote for the depression and general aimlessness after my expulsion from the Party. I knew it was self-destruction, but I didn't know how to stop. Worst of all, I was literally friendless, except for a few Black ex-Party members. Anyone who chose to be friends with me risked getting on the blacklist, too. I was defeated, but I hadn't surrendered.

Turning from the rising cold wind sweeping across Lake Erie, I pulled off my soaking wet, half-frozen glove and wiped my face, unsure if the wetness was tears or sweat or a mingling of both. It was then that the green Ford pulled up alongside me. The passenger-side window rolled down. I glanced at the clean, immaculate, warm, and comfortable crew-cut young FBI agents inside. I could only think they had come to run me off the Manpower job—the end of the line before begging. The anger began to rise within. Adrenaline I hadn't felt since combat began to surge as I half heard, "It's a shame that a man of your intelligence has to do this. Why don't you talk with us . . ."

I lost control. I must have looked insane as I turned toward them. My voice trembled, and I was unable to shout more than half-coherent words: "You goddamn motherfucker. You goddamn white motherfucker."

I heard the shovel bang against the door as the wheels spun, kicking slush and mud into my face. The Ford raced down Ninety-fifth Street toward St. Clair. Wiping my face, I picked up my shovel. Suddenly, the foreman was standing in front of me. "What the hell was that all about?"

"Fuckin' guys pulled up and said something about 'nigger,' and I guess I lost my temper."

The foreman shook his head. "Why they want to do something like that? They must be crazy." Turning to the crew, he shouted, "Let's load up. It's time to quit."

I turned to walk the few blocks home. The FBI never again confronted me. They hadn't won. I didn't bend or beg. I hadn't surrendered, but it was over. I couldn't stay in Cleveland. When I got my pay for the week of shoveling snow, I would have to leave.

The week ended as January turned to February. I received the meager paycheck from Manpower. I sat down with Roberta and discussed my leaving for New York, which was in the midst of a construction boom. We both knew this was the end of our relationship. I told her to keep the house. I would catch up on the delinquent mortgage payments and the bills, then she would be on her own. Characteristically, she said it would be unfair, since we had both worked hard to get the house. But she knew it was the only way for her to survive. With that painful discussion over, I gave her the title to the car and went to get my bag.

I called Armando in New York to inform him that I was coming in. After a few minutes of discussion I mentioned to him that I was pretty broke and needed to know where I could find some cheap lodging. There was a moment's silence. I knew he misunderstood me. Finally he said, "We're not a social agency. . . ."

I became furious that he should think I was trying to live off the organization and said, "It's all right, Armando. Any worker in Harlem will direct me to a rooming house. I'll call you when I'm settled." After an exchange of curt good-byes I hung up the phone.

I hated to think that I was back to hoboing, but that thought or fear guided my hands as I packed my bag with the barest essentials. I long ago learned that traveling light is the key to survival. I chose a jacket instead of an overcoat. Then, closing the door behind me, I walked the two blocks to St. Clair and the bus that would take me to the station.

A winter storm was brewing. The flesh-numbing, wild Canadian wind roared across Lake Erie, strangling Cleveland in its hoary grip. I turned my back and raised the skinny collar of my short leather jacket as the bus, bucking the wind, lurched through the snow to stop on the corner of

Ninety-fifth and St. Clair. I picked up my little canvas satchel and the tool bag. Not much to show for eight years of work and political struggle.

I put such thoughts aside as we pulled into the Greyhound station. A bus labeled "New York City Special" was taking on passengers. I hurried to the ticket window, paid my fare, and barely got aboard before the doors closed and the bus cleared the station, turning in the direction of New York City.

PART III

New York City, 1959

1

The bus pulled into the Port Authority station. I followed the crowd through the terminal and out into the street. The temperature was in the upper thirties, and big flakes of snow were falling, merging into the slush and grime of the city streets. The city seemed ominous and forbidding as I followed the crowd to the subway. With nine dollars in my pocket, I had no idea how I was going to live until I got a job and made a paycheck. I was broke in a strange city in the middle of winter; it was perhaps the worst moment of my life. I thought it best to get to Harlem and figure things out from there.

I left the subway at 125th Street and started walking aimlessly down the street, tool bag and level in one hand and my small satchel in the other. I had to find a place to spend the night and soon realized I would find nothing just walking. I decided to go down to the Bowery, where I knew I could get a clean room for fifty cents. The next morning I could go to the union and explain to them that I was broke and needed a day's work right away. Historically, large numbers of transient bricklayers came through the Manhattan local, and the union was known for giving a helping hand.

As I turned to walk back toward the subway a young man passed me. At that time, Black folks still spoke to one another and I instinctively greeted him with the meaningless "How ya' doin', man?"

Returning the greeting, he glanced at my tool bag and level. "For Christ's sake—Nelson!"

It was Ty from Cleveland. The scene of him sleeping in my car flashed before me. I was never so happy to see anyone in my life. After the embrace and backslapping, I told him why I'd came to New York and that I was broke, in need of a job and a place to stay. Ty looked directly into my eyes. "Man, when I was down and out you took me into your home and fed me and got me a job and taught me the trade. I always said that someday I was gonna pay you back—and I am. You get a room where I stay and they need bricklayers where I work."

The next morning, after a breakfast of grits, gravy, biscuits, and coffee, we drove to St. Albans, Queens, and the construction site of an apartment building. The foreman looked a bit askance as Ty went through his act of assuring him that I was one of the best in the trade and he was going to quit if I didn't get hired. The foreman needed men and agreed to give me a chance. I took out my tools and waited for the whistle to begin the workday. If there was ever a do-or-die moment in my life, it was then. When the whistle blew, as the brickies say, you couldn't see anything of me but ass and elbows.

Apartment and house building is scorned by commercial bricklayers as work for "shoemakers." The commercial bricklayer is faster, neater, and more efficient. I was more skilled than the rest of the crew, and after the lunch break the foreman took me off the line and had me build corners. I had passed the test.

When the workday ended, the foreman came to me with the W-2 forms to be signed. After the paperwork I explained how I had just gotten into town and was flat broke. The foreman had heard that sort of story from every colored man in the crew and barely showed his disdain for guys who couldn't learn to manage their money. My take-home pay for the day was $40. That was almost a week's wage for the average Black worker in Harlem. The foreman handed me $35 as an advance against my pay. I don't know if he heard the sigh of relief.

Full from a big, hot supper at a restaurant on 126th and Lenox, I went back to the rooming house and paid the landlord ten dollars for the week's rent. Back in the room, I lay down on the old-fashioned bed. The mattress was too soft and the bed sagged in the middle, but the room was clean and warm. For the first time in a year I felt a sense of security. In one day my world had changed. I had a job, a place to live and a friend who knew the city.

Although my take-home pay of $200 a week was about four times the average pay in Harlem, I lived frugally, rapidly paying off my Cleveland debts. Finally I was debt free and all my obligations to Roberta were paid off, plus there was money for the divorce. My ties to Cleveland were severed. It was the end of an era. In the next few weeks I saved a little money with which to move to more comfortable quarters.

Time was when 155th and St. Nicholas was the heart of Harlem's Sugar Hill. The big rooming house certainly had seen better days, but it still had a stately if faded elegance compared to the rest of the buildings in the area. A door from the sub-basement opened to the subway. A Chinese carry-out restaurant and a laundry were on the basement level. A handsome bar and lounge was on the street level. My tiny, sixteen-dollar-a-week room on the 3rd floor contained a little refrigerator and hot plate. Best of all, there was a private bath. My immediate neighbor was a friendly, middle-aged southern couple. Thirteen single women occupied the rest of the floor.

I had been in my new home for three days when the furnace went out. It was an unusually cold night for the end of February. There was a soft knock on the door. When I opened it, two young women, their coats pulled tight around them, looked forlornly at me. "We are freezing. Do you have an extra blanket?"

"Sure." I gathered up my blankets and handed them to the women.

"You have some more for yourself?"

"Sure. I'm fine."

"We'll bring them back in the morning."

The next morning I yelled "Come in" to the knock on the door. The two young women saw me lying on my cot huddled under my coat. The word went around the floor that I'd given up my blankets and slept under my coat. I was in. It had taken time and heartbreak, but I'd already learned that women like a kind man.

2

The foreman blew the whistle. Thank God, the workweek had finally ended. The bricklayers cleaned their tools, dusted off their overalls, and started climbing down the scaffold. The foreman signaled for me to wait. Handing me a note, he said, "We need you on a job in the city. Here's the address. Be there on time."

Riding back to the city, I told Ty about the new job. "Sutton Place! Man, you're in! That's gonna to be one of the best jobs in the city."

Monday morning, subway map in hand, I made it to the job site. A small crew was laying out the building. I went to work with a white brick-layer laying out the incinerator, the chimneys, and the elevator shaft.

I don't think anyone anywhere works harder than a New York brickie. The bricklayers' union had just "won" a seven-hour workday. We now had a full hour for lunch and quit work at 4:00 p.m. The catch was we had to do the same amount of work in seven hours as we had previously done in eight. There was no time for getting to know your fellow worker or drink-ing coffee. After exchanging courteous nods, we went to work. During the lunch break I introduced myself. He held out a hairy, red-flecked hand. With a quick smile and a voice heavy with the sound of Ireland he said, "I'm glad to know you. My name is Patrick." The open friendliness about him showed he hadn't been in America long enough to pick up on the racism and suspicions that marked New York's ethnic groupings. In the following few days I got to know Patrick a little. Before work or during lunch he would sit apart from the crew, hands clasped, lost in thought. Sometimes our eyes would meet and I knew he wanted to talk something over with me. That Friday, pay in our pockets, we left the job together. As we neared the subway entrance he turned to me and said, "It's Friday. I'd like you to join me in a drink."

Several times I had started to go into the Blarney Stone tavern, situated as it was at the entrance to the subway, but not knowing what kind of hos-tility might be inside, I'd never entered the place. It would be impolite not to accept Patrick's offer, although I had a feeling he hadn't been here long enough to really know New York.

The tavern seemed warm after seven hours in the raw March winds that blew off the East River. Patrick walked to the bar and shook hands with the bartender, who turned to me. "What'll it be?"

"I guess a beer."

"Stout?"

"Yes, thanks."

He drew a mug of the dark brew, scraped off the foam, and refilled the mug. As he handed it to me he said, "Patrick's my nephew. I brought him over last year. He told me he works with you. Told me you're a gentleman and a good mechanic."

"Thanks very much." I lifted the mug in salute to Patrick and took a long, satisfying drink.

"You're welcome here, lad." The bartender turned to wait on other customers.

Patrick pursed his lips for a moment. "If Kennedy is elected, do you think he will do something for Ireland? He can't forget he's Irish."

I thought it best not to mention the fascist role Kennedy had played in the Senate, his support of the McCarran Act, which set up concentration camps and allowed for holding people without trial. I thought I shouldn't mention his close friendship with Senator Joe McCarthy and that gang. After a moment, to give the impression that I was thinking over a new idea, I said, "I don't think Kennedy will do anything for Ireland. He's a millionaire. He thinks like a millionaire, not like an Irish worker."

After a few sips of stout, Patrick said, "I think you're right, lad. People here don't agree with me, but I think a man's class overcomes everything else."

I finished my beer, shook hands with Patrick, nodded to the barkeep, and left the tavern. I felt a friendship for him, knowing that such thinking was rare and often unwelcome amongst many New York Irish Americans. I wondered how long he would last.

Stopping at the Blarney Stone for an after-work stout became a habit over the next few weeks. Sometimes with Patrick, sometimes alone, I would go in, drink up, and leave. I felt no one was paying any particular attention to me.

The job went well. With the firebrick work done and the elevator shafts up to grade, we were almost ready for a full crew of bricklayers. I transferred to the small gang laying out the building with pink glazed bricks. That Friday when the foreman gave out the pay envelopes he pulled me aside and said, "Monday's St. Patrick's Day. I can't get anybody to come in and finish laying out. I got to have it done by Tuesday—the whole crew is coming in. If you come in on Monday and finish it, I'll give you double time plus you don't have to come in Tuesday and I'll pay you for it. OK?"

A hundred twenty bucks for seven hours sounded good to me. "Sure, I'll come in. See you Monday morning."

St. Pat's Day was cold, crisp and bright. The beginnings of an unforgettable New York spring made me happy, anxious to finish the job and go celebrate payday.

After the last brick was laid, struck up, and cleaned, I turned to our just-finished bricklayers' shanty. Some brickie or perhaps a carpenter had nailed a neatly lettered sign above the doorway: ALL THE WAY INN. It was the standard name for the bricklayers' shack. With my tools stashed in the corner, white overalls hung up, pants dusted, and mortar wiped from my boots, I left 67 Sutton Place and headed for my stout and the subway.

Early evening darkness was settling in as I opened the first set of double doors and looked into the tavern. The place was packed with a noisy, drunken crowd. *Jesus,* I thought, *it's St. Patrick's Day.* I knew this was no place for a Black guy. As I turned to leave, four men crowded into the vestibule. They looked at me as if they couldn't believe their eyes. One of them stepped toward me, hostility hidden by the phony friendly tone that whites use when addressing a cornered Black man. "Ah, you're coming to have a drink to St. Pat, are ya?"

With all the nonchalance I could muster I answered him, "It's too crowded. There must be three hundred people in there. I'll go someplace else."

They didn't answer, but the four of them, moving forward, simply pushed me into the tavern. The place hushed as each set of unsmiling Irish eyes looked me over. I could tell they were thinking, *What the hell is he doing here?* I could sense the growing hostility and glanced around, thinking, *Christ! I'm going to have to cut my way out of here.*

One of my captors turned to the crowd and then to me. "You'll have a drink to St. Pat before you leave. But first we want to hear a song." There was some chuckling from the bar.

I wasn't going to put on a minstrel show for them even if I had to die there. Glancing around for someplace to defend myself, I saw Patrick. He smiled and nodded his head ever so slightly as if to say, *Don't worry.*

"OK. I'll sing a song if you all sing with me."

Again they chuckled between gulps of stout and sips of Irish Mist. "All right. What song will it be?"

I imagine they expected "Old Folks at Home" or "Dixie." I took a breath and said, "Since it's St. Patrick's Day, we'll sing 'Kevin Barry.' " A stunned silence electrified the tavern. I wet my lips thinking, *Thank God the Communists made me learn songs in Chinese, Tagalog, Russian, French, Italian, and Irish.* I took a deep breath and began:

Early on a Sunday morning
High upon a gallows tree
Kevin Barry gave his young life
For the cause of liberty.

The men seated at the bar stood up, and most joined in the song.

Shoot me like an Irish soldier
Do not hang me like a dog.

The singing went on to the end of the verse. I went into the third verse. Most of them stopped singing; I don't think they knew more than the beginning. Patrick had elbowed his way near me. As he paused for breath he said to crowd, "The lad has a true Irish air." Patrick and I finished the last chorus:

All around the little bakery
Where we fought them hand to hand,
Shoot me like an Irish soldier,
For I fought to free Ireland.

If it would have been difficult to get out before, it was impossible now. Incredulous laughter and hands to shake mixed with drinks shoved at me. A mixture of stout, Irish cream, and rye will make you drunk and deathly ill, and I don't know how I got home; perhaps Patrick found my address in my wallet and put me in a cab. I woke up the next morning on the couch in the vestibule of the rooming house. I remained friends with Patrick, but I never went into the Blarney Stone again.

3

After my life got back in order, I called Armando. He seemed a bit surprised to hear from me. Our abrasive phone conversation before I came to New York apparently left him with the idea that I would not contact him. I didn't like his high-handed way of talking to me, but he was the leader of an organization I wanted to belong to. I set aside my apprehensions and we made arrangements to meet that Friday evening so I could be assigned a club. Suddenly the world seemed brighter.

My winter of gloom melted before the brilliant New York springtime sun. Is there a better way to earn a living in the springtime than laying brick in New York? Is there anything better than the balmy warmth of its April sun caressing the bared back and chest, feeling the strong young muscles ripple as you bend for brick and mortar, or lift the heavy lintel stone, setting it across the opening, sensing the young women appraising that strength and wondering if they are wondering? Should one come near, a bricklayer will shout, "Sight that line!" and all the men will turn, splotches of sweat and mortar staining their bare chests and arms, smiling the springtime New York man-smile, laughing when, with hips swaying and nose a-tilt, she turns away. The playful curses between the men and the pusher shouting, "Lay them brick, lay 'em—drop 'em like hot potatoes— lay 'em—raise that line—give 'em hell, boys—get it like it's new pussy!"

The building grew out of the mud a story each day. We were twenty-four stories up, waiting for the foreman's whistle to step onto the hanging scaffold and start the day's work. I went to the edge of the scaffold to look down on the tiny people and toy cars bustling along First Avenue. Jimmy O'Day, the likeable twenty-four-year-old being trained as foreman, stepped from the building onto the scaffold. There was a cracking sound as a hanger snapped. The scaffold sagged and tilted, then snapped back into place. From the outer edge of the scaffold I was thrown into the building. Jimmy, on the inner edge, was thrown past me over the safety barrier, his scream ending suddenly in the mud and debris twenty-four stories down. The men, horrified, stepped back. Somehow, I had his hat. Perhaps I'd tried to grab him as he flew past me. I was afraid of it, as if it proved I had something to do with what happened. Mechanically, I handed it to the foreman. Perhaps he would give it to Jimmy's wife; they had been married eight months. No one spoke. I gathered my tools and followed the men down the stairwell. By the time we got to the ground floor, the ambulance had taken the body away. We walked silently to the subway.

In spite of death, uncertain availability of work, dependency on the weather, and backbreaking labor, there is a charm about laying brick that cannot be found in any other work. There's a warm satisfaction in looking down the column you've built. Perfectly plumb. Not a bump or twist in thirty stories. You did it. It's beautiful. It's your monument, your social contribution and it will stand forever.

4

New York blossomed in the warmth of April 1959. Debt-free, I was ready to explore the other sides of the city. I asked one of the men on the job where I could go to meet some single women. After describing several places, he finally summed it up: "The best place to go is down around Fifth Street and Third Avenue. There are a lot of nightclubs, and women from the university come there."

That night I left the subway and looked up and down Third Avenue. As I started to cross the street the light changed. I stepped back and crossed in the other direction. I stopped for a moment to listen to the music coming from one of the nightclubs. Signed pictures of Miles Davis, Cannonball Adderley, John Coltrane, and a number of other jazz greats adorned the entrance. They seemed to have gotten their start at the Five Spot Café. That night's feature was a Muslim jazz band that seemed to be getting rave reviews around the city. I listened for a moment and then entered the nearly empty club. Taking a small table in front of the band, I ordered a beer, lit the Cuban cigar a friend had given me, and settled into the music.

By nine-thirty the Five Spot was crowded. A few couples were standing along the walls, drinking and chatting. The only empty chair was at my little table. Feeling a bit guilty having two chairs while others stood, I glanced up and saw her. Turning from side to side looking for an empty seat, weaving between the tables, she walked toward me. Solidly built, perhaps five foot seven in high heels, with the shapeliest legs I had ever seen. A New York woman in a stylish spring dress out on the town! She stopped about five feet in front of me and I stole another glance. Shoulder length, dark brown hair with bangs straight across her forehead framed a pretty face accented by the tan skin and epicanthic folds of her eyes. Her lipstick and eye shadow, like everything else, were so perfectly blended they were hardly noticeable. Making up her mind that she would have to share a table with a strange man, she turned to me. The day that makes twenty years, ending the twenty years that hadn't made a day, was in her smile. At that moment I knew every freight train ride I'd taken across this country, every muddy trail I'd foot slogged through the battle-torn Solomons, every lonely drive from job to job, every wrecked relationship and every heartache had prepared me for and led me to this moment. I stood up, crushed out the Cuban cigar, and returned her smile.

"Is this chair taken?"

"No—no, it isn't."

"May I sit here?"

I stood staring at her, forgetting to answer—thinking that anyone else would have said *can* instead of *may*.

"Oh! Yes, yes. I'd be delighted." As she sat down I said, "My name is Nelson."

"Hi, Nelson. I'm Sue Ying Hoyate."

We were both a bit embarrassed by my awkward staring. I was glad when the band started to play another tune. She sat partly turned away from me, so I could safely glance at her. Her perfectly manicured hands were fully shaped and strong, the fingers long and straight.

Man, I thought, *Marxists don't believe in fate, but this is more than an accident. If that traffic light hadn't changed, I'd be in the joint across the street and would have never seen her.*

The music ended. Not wanting to be impolite, she turned to me. I could not let the moment pass. I had to say something. "I couldn't help but notice your hands. They are beautiful. Are you an artist—do you do sculpture?"

"Thank you. Yes, I do art—not enough. I'm still taking classes."

"I haven't been in New York long and I don't know the city, but I was rather struck that a Chinese woman would be interested in jazz from a Negro Muslim band."

She smiled, lowered her eyes for a moment, then looked up and said, "I grew up in Harlem."

"No kidding!"

"The first time Miles Davis played at the Five Spot I was here. I love jazz."

The ice was broken. As we were getting to know each other she said a few words from the Communist lexicon. I let her know that I understood and agreed. The atmosphere was warmer now. She had attended a few Marxist study circles, had a few friends who were dilettante Marxists, and had grown up in the apartment below that of Pettis Perry, an African American leader of the Communist Party. Her father was an immigrant Chinese and her mother an immigrant Norwegian. Her name, Sue Ying, a fairly common Chinese name, meant a soaring eagle.

I skimmed over my past twelve years so she would understand my commitment to the revolutionary movement. When I finished she didn't comment. I ordered drinks. She sipped her gin and tonic slowly and finally said, "It's good to meet a serious Marxist who is a worker. I never got close to the movement because I was disgusted with people who only talk about revolution and go along with the system."

The band played its final selection and the patrons began leaving the club.

"I didn't realize it was so late." She stood up, straightening her dress.

"It's too late for you to take the subway. I'm going in your general direction. Why don't we just grab a cab?"

As we pulled over to the apartment on Riverside Drive, I paid and sent the cab on. We walked without speaking up to the door of her apartment building. I stopped at the door. "Thanks for a wonderful evening. I hope I can see you again."

She looked a little bewildered. "Don't you want to come in for a bit."

"Yes, sure I do. But I shouldn't."

"Why?" She tilted her head as if expecting some crazy answer.

"Well, I've read a couple of these books before. I always started in the middle or at the end and ruined everything. I think this one's important. I think I should mind what my mom told me and take it a page at a time so I don't miss anything."

With a half-incredulous smile she said, "Minnesota must be a strange place. Will your book allow you to come to dinner next Sunday?"

"Sure, but it's *our* book. I want to treat it like it's important."

A light kiss on the cheek, a hug, a "good night," and I turned and walked away. I didn't turn around. I knew she was watching me. She might think me a Minnesota country bumpkin, but she'd walked into the trap, and I knew she was already falling in love.

The next Sunday, Sue Ying, gorgeous in a flowing mandarin orange silk gown, served the dinner—a nine-course feast. I later learned that her father was a cook in Chinatown.

It seemed that half the people in the rooming house were from South Carolina. I readily joined with them in ordering smoke-cured hams and Mason jars of 220-proof "white lightning" corn liquor. I was on my way to visit Sue Ying when the car of runners pulled up, fresh back from the trip to South Carolina and fully loaded. "Hey, man! I got some good shit this time!"

I paid for a ham and refused the corn liquor. Thinking that she would appreciate a real down-home ham, I turned toward Riverside Drive. Passing a flower vendor's pushcart, I decided to buy a rose.

"Look, man," the vendor pleaded, "I only have a few things left. I'll give you this big bunch of gladiolas for two bucks."

It was a lot of flowers, so I took them.

After ringing the bell, I stepped back to see how she would like ham and flowers. She opened the door, looked at me for a moment, then broke out into peals of unrestrained laughter.

I knew that she was thinking her New York thoughts about people from the country. I was on the verge of turning and leaving when, still laughing, she threw her arms about the ham, the flowers, and me.

"Oh, you are such a charming man!" She kissed me, set aside the ham and the flowers, and led me to a table set with Chinese teacups, *ha cao*, *hum bao*, and egg rolls. I briefly had the urge to laugh myself but thought better of it.

She introduced me to her nine-year-old son, Steve, who proudly announced that he was reading *Lady Chatterley's Lover*. I glanced at Sue Ying. She held up her open hands in a pleading manner and said, "I can't tell him not to read."

We sat down to eat, carefully crafting the relationship each knew the other wanted.

During the following weeks, bit by bit, I learned the Chinese names for the various foods. Entering our favorite restaurant on our Sunday morning date for Yum-Cha in Chinatown, all the waiters would gather around to hear me order in Chinese. That always guaranteed the best service and extra portions. I always referred to Sue Ying as *lo-kai* (sweetheart) to the benign smile of the older Chinese ladies.

When I asked for a date, it generally meant going to a distribution, a demonstration, or a bookstore to browse through the latest revolutionary literature from overseas. When she asked for a date we went to one of New York's art museums. Entering the Guggenheim, I told her I had worked on the building. I think from then on she saw me as almost a patron of the arts.

The struggle against colonialism was at a boiling point. Our little organization tried to meet the demands of the times with more meetings, more reports, more distributions. Sue Ying and Armando had a standoff when she asked him if he was going to the distribution the next day. He told her that he had a bad heart and at sixty-four he was too old. A week later she saw him playing baseball and crisply complimented him on his batting style. I was caught between them.

My having meetings three and four times a week was beginning to wear on the relationship. There was more than a bit of irritation in her voice as, night after night, I had to put the defense of Cuba or meeting until midnight to publish our little paper, *The Vanguard,* ahead of our dates. After one particularly emotional outburst, I knew we had come to the inevitable fork in the road. I called and made arrangements for her to come over and talk.

I opened the door to her knock and she walked in, face grim, defiant, and apprehensive. I thought the glass of wine and munchies would be accepted as a peace offering. They weren't. Finally I said as quietly as I could, "I just can't walk away from my assignments and responsibilities. Everything I ever fought for is happening. The whole world is changing. I have to be part of it."

She looked at me, then out the window. "Fine. I get the message."

That was so New York! I suppressed a smile and sat quietly, not wanting to make things worse. I knew she did not want to break off the relationship, but had to assert herself and have some assurance that she was on equal ground with me. She rose and walked about the room looking at the pictures cut from foreign magazines and pasted on the wall. More than decorations, they were my daily reminders that we were winning this great international struggle. She stopped to look at a Chinese woman aviator standing beside her fighter plane.

"Is this from China?"

"Yeah. I cut it out of a magazine called *China Reconstructs.*"

"I didn't know they had women aviators."

"I guess that's what the revolution was all about. They got rid of the old society and are building a new one."

"It was pretty bad. My dad used to tell me about it. I never thought I'd live to see Chinese women flying airplanes."

"Well, she very probably fought against the Americans in Korea."

Sue Ying looked at the photograph again and then sat beside me. "How do I become a revolutionary?"

I embraced her. It was the end of our beginning.

5

As 1959 drew to a close, we tried to keep up with the historic national liberation movement, the bitter fight within the Communist movement symbolized by the conflict between China and Russia, and their mutual struggle against the American intervention in Vietnam.

Between the meetings and demonstrations we found time for the traditional things that lovers in New York do. We took quiet, thought-filled walks through Central Park, sipped French coffee in Greenwich Village, and felt sure we had something important between us. During this time I learned something about the visual arts, not only in the museums but also from the books she gave me in exchange for the Marxist literature I gave her. As I learned more about art I became more spiritual. I became a more determined revolutionary, more convinced of the necessity of creating the material foundation of food, shelter, and clothing from which all humanity—not simply the elite—can live a more cultured and spiritual life.

We had been together for six months when she turned to me and said, "I want to have a baby with you."

I had often thought the same but had never mentioned it. "Good. I'd like that. Let's get married."

"I don't want to get married. It's too painful and doesn't help anything."

That Friday night we went to Coney Island. After I coaxed her to try the parachute jump with me, she finally agreed, providing I would hold on to her. After we were strapped in and began the long ascent to the top, I could feel her body stiffen and saw the fear in her eyes as we were pulled up above the city. "You won't let me fall?"

"Of course not."

Suddenly we were at the top. The cable release snapped, and there was a moment of free fall before the parachute fully opened. Although securely fastened, she screamed and grabbed for me. I held my arms open. "Are you going to marry me?"

"Yes. Yes, damn you—hold me!"

We floated down to a soft landing and laughingly made our way to the boardwalk.

"You did that on purpose."

"Sure—but a promise is a promise."

The next week we went to City Hall for the short ceremony. I left my tiny room on 155th Street, she left her apartment on Riverside Drive, and we moved into her childhood home, a spacious nine-room apartment on 138th and Columbus. Her father, living alone in that huge apartment, welcomed us.

Coming home from work I would exit the subway station on 138th and enter the Siboney Café for one of their delicious blender drinks. The café was always full of young people holding constant, earnest discussion. When the waiter asked what type of drink I wanted, I told him the only tropical fruit I could think of: "I'll take papaya." There were snickers and muffled laughter. I looked around, wondering what I had said wrong. One of the young women leaned out of her booth and, accompanied by the laughter of the rest, explained in a heavy Dominican accent, "In my country that mean *pussy*. You say *fruta bomba*!" I turned to the waiter. "Bring me papaya." When the laughter died down, we all exchanged names and shook hands. Cubans, Dominicans, Puerto Ricans—they were all with the Cuban 26th of July movement founded by Fidel Castro. After years of fighting, the revolutionaries overthrew the dictator Batista in January 1959 and ushered in the era of Cuban socialism. After a few months they insisted that I join them. I did. Even after non-Cubans were asked to resign from the organization, I kept in close contact with them.

Revolutions and revolutionaries were on the upsurge. I felt sure we were building a new kind of Communist Party—a party worthy of the American people. Work was plentiful as the developers rebuilt the Lower

East Side of the city. In mid-April 1960, Sue Ying sat down beside me and said, "I'm pregnant." It was a happy time.

6

The national liberation revolutions in Congo, Angola, South Africa, and Mozambique resonated throughout Harlem in 1960. A groundswell of race consciousness swept through the area. The fact that Black men and women were standing up to and defeating white imperialists inspired them to do the same. Suddenly the irritants of yesterday became unbearable. Eager Black capitalists, hungry for the lucrative trade on 125th Street, joined in the demands of the people that more Blacks be hired or, better still, that the white merchants cease draining the money from the area and leave. Suddenly, everyone was aware of the callous brutality of the police and simply would not take it any more.

The spontaneous outbreaks of fighting with the police, and the increasingly bitter arguments with the white merchants, made it clear to all that Harlem was stumbling toward a major outbreak of street violence. The New York police, with their traditional arrogance, met the growing militancy with increased brutality. I did not want to see street fighting begin. The disorganized, unarmed people were no match for the police, and all the casualties would be on our side. Yet I knew that if there was an uprising, it would be an opportunity for our Provisional Organizing Committee to get its message across. If it happened, I intended to be there and if possible establish an organization in Harlem. I wandered the streets of Harlem talking with the people and feeling the crackling tension. The more I understood the mood of the people the more frustrated I became. It seemed as if no one was doing anything to politicize or organize this growing social unrest. I finally faced the age-old question "If not me, who?" That night after our meetings, Sue Ying and I were settled at the kitchen table for the tea and small talk that comprised the only time we had together. I told her of my frustrations, and we came up with an answer: "Let's put up a soapbox on 125th and talk to the people." It was a scary but exhilarating idea.

The next day we walked down 125th and finally agreed to hold our street corner meeting on 125th and Lenox. I did not realize that the headquarters and bookstore of the Black Muslims were just a half block down the street.

Saturday night we walked to the corner with an armload of our sectarian paper, *The Vanguard*, a milk crate, and a can of soda pop. We agreed that I would talk while Sue, her pregnancy showing, would sell the papers. Getting up on a milk crate to try to speak to a mass of people moving in front of me who were oblivious to my shouts and declarations was terrifying. Of those that stopped, most thought I was a street corner preacher, and moved on when the word *communism* was uttered. Yet, gradually, by ones and twos and threes, a group gathered in front of me, interested in what I had to say about the gathering storm throughout the South, the upheavals taking place in Cleveland, and before our eyes in New York. They were most interested in what we believed to be the cause and the solution to the problem. After two hours on the milk crate and with all our papers sold, we announced that we would be back the following Saturday night, and left the corner. Exhausted and happy, we knew we had struck a raw nerve in Harlem. I was sure of something else: that nothing matures a revolutionary like street agitation—having to answer questions, having to defend one's position in understandable language. Most of all, the soapbox convinces the agitator that he is right.

The second week the police informed us that we had to display the flag in order to talk. Someone came forth with a small flag, which I held during the meeting.

The third week someone from the Muslim temple walked in front of me and demanded, "Get out of here with that Communist shit before I knock you off that box."

By that time we had constructed a little speaker's platform with a railing that held a two-by-four-foot flag. I pushed my finger against the flag as if I were holding a knife, "Cops must have sent you over. You come one step closer and I'll send you back to the police station feet first."

I could afford the bravado. After accusing him of being a cop, I knew the small crowd was with me. A tall, light-skinned young man who had been listening closely to my talk came forward. I recognized Malcolm X.

"Nobody sold this man any woof tickets. You got a right to say what you want. Nobody is going to bother you."

Malcolm had a few words with the man who threatened me, and then the two of them turned and walked toward the Muslim bookstore. The next week the Black Muslims started street corner meetings of their own and kept them going for the next twenty-five years. We moved our soapbox a block away to avoid any abrasive contact.

7

In September 1960, Fidel Castro returned to the United States to address the United Nations. He moved into the Hotel Teresa on 125th Street, thwarting the government's attempt to isolate him. Fidel knew that unity with the African Americans was the most reliable base of support for revolutionary Cuba. At the Siboney, we made plans to demonstrate. After a few phone calls, a conga line of perhaps fifty people formed on 138th and Broadway. Turning and twisting, dancing and singing "Cuba, sí, Cuba, sí, Cuba, sí, sí, sí-sí-sí!" my black-skinned Dominican comrade Alias Balliard led the line. Down Broadway we danced, picking up Latinos at every corner, then turned east on 125th, where the line grew longer and blacker. African Americans were already milling around the hotel as the conga line of several hundred arrived. Shouts of "Lumumba! Lumumba!" merged with "Fidel! Fidel!" Someone began to beat on a set of conga drums. Blacks and Latinos shimmied and danced and hugged. Fidel opened a window, waved, and threw us kisses. It was pandemonium. Even the cops seemed to be doing the conga as they gently urged us to disperse and open 125th Street to traffic.

Shouting slogans, exchanging leaflets, laughing, and hugging one another, we began to disperse toward our respective neighborhoods. Suddenly four or five carloads of white fascists and anti-Castro Cubans drove into the demonstration, leaped from their cars with baseball bats, and attacked anyone within reach. Some of the older men and we veterans rushed to meet them as the women and youngsters scrambled to safety. We got hold of a few of them and worked them over as the cops moved in to break it up. It appeared to the demonstrators that the police were siding with the fascists. The people spread out along 125th Street, throwing rocks at the cops and kicking in a few windows at the stores owned by white merchants. The police escalated the violence, indiscriminately beating and arresting anyone in the area. Two Black men, who I believed to be police agents, told me the cops knew who I was and I should leave the area at once.

It was impossible to organize anything under these conditions, and I was concerned about Sue Ying, so I took the subway home. She met me at the door, her face a mask of anxiety. "I was afraid for you. There's a riot in Harlem!"

"Yeah, I know. I have to go back. I wanted to check on you—make sure you're OK."

"I'm going with you!"

We had our first serious argument. Looking at her, five months pregnant, I told her that if she insisted on going, then I wouldn't go and an opportunity would be lost. She finally gave in, and I ran for the subway to take me back to 125th Street.

Most police departments are somewhat trained to handle crowds, but police often become brutal when they are frightened, and some cops are simply brutal by nature. The New York Police Department was unmatched in its combination of cold efficiency and brutality. Even their horses seemed to enjoy pressing a hapless person against the wall and rolling him along until he was unconscious. The use of their long billy clubs was terrifying. It soon became clear to the people in the street that they could not confront the police. Instead, they turned to breaking the windows of white-owned shops and then some looting began.

As a phalanx of cops charged down 125th I stepped into a coffee shop to avoid their clubs and horses. Two young men stepped in with me. As we sipped our coffee, waiting for the moment to rejoin the crowd in the streets, we tried to assess the situation. They understood the futility of this fight and seemed more interested in resolving the question of our oppression rather than simply fighting back. After a few words I told them about the POC and suggested they come with me to talk to Armando. They were eager to hook up with something serious and agreed to go with me. I called Armando and he agreed to speak with us.

After we were seated in Armando's book-lined living room on Second Street, the three of us gave him a rundown of the situation in Harlem. I expected him to follow the policy of the organization—that the struggle of the African American people is part of the world national liberation movement and that we should counter the growing Black nationalism with an internationalist and revolutionary perspective. Instead I was shocked as he spoke of banal trivialities and completely avoided discussing any revolutionary perspectives. It was clear that he did not want to become involved in anything that might get him into trouble with the law. My two friends saw it, too, and after exchanging a few words rose to leave. I walked with them to the subway, apologizing for the futile meeting. They seemed to understand, and we shook hands as they boarded the A train. I felt crushed and humiliated. I knew that all the time we'd spent on the soapbox, all the leaflets, and all the militant declarations had been compromised. We never met again.

The 1960s was a time of heroes—it was the time of Patrice Lumumba, Che Guevara, and Douglas Bravo, as well as countless unknown and unsung heroes. It was a time when revolutionaries admired and lived to emulate such heroes. I wondered how I would tell Sue Ying that the man we had such confidence in was a coward. By the time I got home I knew Armando and I were on a collision course. I decided the way out was to leave New York and try to build the movement in some other city.

8

The baby was born January 20, 1961. At that time fathers were not allowed to be with the expectant mother at the birth. After six hours in the waiting room, I went home to get some sleep. Becoming a father was no excuse for missing work on a construction gang.

The next day, on the way to the hospital to see Sue Ying and the new baby, the news broadcast announced the assassination of Patrice Lumumba, president of the Democratic Republic of the Congo.* The long and bloody struggle for Congolese freedom climaxed with the order from President Eisenhower to kill Lumumba.

I arrived at the hospital heartsick over the brutal murder of Lumumba, the symbol of African liberation, but eager to see my new son. He lay in his little bassinet staring at his hand as he opened and closed a fist, wondering how he did it. After about twenty minutes a nurse came over and said, "He is an exceptionally beautiful baby." I thanked her and then, a bit embarrassed, went to the maternity ward to visit Sue Ying. I told her first about the murder of Lumumba. She was shocked, and tears formed in her eyes.

"Lumumba is dead? God! What are we going to do?"

"I don't know, but it is going to change things."

She looked at me, a bit hurt and bewildered. "Aren't you going to say anything about the baby?"

"Yes, yes. He is so beautiful. He was born as Lumumba died. I want to name him Patrice."

She smiled her agreement and held out her arms for the embrace that should have already happened.

---

* Patrice Lumumba, leader of the independent Congolese trade union, founder of the Congolese National Movement Party, was elected by an overwhelming majority in Congo's first election in 1960. Independent and nationalistic, Lumumba moved to recover the Congo for the Congolese. To stop this move toward independence, Eisenhower ordered his murder.

PART IV

Los Angeles, 1964

1

Nineteen sixty-three was a year of confusion on the political left. Class conflict in the industrial countries gave way to national and racial struggles in the colonial and semi-colonial world. The white left, afraid of being excluded, deserted the white poor and flocked to the banners of Black liberation. The Black left, afraid that the more broadly connected, better-financed white radicals would outdo them on their own turf, became more nationalistic. POC was drawn into this ideological struggle and it, too, began to swing toward Black and Puerto Rican nationalism. I held fast to my belief in the fundamental decency of the majority of the American people—regardless of color—and the necessity of fighting for their unity. I began to clash more openly with Armando. Again I was faced with a choice: fight for what I believed to be the truth, become isolated, and finally be expelled from the organization, or compromise that truth with the hope of winning the fight when conditions became more favorable. I knew there was no way to compromise truth without attacking it. I resigned myself to the fight.

In the fall of 1964, a small group of radicals in Los Angeles contacted and joined the POC. We were thrilled with the possibility of building a movement on the West Coast. It would mean someone would have to go there to help stabilize the organization. I volunteered, jumping at the opportunity to get out of New York. Eva, a twenty-three-year-old, intelligent, dedicated Puerto Rican comrade, also volunteered and left at once for Los Angeles.

Through November and December I saved our money and prepared to make the move. I purchased a used Corvair van and on the second of January packed up my family and headed out to Los Angeles.

Lurching and swaying with the wind blasting from each passing truck, the Chevy Corvair van chugged north on the Harbor Freeway. Keeping one eye on the upcoming Century Boulevard exit and trying to avoid the maniacs darting in and out, before and behind me, cutting me off. I screwed up the courage to bully my way into the exit lane. The little six-cylinder aluminum motor putted up the ramp to the sanity of the surface streets. For the first time in eight days, I felt the tension evaporate. If I believed in God, I'd have said He was on our side. I'll never have any other explanation for how that Corvair van made it across country through the record cold and blizzards of the winter of 1964–65.

Following the easy directions to Ninety-seventh and Juniper, I tried to visualize what this new chapter of my life and revolutionary work held for me. The idea of working in Los Angeles was exciting. More than that, given the degenerating situation in New York, if we could succeed here, it would give new life to the entire organization.

I pulled over at a one-story stucco building that held a row of apartments. One of them was to be my new home. Comrade Eva, from New York, was waiting for us. After the welcoming hugs and kisses, she helped us carry in the baby and the one trunk that held the total of my life's material accumulation.

I glanced around the tiny apartment—a small entrance area that served as a living room, a combined kitchen and dining area, two bedrooms, and a small area that held the toilet and a stall shower. I assumed that people in Los Angeles didn't spend much time inside. The sun was shining brightly and the warmth was pleasant after our cold journey. Glancing out the window at the two tall palm trees standing on the boulevard between the sidewalk and the curb, I noticed the well-kept lawns, the level and pothole-free streets, and the spacious look of the Jordan Downs housing project across the street. After Harlem and the slums of Cleveland, the Watts area of Los Angeles looked like paradise to me. I didn't say it, but thought, *What in the hell are these people complaining about?*

After our few belongings were put away, I left with Eva to meet the rest of the comrades at the office.

The little Los Angeles POC collective rented a storefront where Firestone and Manchester converged. There, they held their meetings and put together a little paper. After checking the address and noting the police car staked out across the street, I pulled over in front of the building. Two young white comrades came out to greet us. As I went forward to shake hands, I tried to size them up. In the six or seven months that they'd belonged to the POC, they'd became well-known Communists in Los Angeles, receiving wide publicity in the press as dangerous revolutionaries. This didn't sit well with me. The capitalist press has always followed a policy of smothering serious communists in official silence. I shrugged off my apprehensions as a bit of Black nationalism or jealousy conjured up by two middle-class white comrades accomplishing more in a few months than I had in the past few years.

We shook hands warmly, and I introduced myself to Michael Laski, the chair of the area, and Arnold Hoffman, who seemed to be his lieutenant. At thirty-one, Laski was already slightly balding. His sharp face and intense eyes covered by a pair of round glasses gave the impression of a sharp criminal lawyer rather than a revolutionary. Two African American comrades were waiting inside. Vernon, a tall, slender, dark-complexioned thirty-year-old man with slightly protruding large expressive eyes and an intelligent, smiling face, stepped forward to shake hands and welcome us. Hal, twenty-seven years old with light brown skin and hazel eyes, had the erect bearing of the recently discharged soldier. He grasped my hand with both of his in a warm welcome that seemed to say, *Glad you're here, man. We need some colored folks to guide this organization.* I sensed there was friction between him and Laski. Eva stood by, beaming with the revolutionary zeal and confidence that characterized our young Puerto Rican comrades.

During the orientation meeting I tried to understand where the individual comrades were politically. Laski was clever, not really a leader, but a wheeler-dealer who couldn't belong to anything without being in control. With machine-gun bursts of facts about Los Angeles history, the political structure, and its police force, he completely dominated the meeting. The two African American comrades did not speak. Vernon seemed to be the dedicated revolutionary who would put up with anything so long as it contributed in some way to the liberation of his people. Hal fidgeted, trying to get a word in edgewise; finally he gave up and sat staring at the floor. Eva took notes when something new or interesting was said. She seemed to have established a sort of quid pro quo with Laski. She would tolerate his messiah-like ranting and strutting so long as she was in control of the organizational aspects of the work. Hoffman sat quietly, nodding approval whenever Laski summed up or made a point. I sensed rather than understood that he was Laski's gay companion and that I would not be able to grapple with one without struggling with the other. One thing I did know—there was no way for us to create a revolutionary organization without equality of participation. For me, the color of a leading comrade within the Marxist organization was of no consequence, but having working-class Black comrades blocked by articulate, educated, middle-class white comrades could not be tolerated.

Our little collective was paying for the way the revolutionary movement had evolved over the past twenty years. America's expanding imperialism meant the expanding material well-being of especially the white workers. They found such bribery more attractive than the lofty ideals of socialism or working-class solidarity. Consequently, there was a growing tendency for educated middle-class whites to join the movement out of moral considerations and for working-class, poorly educated Blacks to join out of desperation. Creating a unified organization from these contradictory elements was next to impossible.

2

The following week I went every day to the union to see about work. L.A. is not a brick city. Work was slack and the city was full of snowbirds (workers who fled the freezing North for the winter). The union wasn't about to pass over a local brickie and give a drifter a job—and being Black didn't help.

After reporting to the union hall and being told that no jobs were available, I set out to learn about Watts. It was a small Black community. The main street, 103rd, was the shopping area. Actually the people were held captive to the blood-sucking merchants. The public transportation system was so bad and expensive it was almost impossible to shop anywhere else unless a car was available. There was no hospital or movie theater in the area. The poolrooms, storefront churches, and beer halls were side by side down 103rd. It looked not so much like 125th Street in Harlem as the Black slum Soweto in South Africa.

Police occupied the area—state, county, and LAPD. In addition, it seemed that every state or county office, such as the attorney general's office, had a few people in the area. The police let their presence be felt through constantly cruising up and down the street or sitting in their cars at intersections, glaring at people as they crossed in front of them. Police chief William H. Parker created his police force with a core of white college graduates from Alabama, Texas, and Mississippi. Their education did not change them. They feared and hated the people. The people feared and hated them. Minor incidents between the cops and the people were daily occurrences. On the street the tension between the people and the cops was almost visible.

The distinctly southern atmosphere gave Watts a certain charm. As I walked down 103rd, almost everyone I passed gave me some sort of a greeting, even if it was no more than a slurred "What say, man." More of a statement than a question, it was a hangover from the southern Black fireside training that "you don't have to speak to dogs, you do speak to people." Passing a person without speaking implied that you considered him or her a dog.

Sue Ying easily integrated herself into our talkative, friendly, southern-like neighborhood. Steve was in school; Patrice was a happy, healthy baby. I knew I was going to enjoy my stay in Los Angeles.

By the middle of March, I began to know my way around without the grudging assistance of the union. I finally got a job in the jurisdiction of the Long Beach local and joined them. When I went to the union hall to transfer my membership, the young, intelligent business agent assured me, "You're going to be treated same as any other member." The union in Long Beach had more work and was much more democratic on the race question. A mountain of worries fell from my shoulders.

The collective decided to concentrate its propaganda activities in the Jordan Downs housing project. The apartments were bright and cheerful. The spacious lawns between the buildings were neatly trimmed. The tenants either were on public assistance or held low-paying jobs. The project was highly organized and governed by a well-led tenant council. From the outside it seemed to be a nice place. Yet from the inside, the project, like the rest of Watts, was depressing. Isolated from centers of culture, it turned inward, struggling to elevate itself with the material that was dragging it down.

Poor African Americans, especially those in the Watts area, were hardly affected by the anti-Communist hysteria and the witch-hunts. They understood that the communists were for equality and were against the Man. During distributions there, we and our sectarian press were welcome.

The POC's paper, *The Vanguard*, was primarily concerned with the fierce debate going on within the world communist movement. Most of the articles dealt with the latest polemics coming from China or the Soviet Union. It hardly seemed suited for Jordan Downs. Yet there was always an article or two dealing with the struggle of the African American or Puerto Rican people in the United States. That was enough to allow us to distribute in the area. The fact that we sold a large number of papers in the project was an indication of what could have been done with a revolutionary press that dealt with local issues. Even if they did not understand the interparty struggle, the people respected us for trying to do something to better their conditions. One by one we contacted potential revolutionaries in the projects. From the distribution of the paper we formed a small study circle. From the study circle we recruited a few of the local people. In this way, the POC became an integral, if semi-underground, part of Watts.

A few of our contacts were outstanding. Jan and Lev were natural-born communists. Both were well known through their activities in the local PTA and the project's tenant council. A big, husky person, Lev liked to dress in the popular dashiki and put on the threatening air of the Black militant. Beneath that front, he was a loving if stern father to his four children and a serious, intelligent fighter for his people. People gravitated to his and Jan's apartment, and they were an important connecting link to the project as a whole.

Jan was the quintessence of the African American mother. Her life revolved around the children. Deeply aware that the system prevented her children from living a full and wholesome life, she was a militant revolutionary. Her dark complexion highlighted big, clear eyes and a pretty face. Jan was the perfect complement to Lev's sweeping charges against the enemy. She was the meticulous organizer who knew where things were and made things happen.

The entire group walking down 103rd Street Saturday morning selling the paper was an important part of our propaganda effort. On one such occasion I started to go into one of the barbershops when I heard a familiar, stuttering voice calling my name. I turned to see Nat Green, an old friend from Minneapolis. A wheeler and dealer as a teenager, now known as the unofficial mayor of Watts, Nat was forty-five. He had been around the revolutionary youth movement in Minneapolis, and it took just one short discussion to bring him into our group. During our first six months in California we slowly but surely built a political base in a section of Los Angeles society where we were almost invulnerable to Red-baiting or police disruption.

3

Watts, isolated from the more affluent part of Black Los Angeles, could not let off steam by taking part in the demonstrations for civil rights. Instead Watts smoldered. The police stoked the sullen anger with daily reminders of the community's political impotence. My turn came one Tuesday morning in August 1965 as I drove to work. Part of the harassment of Watts was in the form of surprise but frequent "inspection roadblocks." The cops had set up such a roadblock on Central. I knew if I turned off to the side streets to avoid it, they would consider that reason enough to not only stop me but tear the car up and very probably plant something in it. The van was in reasonably good shape, and I just couldn't afford the time to wait in line for the inspection. Not one car was getting through without a ticket. The old van passed the inspection and I prepared to drive away when one of the cops looked up at me and told me to turn on the turn signals. Smiling to one another the cop began writing out a ticket. As politely as possible I asked what the violation was.

"Well, your blinker is too slow."

He knew and I knew there was no regulation concerning the speed of blinker lights. I took the ticket for a "defective blinker" and drove to work. That ticket meant twelve bucks to have a registered mechanic certify that the blinkers passed inspection and missing a day's work to appear in court. Small wonder that any Watts child would tell you that the police slogan "Serve and Protect" meant serve themselves and protect the white folk.

When I returned home from work that evening, Sue Ying was lying down, holding her side and sweating with pain. After feeding the kids, I took her to a doctor on Manchester. He assured us that it was an inflamed ovary and told us to keep hot packs on her stomach. Although I felt a bit apprehensive about his superficial examination, I followed his advice.

August 11 was a hot, hard workday. The official temperature of ninety-five degrees was nothing compared to the double whammy of working in the direct rays of the sun and facing the shimmering heat bouncing off the block wall. When the last lump closed the last block course, we struck up the work, brushed the wall, and, bidding one another good night, left the job, heading out in our respective directions. The few Black guys headed north to Watts and South Central, while the white guys headed west and south to the security of their white neighborhoods.

Approaching Avalon and Imperial, I noticed the unusually large number of people out of doors, sitting on their porches, watering their lawns, or simply standing talking to a neighbor. The heat had brought a larger than usual crowd out of the sweltering houses and into the street to talk and laugh or share a cold beer with a friend. I swung down Imperial to Central and on to 103rd Street. Waving to a few men I knew, I swung over to Ninety-seventh and up to Juniper. Steve, hearing the tinny sound of the Corvair, stepped out to the little porch, his face a mask of worry and fear. I hurried up the steps and looked in at Sue Ying. Her body, hot and bloated, and her face, distorted in pain, left no room for indecision.

"We have to get her to the hospital right away," I told him.

Steve nodded. I ran to the van and backed it over the curb up to the concrete steps and opened the rear doors. I had earlier prepared a military-style cot in the little dining area for her so she could get a breath of air and not be confined to the dark bedroom. With Steve taking one end and I the other, we slid the cot into the van. Leaving Steve to care for the baby, I headed for St. Elizabeth's hospital, across the "Berlin Wall" of the Alameda railroad tracks, into the white enclave of Lynwood. A non-Black cannot know the apprehension a Black person feels in such a situation. There was the probability that the hospital would not accept her since she was from Watts; I was sure she would die before an ambulance could take her to County General or any other hospital. Nevertheless, I swung the van to the emergency dock, opened the rear doors, and called loudly for help. Two men, one Black and one white, ran over and helped lift the cot to the dock. A nurse came out with a hospital gurney, and we lifted Sue Ying onto it. A young, serious-looking doctor glanced at me and then at Sue. After taking her pulse and temperature, he handed me a printed form and a pen.

"You're her husband?"

"Yes."

"You will have to trust us. She is very sick and there is not time for explanations. Just sign, we have to open her up right away."

Two orderlies were pushing the gurney into the elevator. I signed and handed him the paper. The door closed. Shaken, I turned to a nurse standing near.

"What is wrong with her?"

"I don't know. They will have to examine her."

She sounded friendly enough, so I continued, "I know you can only guess, but what do you think it is and how serious do you think it is?"

"I shouldn't say this, but it looks like a ruptured appendix—probably peritonitis and probably bacteremia. It's serious."

I wanted to stay until Sue Ying came out of the operating room, but it was almost 7:00 P.M. and I was afraid to leave the kids alone at home too long. I turned toward the van, its doors ajar and the lights still on.

The African American orderly had been standing quietly by. He came over and put his hand on my shoulder.

"You're lucky. They don't dare try to transfer her to Big County in that condition. That's the only way colored people get into this hospital. That doctor is one of the best surgeons in the state. He came here for a confer-ence and stayed to donate some time. You take care leaving. There's some ratty white folk 'round here."

Those words meant so much to me. I wanted to take the time to thank him from the bottom of my heart, but I had to get back to the kids.

"Thanks, man. That helps."

As I approached Alameda, the Lynwood cops momentarily flashed their spotlight on me. Satisfied that I was Black and heading for the ghetto, they waved me on.

Crossing the tracks at Alameda, I had the clear feeling that something was amiss down Imperial Highway. Toward Imperial Courts, four squad cars were parked, partly blocking the street. Curiosity got the best of me, and I drove slowly down Imperial.

The cops made no effort to stop me but took down my license plate number as I passed them. Suddenly I thought I was back in the war as the shriek of sirens blasted from every direction. The parked squad cars, lights flashing and sirens screaming, burned rubber getting into the street and roared away toward Central. I pulled to the curb to let a solid phalanx of motorcycle cops, six abreast, zoom past me. The people from Imperial Courts, already outside because of the unusually hot night, ran to the street to see what was happening.

After exchanging questions, a few of the young men got into their cars to find out what was going on. As soon as they left, cars started arriving from the west, from Central and Avalon.

"Hey, man! What the hell's going on up there?"

"I don't rightly know, but hell's fixing to bust lose. Looks like two cops raped some woman.* People tried to deal with 'em and they called for backup. Fuckin' laws is beatin' women, children—anybody."

"I'm about sick of them stinkin' motherfuckers. Who the hell they think we are, some kinda dog?"

"You be less than a man lettin' them white bastards beat your women

---

* A few weeks before, in a highly publicized case, Mrs. Beverly Tate was raped by Offi-cer William D. McLeod, while his partner, Officer Thomas B. Roberts, stood by. McLeod was fired, but no criminal charges were pressed.

and children and you don't do nothin' about it. I ain't takin' no more beatin's. I'm gettin' my shit and goin' back there."

Street fighting was in the hot, dry air and hung like a curtain, enveloping the people penned in Jordan Downs, Nickerson Gardens, and Imperial Courts. It enwrapped the dark side streets as Black people felt their way along the rough dirt paths that served as sidewalks. They smelled street fighting and for the first time wondered why Lynwood had lights and cement sidewalks built with their taxes. Street fighting crackled in each rumor that tumbled from each car that sped up and down Imperial Highway and through the projects. It grew with the growth of mass consciousness of inequality. No one organized it. Like a strike wave, it rose when its time was ripe. It spread on the lightning bolts of rumor. Ennobled and emboldened by the frustrations and humiliations and hurt—the pent-up hatreds crammed in, unseen and unheard, for three hundred years—it burst forth, resplendent in its terror.

I smelled it and shuddered, remembering the trepidation embedded by an organized police force bearing down, relentless, invincible, indomitable, beating and shooting, scattering our bravest like elk before a pack of wolves. And as in Harlem, it stoked the adrenaline and drowned the fear and raised the battle cry, "Fuck them motherfuckers! We stick together, they can't whip us!"

For a moment I started to join the group heading for Avalon, where the fighting seemed to have intensified. Then I thought of the kids alone and probably frightened by their mother's illness. I told the few guys I knew that I had to see about the kids and reluctantly headed the old van toward home.

4

The next morning, Thursday, August 12, Watts was quiet. The police and newscasters reported, with a bit of bravado, that the situation was under control. I knew better. I had seen the progression of street fighting in New

York. The lid of fear was off, never to be replaced. Last night had been a battle mainly of teenagers and young adults against the police. As the young
people were shot, beaten, or arrested, the older folk began to be pulled into
the fray trying to protect them. Now they too had a score to settle with the
police. Yes, the morning was quiet. Those with jobs had to go to work. The
rest were sleeping or making caches of rocks in the alleys and biding their
time until darkness gave them some protection.

I was just leaving for work when the phone rang. It was Armando calling from New York. After the usual greetings, he switched to a very formal
tone.

"What is happening there is a riot. There is nothing you can do. Stay
out of it."

I gasped for breath and sat down. I had expected him to give me some
direction, or at least tell me to do the best I could to make connections and
give some leadership to whomever we could influence. "Stay out of it"
sounded like my days in the Communist Party, people sitting in New York
and telling those of us in the field what to do. The anger was rising within
me. I answered him with the same cold formality he had used with me:
"Comrade Armando, what's happening out here is a police riot. They're
shooting and beating women and children. I live in the middle of it. There
is no way for me or anyone else to stay out of it."

There was a moment's silence, followed by, "Nothing can be gained in
this sort of situation. We cannot get into the line of fire. The organization is
too weak."

I breathed deeply, wanting to say, *People are out there fighting with no
organization. We can build one if we are not afraid to.* After a few more cold
exchanges I promised not to allow any provocation on the part of the comrades, and we said good-bye. Hanging up, I realized that every so-called
revolutionary organization in the country had condemned the uprising as
simply a "riot." Only after the Mexican and African press defended it did
they do a 180-degree turn.

Crossing Avalon and Imperial on my way to work, the streets were
quiet and my thoughts turned to the conversation with Armando. I knew
the conversation did not help my precarious position in the organization.
It was unmistakable that Armando was afraid of what might happen to

him should we get involved. The FBI's tactics had been clearly stated by Hoover: "If you want to kill a snake, stomp on its head." Armando was that head, and he wasn't about to go to jail over an uprising that was bound to be crushed. I felt a little sorry for him. It must be a terrible internal ideological contradiction to call yourself a revolutionary and yet be afraid of prison.

Those who had transportation shopped in the well-stocked stores a few blocks away in Lynwood. Watts was the known dumping ground for merchandise and foodstuffs that were ending their shelf life in other areas. To add insult to injury, a few cents were always added to the price. The relations between store owners in Watts and the people were a hated dependency, on one hand, and contemptuous exploitation, on the other. Nevertheless, the supermarket on Imperial was on the way home, and I needed to pick up a few things for the evening meal.

Swinging into the big parking lot, I noticed that there seemed to be an unusually large number of people leaving the store or on the sidewalk, their shopping carts piled high with foodstuffs. Stepping inside the store, I saw what could only be described as a feeding frenzy. People, mostly women, were racing up and down the aisles filling their carts with food of all descriptions. The clerks at the meat counter leaned back calmly watching the sometimes quite polite people empty the displays. The checkout girls were leaning against the cash registers. One woman walked calmly through the checkout aisle and with a charming smile said, "Thank you. Thank you so much!" The clerk smiled back just as sweetly and replied, "Oh, you're welcome."

I asked one of the women leaving the store what was going on.

"You can take whatever you want. They ain't chargin' today."

I started to enter the store, then thought better of it. It would be just my luck to be arrested or shot over two bucks' worth of bread and milk. I could picture the comrades, shocked and disgusted that a veteran revolutionary would stoop to looting.

A few more inquires and I understood that about an hour ago a woman had been a few dollars short of her bill. The clerk waved her through. Apparently the police had advised the merchants that given the shortage of forces, they were going to protect lives but not property. The store owner, believing his choice was giving up the groceries or endangering the lives of the employees, told the clerks not to argue or interfere with anyone. The word soon spread throughout the projects. The people, envisioning a diet beyond the ham hocks and collard greens allowed by the miserable welfare check, flocked to the market. The Watts festival began.

After the kids were fed and settled for the evening, I crossed the street into Jordan Downs to get some assessment of the uprising. The usual group was seated or standing around the front of Lev's apartment. Two young men, still teenagers, were the center of attraction. Arrested the night before along with several hundred other youths and just released by the cops, they were telling their story. Welts and bruises testified to the savage brutality of the police. There was a cavalier but heroic defiance about them. One of them said, "We goin' back. They ain't seen the last of us. We gonna Vietcong their ass tonight."

Kicks and beatings may break an individual who stands alone. It is quite another thing when that individual feels and actually is part of a mass in motion—then the greater the brutality, the greater the resistance. These young people were taking a stand, and nothing more was involved than whether they would allow the police to continue beating and humiliating them simply because they were Black and young. I gave them a salute of a clenched fist across the chest, spoke briefly to Jan and Lev, and hurried back to the apartment, since it was almost visiting hours at the hospital.

At the hospital, not one patient had spoken to Sue Ying because her husband was from Watts. Ignoring the hateful glares of the white patients, I had my first real visit with Sue. She was getting better and was deeply worried about the kids and frightened that I might get caught up in the fighting. I assured her that without organization, I wasn't going to get into a fight with the cops. I left the hospital feeling relieved that she was going to be OK.

Crossing Alameda—the "Berlin Wall"—I could hear gunshots. I drove down as far as Grape Street and for the first time saw the crowds on 103rd. Fires were being set and the looting engulfed 103rd Street. Police cars were speeding through the area with shotguns blasting. I drove home, picked up the baby from Eva, and after the kids were asleep, poured a shot of whiskey and settled in front of the TV, where the fighting was presented to the world.

Our little collective was irreparably split. Laski's constant praise of Armando had gained his support, allowing Laski to move in such a way as to eventually confront the police. The comrades and those close to us were aware of the danger of allowing provocateurs to provoke the police. When the fighting began, I insisted that a meeting be held of all the comrades to agree on what the collective would do. After a bitter discussion, it was basically agreed that the most we could do at this time was to put out a few leaflets that would give some direction to the more politically advanced. We agreed to do what we could to consolidate the poorest section of the working class, who had, for the moment, seized the leadership in the struggle. We also agreed that it was important that the people of Watts understood that they were not fighting alone, that they were part of a worldwide movement of the oppressed. The weak link was that there was little vocal support from any quarter in the United States. After a sharp debate it was agreed that the white comrades would stay out of the areas where the fighting was going on. There were very few attacks against whites walking through the area, for at that moment few in Watts looked upon the struggle as one between Black and white. It was between the cops and the people. Rocks were thrown at some cars because they represented the merchants who drove into Watts, conducted their business, and left with the people's money. We didn't want to give any indication that white revolutionary propagandists were attempting to co-opt the leadership of the struggle.

5

On Friday, August 13, a few of the Black mason tenders did not show up to work. They might have been arrested or just exhausted from the fighting the previous night. I didn't ask about them. I wanted to avoid any discussion with the white brickies about the uprising. The welding crew, from

Mississippi, had other ideas. One of them, a big, ruddy white guy, laid aside his face shield and helmet and walked over to me. "Why you here, fella?"

He didn't sound unfriendly, but just his being from Mississippi was enough to put me on guard. "Got to earn a living, man. I got a family to feed."

"Shit, man! You oughta be out there gettin' yours like everybody else."

"I'd rather earn it. It's safer."

"Shit, man!" he said again. "They took from you for three hundred years, you oughta be able to take back for a few days."

I smiled at him and said something to the effect that, having been in the infantry, I was afraid of getting shot. He turned and walked away. From this and other comments, it seemed clear that a certain percentage of whites, while not supportive of Watts, seemed to give the grudging admiration one gives a dog that, daily beaten, finally bites back.

We left work early because the men delivering the cement blocks would not drive anywhere near the riot area. As I neared the intersection of Wilmington and 103rd I saw Laski and Hoffman passing out leaflets. Two cops stood by, apparently guaranteeing that the rioting Blacks would not interfere with the pair's right of free speech. I sat and watched for a few moments and then walked over to them. Laski was startled when he saw me but merely nodded and handed me a leaflet. It was a garbled set of out-of-context statements by Mao and ended by calling for revolution. Worse, the statement on the bottom said, "Issued by the Watts Area Provisional Organizing Committee." The whole setup reeked of the work of the agent provocateur. I folded the leaflet, put it in my pocket, and gave him a glare that said, *We're going to talk about this tonight.* As I got back into the car one of the cops carefully copied my license number.

I immediately called Armando, informed him of the situation, and demanded that Laski and Hoffman be expelled. There was a moment's hesitation. I knew he was calculating which of us would be more useful to him. In a subdued voice, he agreed. I said good-bye and hung up the phone. The next day, as Laski and Hoffman passed out leaflets around 103rd and Grape, the press took pictures and interviewed them. Later studies on the Watts uprising always included a scene of Laski distributing "Maoist" literature as a caricature of the communist movement. In fact, he had been expelled as an agent. Apparently he thought whatever agency he was working for would continue to protect him. Shortly after the uprising, he was arrested and imprisoned for using the mails to defraud.

Food was becoming scarce for some families in Watts. The stores within walking distance had been emptied. Few of the families in the projects had cars, and many were at the end of their supplies. Diapers and milk were in greatest demand. At first there was a sharing of goods, but when those supplies ran out, the men piled into their cars and headed west and north, where there were still stores. By nightfall they all returned, dividing the goods and taking them to the neediest families in the project. The daily press made no mention of this necessary "looting."

The morning paper sensationalized the looting of the jewelry stores and pawnshops. Nat Green, a natural-born hustler, knew that everybody is after a bargain and the easiest person to cheat is the one who thinks he is going to cheat you. With eight children of his own and always two or three relatives to feed, Nat long ago learned to find the silver lining in any cloud. He hustled a ride to city hall, where he took out a vendor's permit, then walked over to the arts and crafts store and purchased $10 worth of fake diamonds and assorted costume jewelry. After buying a plastic pistol at the toy store, he was ready for business.

Nat stationed himself on the south side of Imperial at Alameda. When the light turned red and traffic stopped, he furtively glanced from side to side, making sure the butt of his "pistol" was showing from his jacket. With a few "diamonds" half concealed in his hand, he would approach the most expensive-looking car. His severe stuttering worked for him. By the time three words were out, the white man behind the wheel understood that here was a real rioter, gun, diamonds, and all. Nat never completed the deal until the traffic light was changing and nervous whites, anxious to cross the "Berlin Wall," honked to move. The deal was quickly made. The white man drove away chuckling that he had taken one of those savages for a ride. Nat, pocketing the fifty bucks, got ready for the next sucker.

Two carloads of cops, alerted to a rioter selling jewelry, converged on Nat, pistols drawn. Stuttering, Nat explained that he was carrying on a legitimate business of selling craft beads, and he showed them his license.

When challenged about the gun, Nat informed them that his lawyer had assured him that it was dangerous but not illegal to carry a toy weapon and that he had threatened no one. The cops, shaking their heads, jumped back into their cars and sped off to the more profitable business of beating kids on 103rd.

6

The military, Nazi-like occupation of Watts, the increasing brutality of the police, the shoot-to-kill orders issued to both soldiers and cops, the rounding up and detention of thousands, and the round-the-clock struggle of the combatants was having its effect. Although fighting continued sporadically along 103rd on Sunday, August 15, the people were worn out and it was beginning to show. The police kept it going, pulling new forces into the fight by shooting randomly into crowds or into homes they might suspect contained snipers.

After my evening visit to the hospital to see Sue Ying, I finally finished the daily routine of feeding and caring for the kids. Sitting them in front of the television and asking Eva to keep an eye out, I crossed Ninety-seventh Street into Jordan Downs. We generally gathered at Lev's place. I would have liked for them to come to my little apartment, but it was too exposed. Any grouping of people in or around a private house was excuse enough for the cops or National Guardsmen to take down everyone on some kind of suspicion. By contrast, not even the soldiers dared invade the projects except in force and with a clear mission. It was safe to meet there.

Five or six men and a few women were in the front room or resting at the front of the building. I was happy to see that they were all alive and uninjured. After the greetings, the conversation turned to the fighting.

"Maybe if we can hold on for a few more days, Chicago or Detroit or New York might blow."

"If three or four cities went at the same time, they'd need the whole damned army to deal with it."

"If we can hold on a little longer, maybe we'll start a revolution."

"Man, wouldn't that be somethin'! Old chickenshit Watts starting a revolution!"

They were expressing sentiments heard throughout the area. Watts was becoming politicized. We were all aware that an army division, on its way to Vietnam, had turned around in midocean in case they were needed for the more important fight here. The Vietnamese National Liberation Front sent a message of thanks to the people of Watts. With 28 percent of American war causalities African American, there were few in Watts who supported the war.

One of the young fighters said, "Well, when this shit is all over, everybody'll know one thing—that them high-yella white mouths downtown don't speak for Watts. We spoke for ourselves."

Lev went inside for drinks, and one of the men, silent until now, mulling over the discussion, looked over the group and said, "For the first time, the field niggers got a word in. From now on, what their house niggers say ain't gonna make no difference."

Lev parceled out the glasses and the conversation halted while everyone poured a drink and thought over what had been said. I knew they understood, even if they could never articulate it, that what was happening in Watts would not only change the African American people but change America forever.

Politics within Watts, as in any Black slum, was complex. The relations between the Black community and the white power structure were based on color. Although little known in the white community, relations inside the Black community were also based on color.

My experience has been that leadership of the Black community developed from a number of factors. On one hand, through a complicated process begun during slavery, the white man picks the Black leader. During slavery, this process was direct. By midcentury it was a more subtle and complicated machine. First, nobody could get anywhere by being a Black militant. The power structure simply refused to deal with them. Since the Black militant couldn't deliver the goods, he could not consolidate a following. Instead, the Man quite openly selected the leader of the Black community and then, to close the circle, selected the opposition. This was done by praising the selected leader as a sensible moderate and labeling the selected opposition as dangerous militants. The reality was that both sides were chosen by and worked for the Man and the people were unable to actually choose their leadership.

The Black press, which had immense influence in the community, was almost always dependent on this power structure. The independent and militant *California Eagle* had been the largest, best-known, and most influential Black paper in the state. When Charlotta Bass, the editor, ran as the vice presidential nominee with Henry Wallace in 1948, the *California Eagle* was crushed by the FBI and Bass politically marginalized.

Between the dealings of the power structure and the propaganda in the Black press, the average African American was resigned to accepting the "leader." This leadership was invariably light-skinned, proud of it, and well educated in accommodation. I remember how irritated I would become reading of the way Walter White, the executive secretary of the NAACP, constantly referred to the fact that he could pass for white. He might as well have. I was never sure whether he was a Black man who could pass for white or a white man who passed for Black. The effect was the same. There was an objective factor here, too. The dawn-to-dark forced labor of the field hands made it almost impossible for any of them to really communicate, let alone emerge as leaders. On the other hand, the slave children of the master were often given preferential treatment that allowed them the time and freedom of movement to take the position of leaders. Thus, almost all the slave rebellions have been led by the light-skinned children of the master, be it Nat Turner, Denmark Vesey, or Toussaint L'Overture. After emancipation, this group, known as the "red men," consolidated in the Caribbean and in the United States. W.E.B. Du Bois and his "talented tenth" were almost all quite light-skinned. I could not help but note that though Du Bois was respected and admired as the outstanding intellectual and principled revolutionary that he was, Paul Robeson was loved. A good part of that was because Robeson was one of the few dark-skinned sons of the working class to rise to the level of moral leadership.

The people of Watts, alienated from this Black-white power structure, felt the color division very deeply. They knew they were the uneducated, unheard, despised field niggers who were now getting the attention of the entire world, and they were proud of it.

• • •

It was ten minutes after curfew when I pulled up to my apartment complex, ran across the yard, and knocked on Eva's door. I could hear the sharp *bam* of rifle fire coming from 103rd. With permission to shoot to kill, the National Guard was running amuck. In one day they had killed more unarmed people than the police had in three days. I felt the apprehension of a soldier awaiting an inevitable attack. Eva finally opened the door and handed me the baby, asleep and wrapped in his blue blanket.

"You better hurry. The Guard is shooting at anyone that's on the street."

"I know. I'll go right home."

She carefully closed the door, and I stepped off the stoop and walked swiftly across the yard. Steve had opened the door. He, too, had heard the reports of the National Guard recklessly firing at anyone outside their house. I was nearly across the lot when the Jeep pulled up. It held three white soldiers. One was a captain; another, who appeared to be about nineteen years old, was manning a mounted .50 caliber machine gun. The captain pulled his .45 and aimed it at me.

"Drop whatever you're carrying and put your hands in the air."

"I'm carrying my baby."

"I said drop it and raise your hands or I'll shoot."

It seemed that time stood still as I watched his hand tighten around the butt of the pistol. I had never come this close to my own death during the war. It seemed that I left my physical body and was watching and listening from outside it. I was calm. I saw Steve standing on the concrete stoop, terrified for my safety. I would set an example for him. My spiritual self knew that my real corporeal self wasn't going to drop the baby; neither was I going to beg this white Nazi son of a bitch for mercy. I had seen other men die, but I had not known that such serenity preceded death.

"I'll tell you what, Captain. I was a damned sight better soldier than you are. I'm not going to drop my baby. You shoot."

There comes a time when principles are more important than life. The Guard had killed so many that day. To bow down would be like betraying the spirit of a dead buddy. I looked calmly at the captain. He glared at me, part of him wanting to pull the trigger, another part of him realizing he would have to justify the murder of a three-year-old and his father. Perhaps it was my Minnesota accent; perhaps it was that I was calm. I did not know that four of my neighbors were witnessing the drama. I watched his hand relax, his eyes livid with hatred as he slid the pistol into its holster.

"Fucking nigger."

I stepped onto our stoop. Suddenly my knees were rubber; my legs seemed unable to hold me up. I took a deep breath and tried to steady myself. All the bravado was gone, and in its place flowed the naked fear of death—not simply my own death, but more important, that of Patrice. Steve held his arms out to me. I handed him his little brother. Steve's face was tense, and he was gulping breaths through his mouth; he was even more frightened than I. We stood together for a moment, waiting for the adrenaline to subside. Then he turned to me and said, "They hate us, don't they?"

It wasn't a question but a sudden deeper understanding of a fact. It was one of those moments when whatever I said would influence his thinking for the rest of his life. "Some of them do, Steve. Mostly they're afraid of us because of what they've done to us. They're afraid we'll get even."

We stepped into the security of the kitchen. Patrice was still asleep. I placed him on his bed, loosened the blanket, and turned back to Steve. "I don't want you to hate them. I don't want you to be like them. Hate the conditions that make them what they are. Then you'll be a good communist."

Steve looked straight into my eyes and I could feel a bonding between us that would last the rest of our lives. Never one to talk when it wasn't necessary, he turned to his chair and opened his book. I turned on the TV to get the white folks' view of the uprising.

Wired up, I did not sleep that night. Half awake, I daydreamed about what one platoon from my old regiment could do here. We could drive them out of Watts. I visualized us—forty-eight strong, battle-hardened, proud Black men—skirmishing down 103rd with 60 mm mortars, Browning automatic rifles, air-cooled machine guns, M1 rifles. If only we had organization, we could do it. Then I thought about dying and leaving a sick wife and two children to fend for themselves. Despite the aching need to get out there and get even, I knew the time wasn't ripe. An uprising without organization and vision could not succeed. We had neither.

I awoke early Saturday, full of apprehension, knowing this would be the day that determined how the Watts rebellion would be settled. The National Guard had moved in. What had started as an uprising of the youth against the police was slowly transforming into a fight between the Black community and the occupying police force.

This would be the first day the majority of the adults would be off work. I was sure a sizeable number of them would be pulled into the fight. Too many children had been beaten or arrested; too many women had been beaten and humiliated by the cops. It had become too much of a Black freedom struggle for the men to stay out of it. My apprehensions grew from my knowledge of the ruthless efficiency of the military as opposed to the simple brutality of the cops. It arose from knowing the effective difference between M1 rifles and machine guns as opposed to the indiscriminate use of pistols and shotguns. I knew Saturday would be a bloody day of decision. It was worse than I feared.

Friday night through Sunday morning had been a slaughter. After listening to the TV and reading the paper, I went back to Lev's to get some assessment of the fighting. Each story was worse than the others: children seven and eight years old picked up, beaten, and jailed, people killed inside their homes or on their porches. More Americans died fighting in Watts Saturday night than in Vietnam that day. Eighteen people killed, hundreds wounded, thousands arrested, and many more thousands beaten. The spoken attitude of the police was that all Blacks were "Commies" and to waste them.

Some seventy thousand people had been out in the streets the night before. They began to be clearly divided into distinct groups. The biggest group was onlookers. The rest divided into those who were there to fight the cops and the Guard and those who were there to loot.

A few things were becoming clear to me. First, the murderous brutality of the cops and the Guard was instilling and deepening a hatred for all whites not only in Watts but also across the country. The Black Muslims easily moved into entrenched positions of ideological leadership. Without some activity on the part of the white progressives, it was not possible to resist the wave of Black nationalism. If only a few whites had spoken out or taken some action on a class basis, history could have changed. Los Angeles is a southern city and in the main populated by whites from the South.* The media was having a field day presenting the cops as law-enforcing heroes and African Americans as the criminals. In fact, most of the police beatings were unlawful assault and battery. Most of the killings were plain hateful murder.

The second thing that became clear to me was that the revolutionary movement in America had its tactics all wrong. The idea of a vanguard organization leading the charge to change America was not going to work. During the Russian Revolution, the military concept of a vanguard was applied to the revolutionary party. Militarily, a vanguard consisting of combat-tested, reliable soldiers moves ahead of and protects the main force. The vanguard makes contact with the enemy and brings them to battle, where they can be overwhelmed by the main force. Within the vast anti-feudal Russian Revolution, the Communist Party, comprising nearly one-seventh of the country's industrial workers, grounded in the army and in the cities, could and did act successfully as a vanguard of the revolution. The Communist Parties in the urban, industrialized West immediately took up this idea, disregarding their actual economic and demographic situations.

The sad decline of the American Communist Party shows how easily and thoroughly such vanguard organizations are penetrated and essentially controlled by political police. They have not only the technology but also the unlimited funds needed to carry this out. American history, especially between Blacks and whites, will not allow the success of such an organization. We revolutionaries knew that the wages of the white workers were increased by the super-exploitation of the Blacks. We could not admit to ourselves that the necessary unity of the working class could not be achieved so long as white workers were fighting for wage increases and Black workers were fighting for equality.

I began to understand the possibility of mass uprising being the form

---

* The Confederacy claimed southern California and sent a few slaves into the area during the Civil War. The Depression-era mass migration from Oklahoma, Arkansas, and Texas strengthened its southern character.

for transition to socialism in America. Watts is a small area, yet it took the city, country, and state police plus a division of infantry—about twenty-four thousand armed men—to contain it. Could there be a widespread—a national, disciplined, politicized—"Watts rebellion"? The answer was before my eyes. Watts was proving one thing I'd always believed: that oppression and exploitation alone are not enough to impel a people into action. That action takes place when an idea takes root, when a vision becomes clear. In Watts the Vietnam War came home. All the talk about freedom and self-determination finally hit a target.

The McCarthy repression and rapidly rising living standards of the organized section of the white workers isolated the revolutionaries. At the same time, the African American freedom struggles were rising. En masse, these revolutionaries shifted from the struggle based on class to that based on color. This retreat of the revolutionaries into the Black community had to halt. There had to be a way to talk to at least the poorest section of white America. It might take another fifty years for the economic conditions to awaken the mass of white workers. If so, we needed to prepare to take those fifty years to educate, little by little, whomever and wherever we could. That would require a different kind of revolutionary organization. It would require an organization that tactically would be part of the current struggles but strategically strive to find ways to educate this decisive sector of the population with a vision of a peaceful, cooperative world.

As the fighting in Watts died out, the Guard left the area and I brought Sue Ying home from the hospital. Despite the pervasive smell of burnt buildings and the occasional confrontation between the people and the police, happiness was again setting out four plates on the kitchen table. My little family had weathered the storm.

7

Quenched with blood, the fires of August smoldered beneath the ashes of defeat. Throughout the winter and early spring of 1966 confrontations periodically broke out between the cops and individuals or small groups of youth hanging out on the streets. On March 15, a minor fight between high school students brought in a phalanx of police who fired indiscriminately, killing one person. Throughout the night the cops beat and arrested anyone in the area. Any resistance to police authority was quickly and brutally crushed with rifle butts, blackjacks, and billy clubs.

In the early part of May, four police roughed up and arrested a suspect. A crowd of two hundred quickly formed and freed the handcuffed suspect. However, the emotional exhaustion of the people and their lack of organization gave the cops an insuperable advantage.

With the last brick laid, the wall joined and brushed down, I bagged my tools, tossed them in the trunk of the old Mercury, waved good-bye to the gang, and set out for home. I only half noticed that more than the usual number of squad cars were parked across from the gas station on Central as well as slowly patrolling "Charcoal Alley." Small groups of sullen young men stood on the corners talking and returning the hateful glares of the police. Lev, dressed in a new orange and blue dashiki, was sitting at the table in our little kitchen. I knew something was amiss; he seldom came to visit during the day. As I opened the screen door and came in, I greeted him with, "Hey, Lev, what's goin' on?"

"You ain't heard the news?"

"Naw, I saw some people on the streets—what happened?"

Lev's face hardened, his lips pressed inward against his teeth. "Fuckin' cops killed a man taking his wife to the hospital. Pulled up alongside him and blew him away with a shotgun."

"Jesus Christ!" I pulled the only other chair up to the table. "When did it happen, Lev?"

" 'Bout two hours ago. Woman having a baby. We can't let 'em get away with this one. God knows what they'll do next."

I didn't have an answer. We could put out a leaflet telling the people what they already knew. It would be nothing less than a provocation, a call to resume the fighting. It was one of those moments when everything depends on organization. It was painful to realize that after all the effort and bloodshed, no such organization existed.

We agreed to call a meeting of the collective that evening to decide a course of action. Lev left to try to get an assessment of the mood of the people in the project. I switched on the TV to hear how city hall would explain this one. The killing of Leonard Deadwyler was the first item on the news. There were no hospitals in Watts, so when Deadwyler's pregnant wife went into labor, they got into their old Buick and sped for the county hospital downtown. Cops, noticing the speeding car, turned on their flashing lights and signaled him to pull over. Deadwyler waved a white rag as a signal of emergency and kept going. After a few blocks of the chase, the cops pulled alongside Deadwyler and killed him with one blast of their 12-gauge shotgun to the head. The car careened down the street, finally jumped the curb, and stopped. Deadwyler's wife, covered with blood and bits of flesh, staggered from the car and fainted. Ironically, she had gone into false labor.

Before the newscast was over, the phone rang.

"Hello?"

"Nelson Peery?"

"Yes, speaking."

"We are holding a meeting of interested individuals tonight. It is important that you attend."

"With whom am I speaking?" I thought I recognized the voice of a leader in the field of public health.

"I'll give you the address."

I started to warn her that my phone was tapped. But she had already given me and the FBI the information.

After supper's dishes were washed and put away, I walked over to the address on Wilmington and 103rd. To my surprise it was the series of temporary buildings that housed the public welfare and county health offices. I was met at the door and ushered into one of the larger offices. Ten or twelve well-dressed people were seated. There were no introductions, but I recognized a few of them. They were among the elite Black professionals who worked in Watts—a lawyer, two administrators from the Health Department, a high school teacher. I wasn't sure what they had in mind, but I knew it was serious, since they were jeopardizing their jobs just coming to a meeting where I was invited. Apparently they were all waiting for me. As soon as I sat down, a tall, angular, light-skinned woman stood up and opened the meeting.

"Since everyone here has already individually said something must be done about the murder of Leonard Deadwyler, we have invited you to join with us in planning that something. We invited you here because you live in Watts and are known as a serious revolutionary. Before going any further, do any of you wish to speak?"

As if it was necessary to everyone there that they go on record denouncing the murder and endorsing some sort of action, they spoke, one after another. The common theme was that this murder was a ploy to see if the people of Watts were capable of taking to the streets again, or if it was safe for the cops to tighten the noose around their necks. A few of them spoke of class and exploitation as if they had learned a smattering of Marxism—perhaps in college. More importantly, for the first time I heard educated, militant people use the term "whitey" and basically follow the general concepts put forward by the Black Muslims.

When my turn came, I tried to stay within their general ideas and yet not compromise my ideology or theory. "I agree with just about everything that has been said. I can only add two things. First, nothing is possible without organization, and second, serious organization is not possible without first clearly identifying who and what is friend and enemy."

The tall light-skinned woman took the floor again.

"I guess it's time to get down to the nitty-gritty." She turned toward me, her features hardened with a determination reminiscent of pictures of Harriet Tubman. "We've come up with a plan. If we are going to do anything, we first have to draw the police out of Watts for a few hours. Then it will be possible for the people to take to the streets again. We have to make that possible and at the same time give them the enthusiasm to carry on the fight. They all know that if the police get away with this no Black person is safe in Los Angeles." She turned and pulled down a map of Los Angeles County. "We know that protecting Mr. Charlie's property is the number one job for the police. That's their weak spot. We believe that if we could get a few teams into the Santa Monica Mountains and set a few fires in strategic places, the police will pull out of Watts to protect those white folks. That will give us our opportunity."

My heart quickened for a moment as I realized why I had been invited. It was already clear that I was expected to provide the teams. There was a moment's silence, and then, looking directly at me, she continued. "Can we do this?"

All the things Lenin had written about petty bourgeois radicalism—their tendency to launch into wild attacks that were inevitably followed by wild retreats—came to mind. I couldn't insult these people. I wanted to win them over. I couldn't help admiring this woman. One of the city's leading Black professionals, she was risking it all in an angry upsurge over the murder of a poor Black man from Mississippi. A part of me wanted to agree with her—to strike back, no matter the consequences, in order to show the cops and the world that we were not defeated. The other part clearly understood it was not possible and that the blood of the people who would be killed would be our responsibility.

I looked up to her and said, "I think it's a good idea. It will take a lot of time to prepare for this. We'll have to determine where it would be best to set fires. We have to scout out ways and means of getting twenty or so Black men through that white area without being seen. We have to guarantee that we get them out of there safely. Most important, we have to prepare the people to respond at the right moment. That will mean dealing with some of the gangs in the area. All this will have to be done without the cops finding out about it—and their stool pigeons are everywhere. The other side of it is, the people are exhausted. It's going to take a lot of education and organization to get them out in the street again. They've suffered around fifty killed, with hundreds wounded and hundreds are still in jail." I thought I had said enough. I didn't want to kill their fighting spirit.

A long moment of silence followed. Finally one of the men said, "We really hadn't considered that side of it. I agree that we can't go off into this thing half cocked."

The woman chairing the meeting said, "We just can't let them get away with this. If this plan is impossible then we have to try something else."

Another long silence followed. Someone asked, "Does anybody have an idea of what to do?"

The meeting was unraveling. Finally, it was agreed that the people who called the meeting would get together and come up with some realistic plan and then we would meet again. I knew nothing could be done until we had organization, and organizations take years to build.

After the handshakes and militant declarations, we left the meeting. We never met again. The murder of Deadwyler was, of course, ruled justified, and the killer cops again stalked the streets of Watts, shotguns at the ready.

In search of closure I walked the few blocks to Mrs. Deadwyler's house to pay my respects. I knocked at the screen door and entered the front room. Two sad-faced women sat quietly near a little table. I placed my ten dollars in the bowl that held other donations. No one had spoken. It would be sacrilege to shatter that pale of grief. Nodding my condolence to the women and turning to leave, I glanced at Mrs. Deadwyler.

She sat numbed, rocking her torso in the straight-backed kitchen chair, hands clasped, lips pursed, crying the lament of our dreary past. *Oh, sweet Jesus, hear my cry.* Rocking, rocking, sorrow too sad for tears. As when she stood frozen in humiliating terror on the auction block. *Sweet Jesus, hear my cry.* As when awaiting the lash, wrists tied tight to the whipping post, dripping blood. *Sweet Jesus, hear my cry.* Rocking, rocking, lips pursed, sorrow too sad for tears. As when her children, tied to the wagon, looked back to their mother, never to be seen again. *Sweet Jesus, hear my cry.* Rocking, rocking, lips pursed, sorrow too sad for tears. As when the baying redbone hounds picked up the scent of her man gone for glory. *Sweet Jesus, hear my cry.* As when she wrapped the greasy sheet around the lashed and bloody body. *Oh, sweet Jesus, hear my cry.* Rocking, rocking, lips pursed, sorrow too sad for tears. As when the drunken howl of the lynch mob celebrated the blood-soaked sacrifice swinging gently beneath the southern sun. *Sweet Jesus, hear my cry.* And when the white-helmeted, hate-crazed cops blasted out the life of her man, she sat numbed, lips pursed, sorrow too sad for tears, rocking, rocking, crying the dirge of the helpless, the lament of our dreary past. *Oh, sweet Jesus, hear my cry!*

Blinking back tears, I turned toward our little apartment. There was work to be done.

Postscript

Watts, isolated and attacked on all sides, turned inward for protection. A wave of Black nationalism swept South-Central Los Angeles, crushing any ideology or organization that stood in its path. In 1968, betrayed and abandoned by the leadership in New York, our organization became one of the casualties. We regrouped as the California Communist League. As it became a national organization, it was reconstituted as the Communist Labor Party (CLP). It played an important role in the revolutionary movement within the United States and internationally.

The Watts uprising was a turning point in American history. Trapped on the horns of world opinion and Cold War demands, the government attempted to resolve the problem by winning over and co-opting the Black upper class at the same time as it moved to crush the aspirations of the Black poor. Mirroring the Black CEOs, generals, and government officials like the portrait of Dorian Gray, every ninth prisoner in the world today is an African American.

Watts was more than a rebellion against intolerable segregation, exploitation, and discrimination. Overwhelmed by the color question, few saw it as a convulsion signaling the beginning of the end of an economy. Today, across the industrial rust belt of America, for the same fundamental reason, a hundred new Watts are forming. This time they are white.

On a more personal level, my son Steve moved to northern Minnesota to become a farmer and worker. Patrice works as a longshoreman in Los

Angeles. Sue Ying passed away on Christmas Eve 2002 after a prolonged illness. Old revolutionaries, like old soldiers, never die—they fade away. I am still staunchly resisting that process by teaching, lecturing, and writing, confident that within the frightful menace of tomorrow lies the wherewithal to build the peaceful, cooperative world we American revolutionaries have given so much to achieve.

Index of Proper Names